S0-BKP-081

11/30/11
$85.00

Critical Race, Feminism, and Education

Palgrave Macmillan's
Postcolonial Studies in Education

Studies utilising the perspectives of postcolonial theory have become established and increasingly widespread in the last few decades. This series embraces and broadly employs the postcolonial approach. As a site of struggle, education has constituted a key vehicle for the 'colonization of the mind'. The 'post' in postcolonialism is both temporal, in the sense of emphasizing the processes of decolonization, and analytical in the sense of probing and contesting the aftermath of colonialism and the imperialism which succeeded it, utilising materialist and discourse analysis. Postcolonial theory is particularly apt for exploring the implications of educational colonialism, decolonization, experimentation, revisioning, contradiction and ambiguity not only for the former colonies, but also for the former colonial powers. This series views education as an important vehicle for both the inculcation and unlearning of colonial ideologies. It complements the diversity that exists in postcolonial studies of political economy, literature, sociology and the interdisciplinary domain of cultural studies. Education is here being viewed in its broadest contexts, and is not confined to institutionalized learning. The aim of this series is to identify and help establish new areas of educational inquiry in postcolonial studies.

Series Editors:

Peter Mayo is Professor and Head of the Department of Education Studies at the University of Malta where he teaches in the areas of Sociology of Education and Adult Continuing Education, as well as in Comparative and International Education and Sociology more generally.

Anne Hickling-Hudson is Associate Professor of Education at Australia's Queensland University of Technology (QUT) where she specializes in cross-cultural and international education.

Antonia Darder is a Distinguished Professor of Educational Policy Studies and Latino/a Studies at the University of Illinois at Urbana-Champaign.

Editorial Advisory Board

Carmel Borg (University of Malta)
John Baldacchino (Teachers College, Columbia University)
Jennifer Chan (University of British Columbia)
Christine Fox (University of Wollongong, Australia)
Zelia Gregoriou (University of Cyprus)
Leon Tikly (University of Bristol, UK)
Birgit Brock-Utne (Emeritus, University of Oslo, Norway)

Titles:

A New Social Contract in a Latin American Education Context
Danilo R. Streck; Foreword by Vítor Westhelle

Education and Gendered Citizenship in Pakistan
M. Ayaz Naseem

Critical Race, Feminism, and Education: A Social Justice Model
Menah A.E. Pratt-Clarke

Critical Race, Feminism, and Education

A Social Justice Model

By Menah A.E. Pratt-Clarke

palgrave
macmillan

CHABOT COLLEGE LIBRARY

LC
196.5
.U6
P73
2010

CRITICAL RACE, FEMINISM, AND EDUCATION
Copyright © Menah A.E. Pratt-Clarke, 2010.

All rights reserved.

First published in 2010 by
PALGRAVE MACMILLAN®
in the United States—a division of St. Martin's Press LLC,
175 Fifth Avenue, New York, NY 10010.

Where this book is distributed in the UK, Europe and the rest of the world, this is by Palgrave Macmillan, a division of Macmillan Publishers Limited, registered in England, company number 785998, of Houndmills, Basingstoke, Hampshire RG21 6XS.

Palgrave Macmillan is the global academic imprint of the above companies and has companies and representatives throughout the world.

Palgrave® and Macmillan® are registered trademarks in the United States, the United Kingdom, Europe and other countries.

ISBN: 978–0–230–10957–5

Library of Congress Cataloging-in-Publication Data

Pratt-Clarke, Menah A.E.
Critical race, feminism, and education : a social justice model / by Menah A.E. Pratt-Clarke.
p. cm.—(Postcolonial studies in education)
Includes bibliographical references.
ISBN 978–0–230–10957–5 (alk. paper)
1. Critical pedagogy—United States. 2. Education—Social aspects—United States. 3. Social justice—United States. 4. Feminism and education—United States. 5. Racism in education—United States. 6. African American students—Education. 7. African American boys—Michigan—Detroit—Social conditions. 8. African American girls—Michigan—Detroit—Social conditions. 9. Single-sex schools—Michigan—Detroit. 10. Educational equalization—Michigan—Detroit. I. Pratt-Clarke, Menah A.E. II. Title.

LC196.5.U6P73 2010
370.11′5—dc22 2010018509

A catalogue record of the book is available from the British Library.

Design by Newgen Imaging Systems (P) Ltd., Chennai, India.

First edition: December 2010

D 10 9 8 7 6 5 4 3

Printed in the United States of America.

Contents

Figures

Acknowledgments

I am indebted to the Spencer Foundation for its support of my work through a $15,000 Dissertation Grant and to Vanderbilt University for its financial assistance through the Dorothy Danforth Compton Fellowship. I gratefully acknowledge the assistance of the Detroit School System; the Detroit law firm of Lewis, White & Clay; the American Civil Liberties Union of Michigan; the National Organization of Women Legal Defense Fund; Detroit Free Press library staff and reporters; and the University of Illinois College of Law and Law Library staff.

Introduction

A Black Girl's Story

I am writing because what I wanted to read was not written. I wanted to read about how to simultaneously work in different academic disciplines and blend the strengths from each discipline to produce a revolutionary and transformative approach to understanding society. I wanted to read about the intersection of academic disciplines and their role in helping to explain the relationship among the interwoven identities of race, class, and gender and the interlocking social institutions of the education system, the legal system, and the media. I wanted to read about how to help transform institutions that perpetuated oppression and injustice. I decided to write because one day I realized I could write what was not yet written. Like Toni Morrison, "I wanted to read that book that I wrote, and couldn't find it anywhere" (quoted in Paul, 2003, p. 25).

There is another reason that I am writing. I am writing this book because I am a Black woman and I have five degrees: a Bachelor's degree, two Master's degrees, a law degree, and a doctorate. I have quietly carried these degrees around trying to find the appropriate use for the responsibility they entail. For almost fifteen years, I have not been able to fully actualize the potential associated with these degrees. Until now, they were unfulfilled potential. But now, I am writing because I must honor the sacrifices of my family, of other African-Americans, and especially of Black women.

My father was born in Freetown, Sierra Leone, in West Africa and became the first citizen of his country to obtain a Ph.D. in nuclear physics. His education quest was pursued on three continents: Africa, Europe, and America. Education was a way for him to move beyond the confines of colonialism. His desire was to improve his country, which was founded as a sanctuary for former enslaved African-Americans.

He studied and taught at Durham College in England; Fourah Bay College in Freetown, Sierra Leone; Hampton University in Virginia; and Carnegie Mellon University in Pittsburgh. It was important to him to gain and share knowledge. He raised his family to be as independent as possible from the "system" and its institutional, organizational, and structural racism. My father was an African man. I saw him fight every day to beat down the "system" and I saw him die from that fight a month after he turned sixty years old. I am writing for my father.

My mother's ancestors were slaves in Texas. My mother grew up picking cotton and sharecropping during the Great Depression in the 1930s. My grandmother, never formally educated past the sixth grade, made sure that her eight children knew the importance of education, speaking properly, memorizing poetry, and knowing scripture. My mother obtained four degrees: a Bachelor's degree in religion from Jarvis Christian College; a Master's degree in religion from Butler University; a Master's degree in social work from Indiana University; and a Ph.D. in social work from the University of Pittsburgh. She is an emeritus faculty member at Illinois State University. My mother knew that education was the only way out of poverty, segregation, and oppression. My mother is a Black woman. I have seen her fight the "system." I used to think she was old-fashioned and out of touch, but now I appreciate the depth of her wisdom, perspective, and understanding about the world that has allowed her to fight and survive with dignity, grace, and conviction of spirit for more than eighty years. I am writing for my mother.

My brother was the first student in the history of the Peabody Music Conservatory to earn certificates in piano, violin, and conducting. He became the first African-American to win a major international piano competition when he won first prize in the Naumburg International Piano Competition in 1992. I know the battles he fought to play classical music on a stage that Black males were only supposed to clean. I heard about the humiliation he endured from flight attendants who refused to believe he should fly first class. I know universities that refused to hire him because of his dreadlocks. He was even arrested because police assumed he was a thief, when he was running late to a music rehearsal with a violin case in his hand. I have seen him conquer and survive. I am writing for my brother.

Most importantly, though, I am writing for myself. I am writing to bring a particular journey to an end—a journey that started when I was a young girl and my father decided his children needed skills so that they could be independent from the "system" and the racism and sexism of America. We learned piano, violin, and tennis. We woke up at 4:00 a.m. every day with a focus on three values: hard work, discipline, and excellence. After graduating from high school at 16, I played professional tennis for two years with my father as my coach. When that season of my life ended, my journey into higher education began. It started at the University of Iowa. I majored in English and minored in philosophy and African-American studies. I learned to love the poetry, the novels, the history, and the philosophy of America. I enjoyed reading the works of American philosophers and reflecting on the relevance of their world view to my life. I absolutely loved learning about African and African-American history: the Egyptian pyramids, slavery, and the Civil Rights movement. I remember thinking that it seemed that the history of African-Americans ended with the Civil Rights movement. I remember wondering what our history was after 1968, after Dr. Martin Luther King, Jr., was assassinated. One of the reasons I am writing is because I know that history is still being created and that stories must still be told.

My education at Iowa taught me much about the role that Black men played in the history of the African-American experience. I remember feeling that Black women seemed like a footnote in the curriculum. My desire to see myself and to know myself led me to explore and examine the stories, the history, and the experiences of Black women through literature. I read Ntozake Shange, Lorraine Hansberry, Nikki Giovanni, Gwendolyn Brooks, Alice Walker, Toni Morrison, and Barbara Christian. As I read, I thought about who I was as a Black girl; what my goals in life should be; who I could influence; and how I could make a difference and improve the life experiences of Black people, and in particular, Black women. I wanted Black women not to be footnotes—marginalized, minimized, disenfranchised, and excluded—in education, in the curriculum, and in classrooms.

I was not sure, however, how to pursue my passion, so I continued my education. Thoughts of being an English professor motivated me to obtain a Master's Degree in literary studies at Iowa. The classic literary analytical approach was so discouraging and disheartening that my love of literature was almost destroyed. Realizing that I could not continue toward the Ph.D. in English, I left Iowa and headed to Vanderbilt University. I enrolled in a joint J.D./Ph.D. program in sociology. After I received a law degree and a Master's degree in sociology, I began to refine my thoughts for my dissertation. I had developed a consciousness around social justice, social policy, and the practical application of law to social issues. I had also begun to experience the challenges of interdisciplinary thought. I recognized the different ways that disciplines ask questions, define problems, and propose solutions. I wanted to combine the theoretical and methodological approaches of law, sociology, and literary analysis in one work. I struggled to find a topic that would enable me to pursue an interdisciplinary approach.

My search for a dissertation topic in the early 1990s led me to Detroit, the Male Academy project, and the Black male "crisis." It led me, though, to ask some questions that no one seemed to be asking: What about the Black girls? Didn't they have a story, a crisis, and a need? How were their issues being addressed? Why were there three Male Academies and no Female Academy? What was happening in Detroit with respect to Black females? In order to answer these questions, an interdisciplinary approach combining literary discourse analysis, legal analysis, and sociology was needed. Yet, as I began to refine my approach, I was greatly disturbed to discover that I had not read the work of a single Black female sociologist, nor had I been presented with the opportunity in any class to contemplate, reflect, or explore the issue of Black feminism. I mentioned my concern to Prof. Yvonne Newsome, my dissertation adviser, who was also an African-American woman. She told me about Prof. Patricia Hill Collins and suggested I read *Black Feminist Thought*. I read the book in two days. I was so excited, I wanted to call Patricia and thank her. Her book was the start of my journey into myself as a Black woman, as a sociologist, as a lawyer, as a teacher, as a wife, as a daughter, and as a mother.

At the same time as I was learning about Black feminism, I was also beginning to learn about Critical Race Theory, Critical Feminism, and Critical Race Feminism. I began to see that there were ways that law and sociology intersected in the study of issues affecting African-Americans. I began to see that race, gender, and class were intersecting concepts. Through a federal court of appeals judicial clerkship with Chief Judge Sam Ervin, III, I was fortunate to learn more about the judicial process, the role of judges, and the role of the law in affecting change in society. The clerkship experience helped informed my dissertation, "Where are the Black Girls: The Marginalization of Black Females in the Single-Sex School Debate in Detroit" (Pratt, 1997). I defended my dissertation, graduated, and started a career as a corporate lawyer—inadvertently setting aside the part of myself that was excited about the scholastic pursuit of knowledge.

Within three years, I was consumed by billable hours, a marriage, a miscarriage, the birth of two children, and the death of my father.

As I tried to become comfortable being a mother and a wife, I left the law firm and joined Vanderbilt University as the Assistant Secretary of the University, University Compliance Officer, and Legal Counsel. I also struggled to keep my passion alive through teaching classes in law, English, Sociology, and African-American history at Vanderbilt and Fisk University as an adjunct professor.

In the fall of 2006, I accepted a position at the University of Illinois in Champaign-Urbana as Assistant Provost and Associate Director in the Office of Equal Opportunity and Access, otherwise known as the Office of Fight for Freedom, according to my then seven-year-old daughter. I was privileged to report to two Black women—women who had navigated the university for almost 30 years and who could help guide me through and around the pitfalls of politics and pettiness. My first week of work I met four minority students who were upset about a stereotype party called "Tacos and Tequilas." Hosted by a White fraternity and White sorority, students dressed up in images that demeaned and dehumanized Latinos and Latinas. In the course of the year, I heard about other theme parties, including "Pimps and Ho's," and "Pilgrims and Indians." I watched the controversy about the University's mascot named Chief Illiniwek unfold as many students and faculty demanded the retirement of the symbol that perpetuated stereotypes about Native Americans, while others fought aggressively to keep it. I heard about religious intolerance, sexual orientation intolerance, and faculty bullying. I struggled to learn about affirmative action, equal employment opportunity, and disability accommodation. I saw and met people dealing with negative employment experiences and needing help. In the late spring, I was given an opportunity to develop a new initiative and create a campus culture of commitment to the values of diversity and inclusivity.

The spring of 2007 represented a turning point for me. In the midst of the cornfields of Champaign and my children's homework—lattice multiplication, partial quotient division, wordly wise, dioramas, coat hanger projects, and shoebox projects—I began again to contemplate my mission and meaning in life. The questions began again in my mind: Who was I? What did I want to do with my life? What did I have an obligation and responsibility to do as a Black woman? While as yet unable to answer these questions, several key events began to unfold around me to guide me to the answer.

First, the Rutgers' women's basketball team made the finals of the NCAA tournament. Their coach was Vivian Stringer, a Black woman whom I so admired when she coached at the University of

Iowa when I was a student there. Don Imus called the team, composed primarily of Black women, "nappy headed ho's" (Farhi, 2007). A few weeks later, I heard about Anucha Browne Sanders, a Black female team executive who successfully sued Isaiah Thomas and the New York Knicks basketball organization for sexual harassment and was awarded $11.6 million in punitive damages. The trial revealed the ways in which Black women were demeaned and dehumanized by Black men and often referred to as "bitches" (M. Martin, 2007). About a month later, the Bounty Hunter, a reality TV actor, called his son's black girlfriend a "nigger" (Dog the Bounty Hunter, 2007). Thus, in the summer of 2007, there were frequent discussions in the media and popular culture about the circumstances under which Black women could be referred to as "ho's, bitches, and niggers." As the children and I went to open house after open house to manage the boredom of small town Champaign, I continued to think about my role in life.

In the early fall, I heard about Anita Hill and learned that Clarence Thomas decided to write a book in which he, again, accused and attacked her (GMA Exclusive, 2007). My husband also asked me to join him in watching C-Span and a panel discussion about the state of Black America. On the panel I saw Tracey Sharpley-Whiting (2007) and learned that she had written a book about Black females and hip hop culture. I had met Tracey just before leaving Vanderbilt and knew that she was a Black woman all about calling life like it was. In the library looking for Tracey's book, I saw that Patricia Hill Collins (2006) had written a book about Black females, Black feminism, nationalism, and the intersecting identities of race, class, and gender. I also noticed that Johnetta Betsch Cole and Beverly Guy-Sheftall (2003) had written a book about Black females and issues of equality in the Black community.

It seemed all of sudden that the energy in the universe was calling me to tell the story of Black girls in Detroit. It was as if Black women were calling to me from the boxes where my dissertation, along with newspapers and journal articles, was buried and moved around for almost fifteen years through four homes and two states. It was as if the Black women were telling me that they still had a story to tell; that their story could still make a difference in the world; and that I needed to use the aloneness, loneliness, and quietness of Champaign-Urbana to begin to write and revise my dissertation to tell their story.

This book is their story, a story about Black females. It is also about Black males. I wrote about Black males because I feel passionate about the ability of Black males, even in the midst of the challenges that exist for them, to actualize their potential. One of the challenges is the criminal justice system. I have had Black men I know get arrested, and as a Black woman, I know what it means to try to gather bail to get them out of jail. I know the challenges that crack addiction and alcoholism present to Black men. I have seen the effects that discrimination in employment opportunities has on Black men's self-esteem and sense of self-worth. I have witnessed the difficulty that Black men with criminal records face in obtaining employment. I have heard Black men share the pain of incarceration when I taught college courses in prison through American Baptist College when inmates were eligible for Pell grants. I know the suffering of Black men because I have been surrounded by Black males as my father, my brother, my husband, my son, my friends, and my colleagues.

But, I also know the suffering of Black women. Black women suffer through their own and Black men's experiences with incarceration, with addiction, and with the consequences of limited employment opportunities. I have seen the suffering of Black women in prison and I have seen the suffering of Black women as visitors to prison to see their sons, their husbands, their boyfriends, their uncles, their grandfathers, and their brothers. Black girls suffer, as do Black boys, from the lack of positive Black male role models. Black women face the effects of emotional and physical abuse, including rape, from Black and White men. We suffer abuse from each other as Black women and from White women. Black women suffer and struggle spiritually, emotionally, and physically as we push forward with an almost unbearable load, often shouldering not only our own trials, but also those of Black men and Black children. It is because of these loads that we, as Black women, often bear alone, that I had to write.

I am writing so that our stories and histories as African-Americans, and in particular as African-American women and girls, can make a difference and influence education and social policy decisions. I am writing so that Black women and Black girls are not silenced, marginalized, and ignored. I am writing because of my responsibility as an educator to participate in the "community" and to contribute to the collective understanding about issues of education, race, class, and gender. Finally, I am writing, at Audre Lorde's (1984) suggestion, to channel my anger at injustice in society against Black women. I am writing to stop spirit murder and spirit injury of Black women (Wing, 1990).

I see myself as part of a long line of revolutionary Black feminist scholar-activists. I am simultaneously positioned in the academy as an insider and outsider (Collins, 1986). I am an administrator in the Office of the Chancellor and the Office of the Provost, working daily as an advocate for social justice in the areas of equal opportunity, affirmative action, and diversity. I am not formally a member of an academic unit. I am an adjunct faculty member in both the College of Law and the College of Liberal Arts and Sciences in the African-American Studies Department. I also work with students in the College of Education in education policy studies. I do not have any formal research support or a faculty mentor. I am unaffiliated and conducting a solitary intellectual pursuit, without the supportive structure of a department, but also without the constraints of such an affiliation. I have been formally trained in three academic disciplines: literary studies, sociology, and law. As a critical race feminist scholar, I am able to overcome the limitations of many scholars who only have formal training in one discipline. My hope is that as an outsider and insider, with an "in-between" status, I can share a unique perspective and approach to social justice scholarship that challenges the rigid disciplinary boundaries to offer a new way of thinking, analyzing, and solving social problems (Rabouin, 2000). My journey is reflected in John Hope Franklin's description of the scholarly path:

> The path of the scholar is at best a lonely one. In [her] search for truth [she] must be the judge of [her] findings and [she] must live with [her] conclusions. The world of the Negro scholar is indescribably lonely; and [she] must, somehow, pursue truth down that lonely path while, at the same time, making certain that [her] conclusions are sanctioned by universal standards developed and maintained by those who frequently do not even recognize [her] (quoted in Paul, 2003, p. 1).

It is this lonely road I have traveled that I hope serves as a bridge across my back for other scholar-activists to travel (Onwuachi-Willig, 2006). The pursuit of truth for women of color scholar-activists requires us to be within and outside of the academy. We recognize that education is a vehicle for social justice through scholarship. We realize, though, that "Black women can't afford to be merely theoretical" (Wing, 1990, p. 198). We must apply transdisciplinary theoretical and methodological work to social justice issues to ensure that the enhanced understanding of these issues in the education classrooms is translated to the policy arena, the classrooms, the churches, the social organizations, the political environment, including federal, state, and local governments, and all locations of oppression in society. An applied transdisciplinary approach incorporates the complexity that exists at the margins of disciplines into a central role to create the possibility for radical transformation of systems and structures that traditionally reproduce and perpetuate domination and oppression. This work, then, hopes to help other scholar-activists who may also be on the same lonely path realize that they are not alone.

This book is dedicated to Black women who have been advocates in big and small ways for social justice, fairness, opportunity, and excellence. Shawn and Crystal Garrett in Detroit (a Black mother and daughter) sacrificed so much for the cause of gender equality and educational opportunity for Black women. I have always admired Anita Hill and wanted to tell her so face-to-face. The awesome, amazing, and powerful spirits of Fannie Lou Hamer and Ida B. Wells have often motivated me. I appreciate Professor Yvonne Newsome, my advisor at Vanderbilt, who showed me by example how to be a Black female sociologist. My sister friend, Alfreda Burnett, a Black woman with a Ph.D. in pharmacology, showed me that Black women can get doctorates in the sciences. I dedicate this book to the Black women closest to me that have touched my life in wonderful and miraculous ways: my daughter, Raebekkah, who continues to inspire me with her spunk and determination to do it all and "be it all,"; and my mother, Mildred Pratt, who is a living example of the power of persistence, discipline, compassion, kindness, and love.

I am so grateful to Iyanla Vanzant, who I read every day and who continually creates the opportunity for me to ask and answer questions about myself on forty-day journeys to spiritual growth and empowerment. I cannot thank Adrien Wing, Professor of Law at the University of Iowa, enough for her encouragement and example of an amazing critical race feminist scholar over the past 25 years that I have known her. Johnetta Cole was a tremendous blessing one day when she took the time to call me and encourage me as a sister scholar. I saved her voicemail message for weeks and played it over and over to motivate myself. My mother's friend and colleague Stephanie Shaw, Professor of History at Ohio State University, took time away from her own scholarship to provide wonderful comments and suggestions. Pearl Cleage was so gracious to email me and tell me to keep writing. Kathleen Hollins, Robbie Loupe, and Debbra Sweat—Black women administrative assistants—inspire me everyday by their own life journeys; the grace that they bring to the workplace; and their willingness to serve. Larine Cowan and Elyne Cole,

Black women administrators at the University of Illinois, created the opportunity for me to share Thanksgiving, Christmas, Mother's Day, overnight sleepovers, and great parties with my mother. I thank them for bringing me to the quiet town of Champaign, where I could emerge from my self-absorbed, life-consumed routine to push and birth a story.

I also thank the Black men who have been an inspiration and strength for me. Several pastors prayed for me and my family: Reverend Edwin Sanders, Minister Kevin Colon, Pastor Claude Shelby, and Pastor B.J. Tatum. Two Black male law professors at Vanderbilt, Charles Watts and Robert Belton, encouraged me tremendously and were instrumental in the development of my legal career. Victor Rodgers, a Black chemical engineering professor at University of California Riverside, and his twin brother, Vincent Rodgers, a physics professor at Iowa, provided so much motivation by just doing their own thing. I appreciate my brother, Awadagin, for his life inspiration and example of being disciplined, having perseverance, and feeling obligated and responsible for developing and mastering a talent. My son, Emmanuel, always reminds me that God is with us. This journey would not be possible but for the constant presence, love, and support of Obadiah, my husband of 16 years. I thank him for all the amazing, wonderful, and perplexing ways in which he challenges my Black feminist self to be real! I thank him for cooking, for doing laundry, for washing my car, for picking our children up from school, and for loving me unconditionally.

Finally, I thank the many friends and colleagues who have assisted me along my higher education and legal career path. I am particularly grateful to Judge Sam Ervin, III, who created the opportunity for me to learn about the federal court system during my Fourth Circuit Court of Appeals clerkship. I also thank my fellow John Wade Scholars at Vanderbilt for their example of academic excellence. Sandy Barkan from the University of Iowa Honors Center gave me a personal loan to help me stay in school during a particularly difficult time at the University of Iowa and I am eternally grateful to her. Several colleagues at the University of Illinois have been extremely supportive: Antonia Darder, Jennifer Hamer, Cris Mayo, Wendy Haight, Chris Span, James Anderson, and Chris Benson. I must also extend my deepest gratitude to Burke Gertenschlager, editor, and Samantha Hasey, editorial assistant, at Palgrave Macmillan. But for Burke's willingness to act on my submission, this work would not have come to life. So, here it is. This is a story of why we must continue lifting as we climb, in order to uplift the race as a whole. This is a story about why we must study and think strategically and historically about how to empower and advance both Black men and Black women by lifting everyone collectively, and not sacrificing anyone. It is a call for activism to be informed by scholars and scholars to be informed by activism to ensure that social justice liberates without oppressing.

1.1 Overview

In 1991, the Detroit Public School system decided to implement an ambitious and aggressive education policy reform initiative for Black boys: three all-male Academies. The Academies, designed to serve boys from pre-school to fifth grade, had many unique programs. They included male role models, a rites of passage program, an Afrocentric curriculum, an emphasis on male responsibility, Saturday classes, extended hours, and student uniforms. The excitement and support of the Detroit community was reflected by over 1200 applications submitted for a total of 560 seats in the three Academies (Ray, 1991). Concerned that gender was being used as a discriminatory label for determining eligibility for enrollment, the National Organization for Women Legal Defense Fund (NOWLDF) and the American Civil Liberties Union (ACLU) filed a lawsuit on behalf of a Black mother and her daughter. Shawn and Crystal Garrett. In the *Garrett v. Detroit School Board* (1991) case, the organizations requested that the schools be prohibited from opening because they were unconstitutional. The federal district judge agreed and issued a preliminary injunction preventing the schools from opening. A settlement agreement, however, between the Detroit School Board and the plaintiffs allotted 136 out of 560 seats for girls (School board vows to fight for all-male school, 1991). After the settlement was publicly announced, an aggressive media campaign by the Detroit Male Academy supporters was launched. The campaign urged parents not to send their girls and to keep their girls at home. As of September 4, only 27 girls had applied (Wolffe, 1991; Twenty-seven female applicants, 1991; Walters, 1991). By the end of the first semester, only 39 girls were enrolled (Moore & Associates, 1993).

This book examines why only 39 girls enrolled. In the process, it asks and explores the following broad sociological and legal questions:

1. What factors should be considered in developing education policy reform initiatives involving access and opportunity?

2. What role do intersecting race, class, and gender identities play in social justice advocacy?
3. What is the relationship among the education system, the legal system, and the media in education policy reform initiatives?
4. How does the framing of a social issue, including the definition of a problem and the causes attributed, influence the outcome of social justice activism?
5. What strategies should individuals and organizations use to optimize the likelihood of success when engaging in social justice advocacy on behalf of a marginalized group?

This book also examines specific questions involving the relationship between Black males and Black females in the Detroit community. These questions include the following: Why was a legal right for Black girls not fully actualized? What role did the main actors—individuals and organizations involved in the Male Academy Project—play in the outcome? Why was the outcome seen by many as a victory for Black boys and the Black community? How could there be a "victory" for the "Black community" when others saw a loss of opportunities for Black girls? What lessons can be learned from the Male Academy initiative to inform social justice activism today?

In order to effectively explore answers to these questions and to understand what happened in Detroit, the lenses of different academic disciplines are required. This study fuses the theoretical and methodological tools from multiple disciplines to create a transdisciplinary analytical framework. The framework is used to analyze the Detroit Male Academy (DMA) initiative to demonstrate the power of language, words, arguments, and discourse to influence social and political outcomes.

This book is organized into two parts. The first part sets forth the transdisciplinary applied social justice model and the second part applies the model to the DMA initiative. In the first chapter, the relationship between the academic disciplines of law, sociology, political science, and history is explored. The synthesis of critical race theory, critical race feminism, feminist theory, social movement theory, collective action theory, and discourse analysis provides the theoretical and methodological tools for the model. The concepts of interwoven identities, interlocking social structures, power domains, and collective action frames constitute the key components of the model. Part I concludes with a detailed discussion of the DMA initiative, the narratives arising out of the discourse, and the relevance of transdisciplinary social justice to the initiative.

Part II is the application of the model to the DMA initiative. Chapter 2 examines the definition of the social problem in Detroit. The analysis reflects that the social problem was defined as the Black male crisis in society and within the education system, particularly as it was perceived in Detroit in the early 1990s. In the process of examining the problem, the social construction of race, gender, and class around issues of masculinity, patriarchy, and manhood is discussed. Federal and state education laws as they were in 1991 are also examined.

The third chapter discusses the causes of the social problem as reflected by the discourse of various social actors in Detroit. The causal attribution analysis of the discourse reveals the complex intersection of race, class, and gender issues. Females, as students, teachers, and mothers, were explicitly and implicitly mentioned as a cause of the social problem. Additionally, because of the advocacy role of the ACLU and NOWLDF in the legal case, White privilege and feminism were also implicated in the discourse. This chapter discusses the historical stereotypical portrayal of African-American women as matriarchs and saffires, the tension between race loyalty and gender advocacy for Black women, and the relationship between class and school choice.

The fourth chapter examines the proposed solution to the problem and the cause. The solution was essentially an all male, all-Black Academy. To achieve this end, the Detroit School Board, on one hand, entered into a settlement agreement with the ACLU and NOWLDF to permit girls to attend the Male Academies. At the same time, the Board and the Male Academy supporters participated in a communications initiative that asked the community to not honor the settlement agreement and to not send their girls to the school. This chapter analyzes the settlement agreement terms, the resulting media discourse, and the community's response to the proposed solution. The theme of Black nationalism and self-determination is also addressed as a response to the attributed causes of the problem: feminism and White privilege.

The final chapter focuses on the outcome. This chapter demonstrates how the social construction of race, class, and gender categories influenced the discourse and ultimately the outcome. This chapter illustrates how the exclusion of Black girls from the Male Academy justified and legitimized the supremacy and dominance of Black male interests. It documents the inability of political, civil rights, and feminist organizations to effectively challenge the racialized patriarchy and represent the interests of the Black mothers and their daughters.

This chapter also demonstrates that an understanding and recognition of the complex dynamics of race, class, and gender politics in the Black community is necessary for the interests of Black females to be effectively represented and protected. The antagonism of Black males and Black females to "feminism" and the absence of politically powerful Black feminist organizations contributed to the marginalization, disenfranchisement, and exclusion of Black women from an educational opportunity based not on their qualifications, but on their race, gender, and class status. This chapter shows that even after 20 years, the rhetoric and discourse about girls and boys in the education system continues to perpetuate long-standing ideologies about power and privilege. Although Detroit now has public single-sex college preparatory high schools—one for boys and one for girls—the on-going debate about single-sex schools requires continued vigilance to ensure that education policy reform debates promote equal opportunity regardless of intersecting race, gender, and class status. Transdisciplinary applied social justice model is a tool for social justice scholar-activists to use to implement successful strategies to address injustice and oppression in society. By remembering the Black girls in Detroit, this work encourages political and community activists, students and scholars, and other key players in local, regional, and national social policy debates to have increased sensitivity about the effect of discourse on the daily lives of politically and socially marginalized and disenfranchised groups.

PART I

SOCIAL JUSTICE IN THEORY: FRAMEWORK AND FOUNDATION

1

Transdisciplinarity

In the process of pursuing five degrees, working in higher education, and sending children to public schools, I have spent a great deal of time thinking about education system's structure and method of operation. As a result of conversations and personal experience, I have come to believe that the education system, both at the secondary and post-secondary level, is at a critical stage of justification and relevance. With significant technological advances every few months, former ways of doing, thinking, and being become obsolete not in decades, but in weeks. The information age of the Internet has made the current education system in America seem old and outdated, as existing textbooks fail to meaningfully address important and timely issues. Access to information is no longer limited to a select few educated teachers. It is available to anyone with cable TV or access to a computer and the Internet. Although minorities certainly lag behind in the digital age, on the whole, there is another level of expectation by students about their educational experience, and in particular, their higher education experience.

The relevance of education is challenged when the experience in the classroom fails to incorporate current events, new technologies, and new theories that are being analyzed and discussed daily in the media (Russell, Wickson, & Carew, 2008). The agility, flexibility, creativity, and versatility of the business and technology environment, where competition and profits drive innovation and serve as a propelling force for new ideas, can be contrasted with the inflexible bureaucracy of the education system. The education system, particularly higher education, often sits quietly, yet imposingly, and surprisingly content, with its rigid conformity to structure and status quo (Becher, 1989). This heavy bureaucratic monster is difficult to maneuver, difficult to change, and reluctant to explore transformative initiatives (McWilliam, Hearn, & Haseman, 2008). Its reluctance to incorporate change is reflected in the military-related language used to refer to disciplinary interactions in higher education: "turf wars; territories; bastions, fiefdoms; jealously guard; police; border traffic; intellectual migration; boundary crossing" (Tatar, 2005). As a result, higher education is often ill-equipped and slow to adapt to social problems, technological advances, or unfolding history (Webb, 2006). It also struggles with the best way to prepare its graduates for the responsibilities of a complex society and world that is integrated, interdisciplinary, and intertwined on many levels.

As a new generation of students pursues higher education, they expect that the knowledge they are receiving will be relevant and useful—that it will provide them with skills and ways of analyzing issues that can transform the world and not just affirm the status quo (Russell, Wickson, & Carew, 2008). Today's students do not just want history of hundreds and thousands of years ago; they want the history of last year, last month, and even last week when dynamic changes in climate, politics, business, and technology were occurring. They want a new theory and new way of understanding and explaining their world. As a result, the education system is struggling to respond to the speed demanded to keep education relevant and meaningful in today's media and Internet-driven society (Irvine, 1990).

The move within colleges and universities toward required study abroad programs, living-learning communities, public engagement, and community service reflects universities' slow and belabored response to the demand by its students to create a more meaningful relevance to the educational experience, integrating education with life experiences (Lattuca & Stark, 1995). Joint appointments represent another attempt to respond to new scholars who have interests in more than one discipline, because interdisciplinary departments and units rarely exist. These joint appointment scholars struggle to meet different, and at times, competing and conflicting requirements. Because the education system considers publication as legitimation, it is critical that the work of these interdisciplinary scholars is published (Buanes & Jentoft, 2009). However, university and other academic presses rarely have an interdisciplinary editor. Thus, interdisciplinary scholars are forced to define and limit their work to a particular discipline to be reviewed for publication, hoping that the selected disciplinary editor is familiar enough with multidisciplinary analysis to appreciate the intersecting boundaries and the scholarship used.

Even when universities want to encourage collaboration, the bureaucratic structure of how units are financed and funded often becomes a barrier to such multi-unit collaboration. These structural challenges, then, often prevent the higher education system from serving as a true conduit of social change.

Complicated and intertwined dynamics of social situations and problems cannot be comprehensively addressed with a uni-disciplinary approach. Although such an approach can advance understanding of particular aspects of a social problem, other perspectives and approaches that could inform problem solving are often ignored (Buanes & Jentoft, 2009; Francois, 2006; Webb, 2006). Understanding is limited and constrained by the theoretical and methodological constructs of a single discipline. Transdisciplinarity, however, is a potential solution. It is the use of multiple theories, methods, approaches, frameworks, and disciplines to understand, strategize, and implement transformative initiatives in society. The following section begins the discussion of transdisciplinarity.

1.1 Academic Disciplines

"Without knowledge from several academic disciplines, important problems in contemporary society cannot be solved" (Buanes & Jentoft, 2009). "Many of the most interesting and pressing problems can no longer be addressed exclusively from within established disciplines" (Webb, 2006). The "problem" of race, class, and gender is such a problem, requiring contributions from several disciplines. To appreciate the role of academic disciplines in contributing to problem-solving, we must first understand academic disciplines and the way in which they have been categorized (See Becher, 1989; Biglan, 1973; and Kolb, 1981 for an extensive discussion of different disciplines, professions, and how they can be categorized). Academic disciplines can be broadly categorized into three large groups: the natural and physical sciences, such as biology, chemistry, and physics; the social sciences, such as sociology, anthropology, political science, and psychology; and the humanities, such as philosophy, literature, languages, history, and religion (Becher, 1989; Lattuca & Stark, 1995). Arising from these disciplines are professions that utilize the knowledge from each discipline. For example, the profession of medicine utilizes knowledge from the sciences. The social work profession utilizes knowledge primarily from the social sciences and occasionally the sciences; law utilizes knowledge from humanities and the social sciences; and education utilizes knowledge from all disciplines and focuses on the application of knowledge in society. Spector and Kitsuse (1987, p. 65) suggest that sociology, psychology, social psychiatry, economics, and social work can be viewed as "ambitious social movements" and historical institutions. As such, the products of knowledge from these movements should not be seen as "reflections of the phenomena they purport to describe and explain" as much as products of the social movement and the objectives they seek to promote (Spector & Kitsuse, 1987, p. 67).

Disciplines, then, can be seen as institutions and as "powerful self-organising systems of signification and communication" that are socially constructed and maintained with regulatory, cognitive, and normative structures, systems, and activities (Webb, 2006; Buanes & Jentoft, 2009, p. 447). The regulatory system within an academic discipline involves the rules that govern the discipline. This includes length of study requirements, funding systems, publication requirements, the peer review process, career paths, and recruitment procedures. The rules, both formal and informal, are often perpetuated through a long training process (Buanes & Jentoft, 2009). The cognitive system relates to the knowledge foundation within a discipline, such as the unit of analysis, the cause and effect relationships, and the concepts, theories, and models of the discipline (Buanes & Jentoft, 2009, p. 449). This principle focuses on the theoretical and methodological foundations of the discipline. If a discipline is also a profession, disciplinary hegemony can form where the knowledge is not only created within a discipline, but also perpetuated through its practice in society, thereby serving to legitimate and validate the discipline. The normative element involves the norms and values undergirding the discipline. These are expectations of conduct as communicated through formal and informal mechanisms, such as mentoring relationships, collegial relationships, associations, and organizations. This element maintains the unique identity of the discipline. This maintenance of identity is critical for the perpetuation of the discipline. The academic disciplines are essentially structures within structures. They exist within the larger structures of academic departments, colleges, universities, and the higher education system. Their existence within the higher education system, however, creates an interesting paradox.

The paradox of higher education is that though ostensibly a portal to "unlimited" knowledge, it is structured in a way that limits and constrains access to knowledge for students and faculty. Rigid degree requirements, including required classes for majors in academic disciplines, general education credits, and college-level residency requirements often create an educational experience for students that legitimizes and affirms existing paradigms of thought, rather than encouraging the development of new paradigms that could challenge and dismantle traditional boundaries. Similarly for faculty, there are few opportunities within the academy for the creation of transformative knowledge based on the integration of academic disciplines. The relative inflexibility of academia perpetuates existing standards and traditions. This includes the curricula, the teaching methods, the program operations, and the academic leadership structure of deans, tenured faculty, and department heads. According to Becher (1989, p. 71), the "jealous guardianship of the status quo, especially among the more senior...colleagues, acted as a barrier against promising innovations." These senior colleagues are members of an elite, powerful, and exclusive society. The membership criteria is based on being validated by existing members, similar to a sorority or fraternity. New potential members must be legitimized and affirmed by existing members based on their ability to speak the language of the society or discipline and their ability to look, act, and think the way of the current members. If the new proposed initiates are willing to be inculcated by the existing members and are able to meet the criteria, they, too, become members. If not, they are forced to leave the institution, and sometimes, the academic discipline (J. Lee, 2004).

Socialization into this community begins in the undergraduate years and continues through the graduate process, where the new initiate learns to be technically competent within the discipline, loyal to colleagues in the discipline, and committed to the norms, traditions, values, beliefs, rules of conduct, and the communication styles of the discipline and the academy (Lattuca & Stark, 1995). The culture of the academy includes a commitment to the existing validation structure and the constraints of the tenure system. The tenure system rarely encourages scholars to step outside of the norms of a discipline and its well-established, theoretical, and methodological paradigms. It controls and defines through impermeable and inflexible rules who advances and what theories are legitimated. This structure involves senior scholars who communicate with peer senior scholars through letters of reference, scholarly research, and participation in scholarly communities, societies, and organizations. These senior scholars, in turn, train junior scholars, who in turn, train graduate and undergraduate students to think, write, teach, and work in the narrow, prescribed, legitimized, and verified ways of the discipline. Through this system, scholars are created, recognized, and accepted as members of the community based on their ability to demonstrate mastery of the genre and the "disciplinary voice" (Matsuda & Tary, 2007). In this way, they legitimize their "disciplinary identity" and "disciplinary becoming" (Dressen-Hammouda, 2008, p. 234). A seven-year tenure system, preceded by a five- to seven-year doctoral process, perpetuates an academic discipline by training new members who must justify their membership and demonstrate their mastery through publications.

According to Whitley (1984), this structure does not, by definition, create the possibility of radical change. "Radical intellectual change—such as is implied by the term 'revolution'—is improbably where work goals and procedures are relatively uniform and stable and the hierarchy of problems and areas is reproduced and controlled by a strong authority structure" (quoted in Becher, 1989, p. 71). Revolutionary change within an existing discipline must meet five requirements, according to economist Johnson (quoted in Becher, 1989, p. 73). First, it must attack and reverse the current theory "with a new but academically acceptable analysis" (Becher, 1989, p. 73). It must also appear new, while still retaining as much as possible the validated components of the existing theory. It must be presented in a manner that appeals to both senior and junior colleagues in the discipline, despite the differences between their years of experience and approach to the discipline. It must offer a new methodology "more appealing than those currently available," and "provide a new and important empirical relationship" (Becher, 1989, p. 73). These requirements, if met, have the potential for transforming not only scholarship, but society.

The desire to push the limits of disciplines has resulted in three different yet often intermingled concepts: interdisciplinarity, multidisciplinarity, and transdisciplinarity. According to Francois (2006, p. 618), interdisciplinarity "should better be used to describe a specific, more or less integrative, interrelation between two disciplines." Biochemistry and astrophysics are two separate disciplines whose expert knowledge is critical to advancing scientific knowledge and creating a synthesis between the disciplines (Webb, 2006). The evolutionary progression moves from interdisciplinarity to multidisciplinarity. Multidisciplinarity involves collaboration among specialists in different disciplines who may come together to solve a particularly complex problem, necessitating input from varying disciplines and approaches (Francois, 2006; Russell, Wickson, & Carew, 2008).

Environmental challenges, for example, must often be addressed by both scientist and social scientist. Finally, transdisciplinarity represents the most comprehensive approach, involving "a growing set of growingly interconnected concepts and models, mainly about ways of interactions among elements and the resulting coherence in complex situations and systems" (Francois, 2006, p. 619). It is an approach that cuts across traditional academic boundaries.

A transdisciplinary approach is an applied, problem-solving, and heterogeneous approach, as contrasted to an academic and homogeneous approach (Webb, 2006). The goal is to "test the boundaries; to find openings that are themselves immanent in the creative tensions that exist between the disciplinary flows and networks of information; and in the interstices and `undecidables' that emerge within a disciplinary knowledge" (Webb, 2006). Transdisciplinary research requires comprehensive mastery of multiple disciplines. To be a true practitioner of transdisciplinary research, one must know each field through disciplinary and genre mastery, and be able to apply foundational concepts from different disciplines to phenomena in society (Dressen-Hammond, 2004). Transdiciplinarity breaks, "transgresses and transcends disciplinary boundaries," with the potential for creativity and innovation (Buanes & Jentoft, 2009, p. 461; McWilliam, Hearn, & Haseman, 2008). The field of critical race studies is an ideal area for transdisciplinary research.

Critical race studies is a multi-disciplinary activist-oriented approach to law exploring the possibility of the legal system serving as a mechanism for radical and transformative social and economic change (Crenshaw, Gotanda, Peller, & Thomas, 1995). Critical race studies incorporates critical race theory (CRT). CRT examines racism in the American legal system and the "legal manifestation of white supremacy and the perpetuation of the subordination of people of color" (Wing, 2003, p. 5), including the social construction of race and racism in the legal system. There are several common themes in critical race theory. It recognizes the permanence and pervasiveness of racism in American society. Dominant claims of ahistoricism, objectivity, neutrality, colorblindness, and merit in the law are challenged. The experiential knowledge of people of color is affirmed and acknowledged through a contextual and historical analysis of the law and its operation within society.

CRT has as its objective working toward eliminating racial oppression as part of a broader goal of ending all forms of oppression (Dixson & Rousseau, 2006, p. 4). It has a social critique focus and commitment to transformation and emancipation (Guba & Lincoln, 1994; Creamer, 2003; Toma, 1996). It encourages the building of social movements and connecting scholar and community (Onwuachi-Willig, 2009). CRT emphasizes discourse, stories, words, language, and narrative. Although CRT has its roots in the law, it is being extended to other disciplines and professions. CRT is informing education theory, research, pedagogy, curriculum, and policy (Yosso, 2006, p. 171).

Critical race feminism (CRF) builds on critical race theory. It places the role, experiences, and narratives of women of color in the legal system in the center of the analysis. It focuses on the multiple identities of women and how their experiences are a product of those identities. Critical race feminism, in fact, can be seen as a field of study that blends several other related fields of study: critical legal studies, critical race theory, gender studies, race and ethnic studies, and communications studies. Critical race and critical race feminist scholarship provide a legal framework for examining the complex effects of race, class, and gender categories on women of color (Austin, 1989, 1992; Barnes, 1990; Crenshaw, 1989; Delgado & Stefancic, 1993; Harris, 1990; Herbert, 1988; Scales-Trent, 1989; P. Smith, 1992; J. Williams, 1991). CRF challenges the traditional legal scholarship's focus on analyzing a legal case based on the outcomes of prior related court cases, ascertaining and examining the nuanced differences of each analysis based on the unique facts of those cases, and then applying the constitutional and statutory interpretations reflected in the past decisions to the new facts. This process rarely discusses the operation of power, systems of domination, or social justice activism. Thus, a legal approach alone to a complex social problem will rarely result in a full understanding of the dynamics necessary to create transformative change. In fact, the field of law has historically been structured to allow only for minimal and marginal advances and changes. It is because of the limitations of traditional legal analysis that CRF emerged as a necessary lens to analyze the experiences of women of color.

CRF often incorporates a narrative or storytelling component and a focus on praxis—being involved in the solutions to problems that affect women of color through creating "comprehensive and practical strategies" (Wing & Willis, 1999; Wing, 2003). Wing and Willis (1999) note "Critical race feminists are concerned with practice, not just theory. They address actual needs and emphasize practical applications in an effort to bring about change and progress within society." African-American critical race feminist scholars recognize that their outsider status in the academy allows them to "infuse legal constructs with new power and meaning" (Rabouin, 2000, p. 597) and to encourage the law to be used to focus on justice with a moral sensitivity. CRF endorses a multidisciplinary and interdisciplinary approach with a critical historical methodology.

> Critical race feminism is also multi-disciplinary, drawing from a wide array of legal and non-legal fields. One goal of critical race feminism is to synthesize and utilize these bodies of knowledge in a theoretical analysis to create comprehensive and practical strategies which address the needs of our communities. (Wing & Willis, 1999)

The challenge, however, of interdisciplinarity is reflected by Wing's (2003, p. 6) acknowledgement that the use of other academic disciplines is "still embryonic in nature as most legal scholars only hold law degrees and may be self taught in other fields."Critical race feminism does, however, draw heavily from Black feminism, which has foundations in sociology and literary studies.

Black feminist scholarship examines the multiple oppressions that Black women experience as a result of their race, gender, and class statuses and the consequences of those oppressions, including exclusion and the silencing of their voices (Barnett, 1993; Collins, 1991; Guy-Sheftall, 1995; hooks, 1981, 1990; King, 1992; Marable, 1983). Black feminism emphasizes that the multiple, varied, and dynamic oppressions faced by Black women must be viewed in an interlocking, intersecting, matrix-like manner, rather than as simply additive and hierarchical (Brewer, 1989, 1993; Collins, 1991, Deitch, 1993; Ferguson, 1990; Gregory, 1993; Griffin & Korstad, 1995; Hamer & Neville, 2001; hooks, 1981, 1984; Howard-Hamilton, 2003; Hull, Scott, & Smith, 1982; King, 1988, 1992; Sacks, 1989; L. Williams, 1984). Black feminism incorporates concepts of intersecting identities, interlocking social structures and systems, and personal experiences and stories into its analytical framework. The strength of a Black feminist framework lies in its ability to facilitate an analysis of the experiences of Black women as reflected by the text, language, discourse, and words used in particular events or contexts. It also recognizes the importance of examining the "local and historical context" in which experiences unfold (Ken, 2008, p. 171).

Black feminism draws heavily from sociology, history, and political science. The discipline of history is often incorporated into both sociology and political science (Griffin, 1995; American Historical Association, 1998). Political science and sociology frequently use historical events and perspectives to explain current phenomena, as well as structural and systemic changes in society. Sociology provides a method for analyzing the relationship among individuals, groups, and organizations as influenced and affected by the intersection of race, gender, and class. Sociology and political science facilitate an examination of the relationship between power and outcomes, both social and political, within systems and structures in society (American Political Science Association, n.d.; American Sociological Association, n.d.). Both disciplines are used to examine issues of oppression, including those based on race, gender, class, religion, ethnicity, and nationality, among others. These are disciplines with roots in praxis and action (Pascale, 2006). A transdisciplinary approach through CRF using multiple disciplines furthers the objectives of Black feminism through revolutionary transformative scholarship that challenges rigid boundaries, exposes the artificial lines, forces questions to be asked from a different standpoint, and produces answers that have the opportunity to transform society by informing both scholarship and the professions that can apply the scholarship, such as education, social work, and law. Black feminism's goal is to change society through theory and praxis (Zerai & Salime, 2006). A transdisciplinary approach to social justice, however, cannot merely be "rebellion against orthodoxy" (Buanes & Jentoft, 2009, p. 453). It must be "legitimate, meaningful, and inspirational for both producers and users of research" (Buanes & Jentoft, 2009, p. 453). It requires the tools of a scholar-activist.

Transdisciplinary scholar-activists must have courage and maturity (Buanes & Jentoft, 2009). They must have ambition and passion about developing new ways of seeing ideas, "either a syntheses of existing perspectives or as genuinely novel ones" (Buanes & Jentoft, 2009, p. 451). Scholar-activists must incorporate the concept of "innovative action," and a real-world problem focus through an evolving methodology (Buanes & Jentoft, 2009; Russell, Wickson, & Carew, 2008). A scholar-activist must "unearth, disrupt, and transform existing ideological and/or institutional arrangements" (Theoharis, 2007, p. 224). A social justice activist or lawyer must not only understand the law and relevant cases, but also the history, values, and power dynamics of the community and the way racism, sexism, and classism operate within the community. All of this is consistent with the goal of "transformative pedagogy," which is to "emasculate the legal imbalance resulting from giving effect to the bad faith of unspoken privilege" through the consideration of the social context in which the legal problem is asserted (Rabouin, 2000).

Critical race scholars recognize the value of multi-consciousness—seeing what others claim doesn't exist, recognizing different facts, and raising issues previously ignored (Rabouin, 2000, p. 610–611). The value of this multi-consciousness is in "being able to see and use multiple perspectives, including that of the oppressed, to build creative and transforming praxis" (Rabouin, 2000, p. 611). Black women, particularly Black women law professors, have often felt a heightened level of responsibility to "create new frameworks of legal relevance" and to use our "experience to fashion meaningful praxis" and social policy (Rabouin, 2000, p. 600; Wing, 1990).

Black women law professors are also uniquely positioned to undertake this challenge because of our outsider status in the academy and experiences of multi-consciousness that "enable us to discern meaning from not only the written text, but also the often unspoken subtext." We can use these insights to inform scholarship and practice (Rabouin, 2000, p. 597). Additionally, our lived experiences require negotiating boundaries and borders, challenging the status quo of institutional systems and structures, being creative and innovative, and thinking strategically and practically to achieve social and political outcomes. On the micro and macro levels, our multiplicative identity informs both scholarship and activism. This is also consistent with the charge of Black feminists. Black Radical Feminism (Hamer & Neville, 2001) calls on feminists to offer theoretically grounded strategies with the objective of eliminating oppression through an "integrated analysis and practice" (Ransby, 2000). Transdisciplinary applied social justice (TASJ) is one such strategy using race, gender, and class studies; critical race studies; critical race feminism; and Black feminism (Dolling & Hark, 2000). TASJ is the application of concepts, theories, and methodologies from multiple academic disciplines to social problems with the goal of addressing injustice in society and improving the experiences of marginalized individuals and groups. The next section sets forth a TASJ model.

1.2 A Social Justice Model

Social justice involves "disrupting and subverting arrangements that promote marginalization and exclusionary processes" (Theoharis, 2007). According to Goldfarb and Grinberg, this can involve "actively engaging in reclaiming, appropriating, sustaining, and advancing inherent human rights of equity, equality, and fairness in social, economic, education, and personal dimensions" (quoted in Theoharis, 2007, p. 223). It involves the implementation of strategic solutions, informed by multiple disciplines, to minimize the effects of injustice toward individuals and groups based on their intersecting identities as a result of the operation of systems and structures of oppression and power. It affirms the value of the "search for justice at the margins of the legal epicenter" (Rabouin, 2000, p. 594).

By blending historical, political, legal, and sociological analysis, a framework can be created for social justice activism. The framework must take into consideration differences in "purposes, standards, methods, frameworks, values, audiences, vocabulary, etc., between and among scholars working in various paradigms" (Toma, 1996, p. 30–31). A paradigm can be seen as a framework that specifies "appropriate problems for study and appropriate methods for studying those problems" (Lattuca & Starks, 1995, p. 317). Recognizing the application of common paradigms among different disciplines creates an approach to transdisciplinary work that can lay a "foundation for change" (Toma, 1996, p. 31). The paradigm of TASJ includes a theoretical foundation, a methodological approach, and a component of praxis. The theoretical foundation draws heavily from history, sociology, and political science, recognizing that social justice often involves advocacy on behalf of historically disenfranchised and marginalized populations (Pascale, 2006). It includes the concepts of power, individual and group interwoven identities, and interlocking social structures, institutions, and systems. Analyzing these concepts requires a flexible methodology. Methodology can be defined as "the process or approach to creating or discovering knowledge" (Creamer, 2003, p. 450). Because experiences are often institutionalized through discursive structures (Ken, 2008), discourse analysis is one method by which these experiences can be examined. Discourse analysis allows the voices of those engaged in experiences of activism and oppression to tell their story. Finally, praxis is the concept of theory in action. Social movement theory and the concept of collective action frames informs the praxis component of TASJ.

The foundational component of TASJ is theory. The central component of the theory involves individuals. The individuals who are often most in need of social justice activism are minorities and females with lower income levels, marginal family relationships, fewer employment opportunities, and lower educational attainment. Individuals have membership status in multiple groups based on their identities. The historical experiences of these individuals reflects their marginalized treatment as a result of their multiple status memberships within one or more of the following categories: race, gender, class, ethnicity, family relationships, language ability, disability, residential location, employment and education levels, and other factors by which individuals identify or are identified by others (Scott, 1986). Race, gender, class, nationality, and religion are frequently the most salient issues in social justice as these categories and identities are associated with particular ideologies, perspectives, values, beliefs, and stereotypes. Ken (2007) notes that race, class, and gender have assumed a dominance and primacy in both sociology and women's studies, often marginalizing other equally important identities. This marginalization, however, does not mean that the principles applied to race, class, and gender cannot also be transferred to other identities.

Because identities are socially constructed, they have varied meanings, effects, and salience in different social contexts (Anthias, 1990; Griffin & Korstad, 1995; Higginbotham, 1992; Ken, 2007; Lei, 2003; Omi & Winant, 1986). The dynamic nature of these categories is reflected by concepts such as "gendered ethnicity" and the "racialization of gender" (Anthias & Yuval-Davis, 1992). Class can be experienced in racially specific or gender specific ways (Sacks, 1989). Gender can be racially specified and race can be gender specified (Ferguson, 1990). For example, Hunter and Davis (1992) and Whitehead and Reid (1992) examined the construction of gender with respect to Black men's conceptions of manhood and the relationship between gender constructs and social issues. Understanding race, class and gender as dynamic, "mutually constituting," fluid, interdependent, historical social constructions, social locations, intersecting processes, and structures is important for effectively addressing the implications of racism, sexism, and classism on the life changes of oppressed groups (Ferguson, 1990; James & Busia, 1993; Ken, 2007; Omi & Winant, 1987; Ransby, 2000, p. 1219). Implicitly embedded within these identities are the concepts of power relations, privilege, entitlement-conferred dominance, unearned advantage for particular groups, and a corresponding disadvantage for other groups. Ken (2008) uses sugar as a metaphor for race, class, and gender issues, recognizing that like sugar, race, class, and gender are products. As products, they "encompass categorization schematas, processes, sets of embedded relations, histories, structural locations, practices, social institutions, distortions, products of discourse, elements of symbolic representations, structural arrangements, tropes, dimensions of identity, and opportunities to express power, get produced, used, occasionally in isolation but usually in interconnected ways" (Ken, 2008, p. 153). Race, class, and gender are also a tool for delineating boundaries in society (Vojdik, 2002).

Understanding these identities is important because the life experiences of people of color often involve the denial of a social, political, or legal right based on their multiple, socially constructed, and interwoven identities. Their experiences are affected by the operation of power domains. Effective social justice activism requires a clear understanding of power and the way in which power operates at the macro and micro levels. Collins (2000) notes that one model of understanding power involves a dominant group oppressing another group. It is a model of "permanent oppressors and perpetual victims" (Collins, 2000, p. 274). This model, however, fails to incorporate the complex way power is used and operates. Power can also be viewed "not as something that groups possess, but as an intangible entity that circulates within a particular matrix of domination and to which individuals stand in varying relationships" (Collins, 2000, p. 274). Collins encourages seeing these as complementary approaches, rather than competing ones.

There are four interrelated domains of power, with each serving a particular purpose: the structural, the disciplinary, the hegemonic, and the interpersonal. The structural domain focuses on the organizational aspects of power, the disciplinary domain focuses on the management of power, the hegemonic domain serves to legitimize and justify oppression, and the interpersonal domain influences the day-to-day micro-level interactions between individuals (Collins, 2006, p. 276). The relevance of these domains lies in their ability to explain the experiences of individuals and consequently to inform activism and social justice.

The structural domain focuses on macro-level interlocking social institutions in society. These institutions include the education system, the legal system, the political system, the economic system, the financial system, and the media and communications industry, as well as family and religious institutions. These institutions are sites where domination and subordination of groups and individuals occurs. Though they are sites of oppression, they also represent opportunities for activism. These institutions do not operate in isolation from one another. They operate as an integrated system with varying levels of influence in different contexts. Social justice activism must understand this domain of power to determine the effectiveness of particular initiatives. Given the permanence and strength of these institutions, societal change occurs most often through large-scale social movements, such as the civil rights movement, war, or revolutions. Effective change at this level requires a detailed and specific understanding of each social institution and its relationship to other social institutions and their operational structures.

The operational structure of a social institution is associated with the disciplinary domain of power. The disciplinary domain of power refers to the bureaucratic and internal structure of institutions designed to discipline, control, and monitor individuals and groups who operate within social institutions (Collins, 2000). This domain includes automated systems that impersonally operate, and protocols, procedures, rules, by-laws, and practices that are often difficult to find and access and, as a result, difficult to challenge. The disciplinary domain embodies the laws and regulations that control and manage individuals, organizations, and society by defining consequences for conduct that is inconsistent with defined norms. This domain also includes the organizational hierarchy of individuals with varying levels of decision-making authority within an organization or institution. In the education institution, these decision makers include teachers, principals, PTA presidents, school superintendents, school board members, school social workers, and school counselors. In other contexts, they can include preachers, legislators, chief executive officers, foremen, team leaders, and managers. These individuals have authority to create and implement rules, codes of conduct, and written and unwritten operational protocols, practices, and procedures within their institutions. Intermediaries within the same domains can serve as access barriers to those with ultimate decision-making authority. These intermediaries are often the assistant to the director, the administrative secretary, the middle manager, the associate director, or even an assistant director. Many of these individuals exercise a great deal of authority, often delegated by senior management to implement formal and informal policies, practices, and procedures.

The disciplinary domain is designed to perpetuate, advance, and institutionalize relationships of power, privilege, dominance, and advantage. Consequently, it is also designed to discourage and dissuade those interested in social justice activism by making it difficult to know where and how to enter the fight, to know the opponent, and to understand the rules of engagement. As a result, challenges to this domain remain extremely difficult. The disciplinary domain is implemented through the operation of the interpersonal domain.

The interpersonal domain is the micro-level "day-to-day practices of how people treat one another" (Collins, 2000, p. 286). This domain includes one-on-one relationships within social institutions: student-student and student-teacher interactions in schools; doctor-patient and nurse-patient interactions in hospitals; spousal, sibling, and parental relationships in families; and co-worker and supervisor relationships in the workplace. These interactions often involve those in authority and those who are marginalized based on their interwoven identities and membership status in social groups. Policies, procedures, and practices are implemented by individuals in the interpersonal domain. This domain also involves the opportunity to perpetuate, mitigate, substantiate, undermine, legitimate, or challenge particular values, ideas, ideologies, and attitudes that are part of the hegemonic domain of power.

The hegemonic domain of power justifies the practices and operations within the structural and disciplinary domains through the perpetuation of dominant ideology, culture, and consciousness (Collins, 2000). The dominant ideology often includes values, beliefs, ideas, and stereotypes about particular groups in society. This domain can be seen through the operation of religious institutions and ideologies related to the value and roles of men and women in society. It can also be seen in school curriculum and the ideas that are taught and perpetuated in schools, including what is often omitted related to the achievements of women and minorities, and what is included about dominant cultures and their role in society, history, and culture. The operation of this domain is reflected by the way in which the media perpetuates, communicates, directs, influences, and often distorts the reality of particular social groups and influences ways of thinking. Families are another mechanism through which this domain of power operates, as families perpetuate and pass down values, ideas, and expectations from one generation to another.

It is within this domain that the role of history is critical. The academic field of history intersects with the hegemonic domain by serving as a vehicle through which values, ideas, and ideologies are perpetuated and legitimated through time. The domain is an intangible space that is impacted and defined by past events, ideas, and beliefs that have been given credence and are often labeled as "common sense" (Pascale, 2006). Embedded within this domain is the global history related to supremacy, imperialism, colonialism, and slavery. It includes the ideologies of separation and superiority between dominant and subordinate groups, such as racism and sexism. "The significance of the hegemonic domain of power lies in its ability to shape consciousness via the manipulation of ideas, images, symbols, and ideologies" (Collins, 2000, p. 284). Social justice activism within this domain is about dismantling and challenging existing ideologies, as well as constructing new ideologies and viewpoints. These four domains of power play a critical role in social justice activism by revealing the complexity of the relationship among individuals, their life experiences, social institutions, and their operational structures.

These domains also inform our understanding of academic disciplines. Disciplines can be viewed as institutions located within the structural domain of power. The domains match well with three pillars identified by Buanes and Jentoft (2009): the regulatory pillar, the rules that govern disciplines, serves as the disciplinary domain; the cognitive pillar, involving the knowledge foundation of disciplines, is consistent with the hegemonic domain; and the normative pillar of norms and values of disciplines is influenced by the interpersonal domain of collegial and professional relationships. The power of these domains illustrates the difficulty associated with transdisciplinarity, which must try to break through multiple domains to facilitate the potential for radical transformation through a comprehensive theoretical and methodological approach. The theoretical foundation is grounded in sociological concepts of individuals and groups with intersecting identities influencing and influenced by domains of power. It requires an appropriate and complementary methodological strategy that can analyze both the experiences of individuals in institutions as a result of their race, class, and gender status, as well as the operation of power domains (Ken, 2008).

Discourse analysis is a qualitative methodological technique that supports TASJ. Discourse analysis is a tool that can be used for historical, sociological, and legal analysis of texts because it focuses on the structure of arguments, the categories constructed, the meanings invoked, and the historical context in which the text was produced (Deitch, 1993). Noting the "broad multidisciplinary relevance of discourse analysis," Van Dijk (1993, p. 93) discusses the role of discourse in political science, law, sociology, anthropology, communication studies, and psychology. Discourse analysis provides a theoretical and descriptive account of the structures and strategies of discourse, and their relationship to cognitive, social, cultural, and historical context (Van Dijk, 1993, p. 96). The strength of discourse analysis is that it enables a researcher to deconstruct language to expose "what is or is not said," to look "at silences and gaps," to dismantle dichotomies, and to analyze disruptions (Feldman, 1995, p. 51).

Scholars have used discourse analysis to understand the relationship between intersecting categories of oppression within a specific social context. It is especially useful for studying groups situated at the bottom of social hierarchies. It allows a researcher to deconstruct language on "power abuse" by dominant groups by analyzing discriminatory discourse—the "derogation, intimidation, inferiorization, and exclusion in everyday conversations, institutional dialogues, letters, evaluative reports, laws, and other forms of institutional text and talk" (Anthias, 1990; Anthias & Yuval-Davis, 1992; Higginbotham, 1992; Van Dijk, 1993, p. 101). For example, Van Dijk (1993, p. 94) stresses the importance of studying political, educational, legal, and media discourse as a means to "express, signal, confirm, describe, legitimate, or enact ethnic dominance."

> Minorities can be excluded from the communication context, inferiorized, problematized, falsely accused, threatened, marginalized, or derogated in majority discourse about them, for instance, by expressing and persuasively conveying at all levels of discourse models that feature lack of respect, the misattribution of negative properties, and general instantiations of ethnic stereotypes and prejudice. (Van Dijk, 1993, p. 118)

The use of discourse analysis is not limited to the ethnic context. It can be used to study gender and class dominance, as well as the interactive effects of race, gender, and class. For example, scholarly writing on Clarence Thomas and Anita Hill analyzed the content of the congressional hearings and the media coverage to shed light on the complex race and gender dynamics between Black males and Black females (Chrisman and Allen, 1992; Morrison, 1992; Smitherman, 1995). Similarly, Deitch (1993) conducted a textual analysis of the congressional debate on the gender amendment to Title VII, analyzing the content and presentation of arguments, and exploring the manner in which race, class, and gender operated in complex and contradictory patterns to shape social policy. She noted

> The way in which race, gender, and class categories are constructed in political discourse reinforces inequalities, obscures common interests, and denies the experience of many women (and men). When the dominant and the oppositional discourse tend to construct women,

> Blacks, and labor as separate and distinct categories or constituencies, the underlying interconnections are distorted. Part of the task of a feminist analysis of interlocking systems is to deconstruct that discourse. (Dietch, 1993, p. 21)

Discourse analysis has been used to detail the instability and heterogeneity of racial categories and meanings (Dominguez, 1987; Gates, 1987; Goldberg, 1990; Gregory, 1993) and the complex ways in which ideologies of race, class, gender, and nationalism intersect in the construction of social identities and hierarchies (Anthias, 1990; Balibar, 1990; Hall, 1980; hooks, 1990; Sacks, 1989; B. Williams, 1989). In Gregory's (1993, p. 32) study of the community activism by Black mothers in a housing project, he argued that "the manner in which they [the residents] were discursively framed and strategically addressed hindered, if not precluded, the active participation of the residents as subjects in the process of 'neighborhood stabilization'." Gregory illustrated how complex, conflicting, and contradictory race and gender ideologies often positioned Black women in the equivocal situation of both resisting and supporting existing power relations. Studying the "local" context informs the larger global dominant perspective (Ken, 2007). It facilitates understanding about how "hegemonic notions of race, class, and gender are embedded in our cultural discourse in ways that continually reproduce conditions of exploitation and inequality" (Ore, 2006, referencing Pascale, 2006). Interpreting and deconstructing discourse about race, gender, and class provides insights into the interlocking nature of systems and ideologies of oppression and exclusion. By focusing on hidden meanings, researchers are able to document the varied, intertwined, and even contradictory responses to the multiple oppressions of race, class, and gender. These responses are often evident in discourse about policy, particularly policy involving the experiences of marginalized groups within social institutions.

Policy discourse analysis is a particular type of discourse analysis designed to "respond to research questions related to the discursive shaping to policy problems, solutions, and images; and the ways in which discourses shape and re/produce subject positions" (Allan, 2008, p. 54). Policy discourse analysis is uniquely suited to examine policy texts and respond to the following research questions: (1) "What are the policy problems and solutions identified in the policy documents? (2) What images emerge related to constituencies affected by the policy? (3) What are the discourses employed to produce particular images? and (4) What subject positions are re/produced via these discourses?" (Allan, 2008, p. 163). Policy discourse analysis is informed by three "frames of inquiry." The interpretive frame seeks to understand policy through a textual analysis of policy documents. The critical frame seeks to understand and critique social inequality based on race, gender, ethnicity, and other differences between individuals with the objective of achieving social and political change. The post-structural frame focuses on the social construction of problems, rather than the uncritical acceptance of the problem, and proposed resolution through policy (Allan, 2008, p. 40).

The power of policy discourse analysis lies in its ability to shape and reframe concepts, ideologies, and dominant themes embedded within policy discourse documents, particularly when they undermine and devalue the intended beneficiary of the policy. Dominant discourses embedded in policy discourse are often normalized to such an extent they are rarely called into question. Policy discourse analysis can often indicate "some surprising ways in which equity-related efforts may unwittingly contribute to inequity by taking up discourses that shape subject positions that portray women or members of historically disadvantaged groups in disempowering ways and re/produce dominant power structures and hierarchies of social relationships" (Allan, 2008, p. 165; Iverson, 2005). Policy discourse analysis, as a methodological tool, is ideal for TASJ because it enables a researcher to easily connect method with praxis. A critical strategy in policy debates is understanding how groups and individuals define, describe, and frame their group interests in order to achieve political and social objectives.

The structuring and framing of group interests involves the assignment of meaning to and the interpretation of particular events by various social actors (Snow, Rochford, Worden, & Benford, 1986) for the purpose of mobilizing constituents and demobilizing antagonists (Klandermans, 1992). Framing is a critical concept in TASJ as it combines theory, method, and praxis. Frames, in the social movement context, are ways in which individuals and groups interpret, explain, and organize issues and concepts to achieve a particular outcome (Snow & Benford, 2000). "The concept of issue-framing in social movement research implies that it is a purposive interpretation of some sociopolitical issue by a particular entity that wishes to mobilize support by conveying this interpretation to other entities, thereby hoping to guide subsequent beliefs and/or actions related to the issue" (Dardis, 2007, p. 249).

A frame, therefore, is "an interpretive schemata that simplifies and condenses the 'world out there' by selectively punctuating and encoding objects, situations, events, experiences, and sequences of actions within one's present or past environment" (Snow & Benford, 1992, p. 137). Successful collective action is based on the extent to which a particular interpretation or frame "resonates" with, coincides with, and is relevant to the "life world" and belief system of the potential participants (Klandermans, 1992, p. 80). In fact, the frames created by organizers or proponents of collective action are designed to motivate social actors on the basis of several factors, including socially constructed identities. To mobilize such identities, organizers often draw on available cultural themes by using and redefining existing images, institutions, and beliefs in the hegemonic domain (Nagel, 1984, p. 165; Tilly, 1978). Collective action frames, according to Snow and Benford, are "emergent action-oriented sets of beliefs and meanings that inspire and legitimate social movement activities and campaigns" (cited in Gamson, 1992, p. 67).

Collective action frames are the result of combining the methodological tool of discourse analysis with theoretical lenses from different academic disciplines. Collective action framing allows events to be interpreted, deconstructed, and reconstructed with the objective of analyzing the effectiveness of social justice activism. This blend between theory and methodology is critical for understanding issues of inequity and injustice involving marginalized groups, particularly when these groups may find themselves in conflict with each other.

Social movement and communication scholars have conceptualized three stages of framing: diagnostic, prognostic, and motivational. Diagnostic framing is defining a problem and attributing blame or causality. Prognostic framing involves suggesting solutions and identifying strategies, tactics, and targets. Motivational framing is a call to arms or incentives to actually urge people to act on behalf of the movement, usually based on a moral appeal (Dardis, 2007, p. 249). These three types of framing incorporate three key elements of the collective action framework: punctuation, attribution, and articulation. Punctuation is defining a particular social condition as unjust and immoral, as opposed to unfortunate but tolerable. Attribution is placing blame or causality on culpable agents, such as structures, individuals, or collective processes. Articulation is meaningfully interconnecting diverse events and experiences to encourage social action. The success of a frame can be measured by frame alignment—the degree to which social movement participants agree or accept the frame and are motivated to act in accordance with the frame.

Understanding how social problems are defined, then, is critical to understanding framing and social justice activism. Spencer and Kitsuse (1987, p. 75) define social problems as "the activities of individuals or groups making assertions of grievances and claims with respect to some putative conditions." They note that "social problems are constructed by members of society who attempt to call attention to situations they find repugnant and who try to mobilize the institutions to do something about them" (p. 78). Issues of motives and values are also relevant to understanding how social problems are constructed (p. 96) and the implications of the constructions. Sociologists note that social problems seem to have a natural process of development that leads to action (Spencer & Kitsuse, 1987, p. 142). These stages can include defining a condition as unjust and creating publicity about the problem, gaining supporters, developing a plan of action, and implementing the plan. There may often be alternative strategies based on the success or challenges of implementing the plan.

McCammon, Newman, Muse, and Terrell (2007) explore how social movement participants can effect social change through framing and how frames that are grounded in social contexts and resonate with dominant hegemonic discourse are likely to be more effective. Their work examines the cultural and structural context of women's jury movements and the use of frames to persuade lawmakers to alter jury law that prohibited women from serving on juries. McCammon et al. illustrate six "discursive opportunity structures" that were used to try to influence the decision-making process: a legal discursive opportunity structure, a traditional gendered discursive opportunity structure, women in the legal profession discursive opportunity structure, women in the state legislatures as a discursive opportunity structure, opposition framing as a discursive opportunity structure, and a wartime discursive opportunity structure. These discursive opportunity structures at times are dominant hegemonic discourse and, at other times, revolutionary discourse. Yet, McCammon et al. (2007, p. 730) note that "empirical investigations of how movement framing succeeds in winning legal change remain quite limited, and few researchers consider in any depth how framing and the cultural and political context combine to produce change."

These comments reveal the importance of TASJ because it incorporates theory, methodology, and an applied component to affect transformative change in society. Its goal is to understand the manner in which the life experiences of individuals and groups are entangled and influenced by the operation of systems of power with the objective of designing effective intervention strategies. TASJ asks the following questions: What is the social problem? What form should social justice activism take? What is the best strategy to ensure success? With what theory and with what argument can transformative change be achieved? On which institutions, individuals, and/or domains should the strategy focus? TASJ recognizes the role of the definition of the problem on social activism.

The TASJ model, then, is a theoretical and methodological tool for engaging in transdisciplinary applied social justice research and practice. Figure 1 is an illustration of the transdisciplinary applied social justice model.

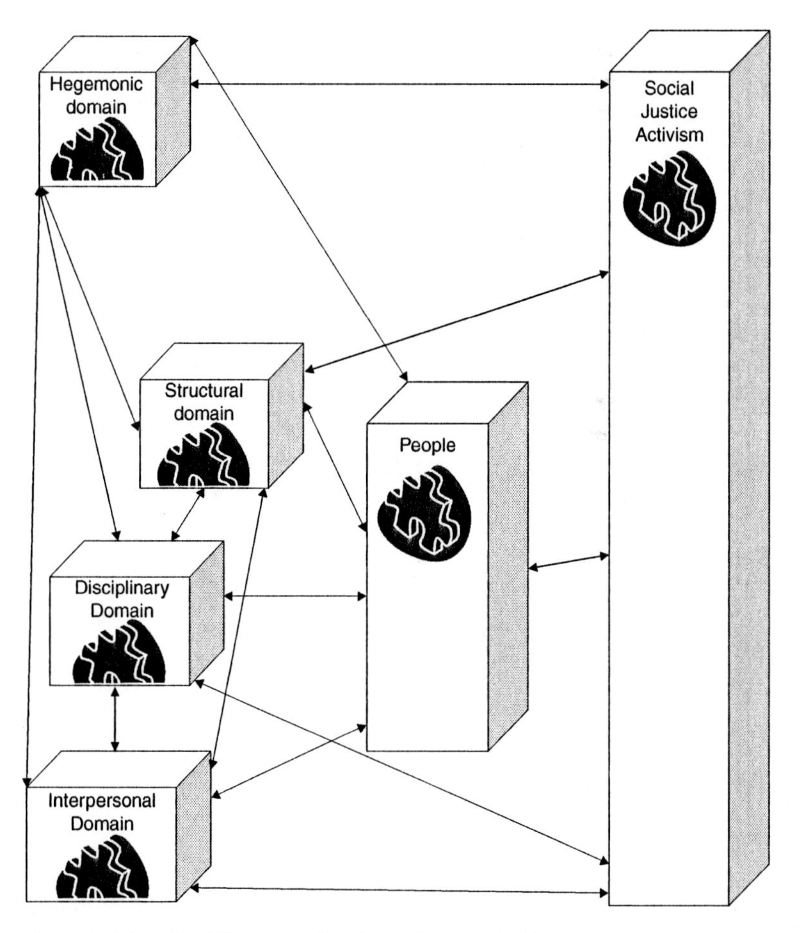

Figure 1 Transdisciplinary Applied Social Justice Model

This model demonstrates the complexity of transdisciplinarity in a social justice context. It includes the four domains of power: hegemonic, structural, disciplinary, and interpersonal. The hegemonic domain represents systems of thoughts, ideology, perspectives, values, beliefs, and stereotypes, often shaped by history. This domain includes racism, sexism, classism, and other systems of oppression rooted in ideologies about individuals based on their interwoven identities. It also includes oppositional ideologies that challenge the dominant standpoint. The disciplinary domain represents invisible and visible policies, practices, procedures, preferences, rules, regulations, and laws. This domain is the operational and organizational domain. It includes strategies that are consistent with ideas and ideologies from the hegemonic domain. It reinforces and legitimizes the hegemonic domain by transforming intangible ideologies into tangible policies and practices. The disciplinary domain is implemented within the structural domain of institutions, systems, and structures. The structural domain includes both broad and specific concepts. For example, it includes the "state," and systems within the state, such as the education system and the legal system. It also includes organizations, schools, courts, and families. It is within these specific structures that the disciplinary domain is implemented through the interpersonal domain. The interpersonal domain is the domain of daily interactions among individuals. It includes individuals who are leaders and gatekeepers—individuals directly or indirectly empowered to implement policies and procedures in the disciplinary domain. All these domains shape and are shaped by individuals and groups with interwoven identities. These identities do not merely intersect with one another, but are often interwoven and dynamic, assuming different levels of saliency and relevance. The identities can be influenced by race, gender, class, ethnicity, nationality, color, sexuality, language, family relationship, disability, and social location, among others. These identities can have varying degrees of privilege, entitlement, conferred dominance, and unearned advantage associated with them. These identities often shape the experiences of individuals as reflected in their narratives, discourses, stories, and life experiences.

These narratives and life stories occur within specific contexts and the legitimacy of these narratives, particularly of oppression, are often challenged, silenced, or re-created with different voices and versions. These narratives are the key to social justice activism. The words, the stories, the experiences must inform the social justice activism strategy. The arrows in Figure 1 show the dynamic, interactive, and interwoven relationship between the power domains, individuals, and social justice activism. The relationship and interaction between domains and individuals influences political and social outcomes. These outcomes can result in personal or group liberation or oppression. Social structures may be strengthened or weakened and ideologies may be challenged or legitimated. It is the responsibility of social justice scholar-activists to engage in discourse analysis, to deconstruct the discourse, and to strategically determine the most effective method of intervention to have a transformative impact on the lives of individuals.

The objective of social justice activism is to directly or indirectly improve individual lives through strategic initiatives that impact the domains of power. The TASJ model reveals that "understanding how our lives are governed not primarily by individuals, but more powerfully by institutions, conceptual schemes, and their texts...is crucial for designing effective projects of social transformation" (Harding & Norberg, 2005). Given the interrelatedness of social institutions, the allocation of legal, social, or political rights for one group will often affect other groups and individuals. The model incorporates concepts from critical race theory, critical race feminism, feminist theory, sociology, gender and women's studies, ethnic studies, history, political science, and communication studies. It combines the concept of framing and discourse analysis to document the way in which race, class, and gender are socially constructed, and how those constructions affect individuals and social groups. It is a powerful tool for analyzing social problems and social activism.

The next section begins this analysis using the Detroit Male Academy as a case study.

1.3 Case Study

A case study can be used to test, prove, or invalidate a theory or hypothesis. It can also be used to illustrate a concept or exemplify a key finding (Creamer, 2008). The Detroit Male Academy (DMA) initiative is an ideal case study for TASJ because the debate was very public. As a result, there is a wealth of material available for analyzing the way in which discourse, words, and arguments influenced the outcome. As the DMA story unfolded, it was documented by the media, by organizations as part of their records, and by the federal court system as part of the *Garrett v. Board of Education* (1991) case.

The primary local media sources were the three Detroit newspapers, including the *Detroit News*, the *Detroit Free Press*, and the *Michigan Chronicle*. The *Detroit Free Press* library staff provided a computerized printout of all the articles mentioning the Male Academy from October 1990 through December 1992. The attorneys' files also contained local and national newspaper articles. The LEXIS-NEXIS computer database was used to obtain national newspapers, national newswires, and transcripts of national television programs, such as *ABC Nightline* and *CNN Crossfire* for the period from October 1990 through December 1992.

The legal briefs consisted of documents written by the Detroit School Board's attorneys, the ACLU, and NOWLDF. The law firm of Lewis, White and Clay (which represented the Board) graciously provided a copy of most of their entire internal file on the *Garrett* case. Their file contained not only legal briefs and memos, but also School Board documents and information about the Detroit School System, as well as copies of newspaper articles. The Michigan chapter of the ACLU was equally generous in opening their internal file. Their file consisted of all of the legal briefs and memos generated by the ACLU and NOWLDF, as well as organization documents and position papers. The United States District Court, Eastern District of Michigan, Southern Division, provided the transcript of the oral argument, as well as a copy of the judge's opinion in the case. The Board's legal discourse consists of its reply to the *Complaint and Motion for Temporary Restraining Order and Preliminary Injunction* filed by NOWLDF and the ACLU, on behalf of Shawn Garrett and Nancy Doe. The Board's response contains several documents: *Answer to Complaint*, *Answer to Plaintiff's Motion for Temporary Restraining Order and Preliminary Injunction*, *Memorandum of Law in Opposition to Plaintiff's Motion for Temporary Restraining Order and Preliminary Injunction* (with Exhibits and Affidavits of experts, Board members, and Male Academy principals), and *Affirmative Defenses*. The Board's principal position is contained in the *Memorandum of Law* The plaintiffs' position was set forth in (a) the *Preliminary Statement* , with Exhibits A through H; (b) the *Motion for Temporary Restraining Order and Preliminary Injunction*; (c) the *Memorandum of Law in Support of Plaintiff's Motion*, with the *Affidavits of Diane Scott-Jones, Pamela Reid, and Charles Willie*; (d) the *Affidavit* of *Martha Davis*, with Exhibits A through D; (e) the *Declaration of Martha Davis*; (f) *the Affidavits of Nancy Doe and Shawn Garrett*; and (g) the *Reply Brief* with Exhibits A and B.

The legal and media discourse included the experiences of individuals and organizations that supported and opposed the DMA. Within the discourse, several narratives emerge. One version of the story is the master narrative, a historical timeline of major events. This version begins in the late 1980s and early 1990s when there was extensive debate in books, newspapers, and conferences about Black males and their social "crisis" (Barriers and Opportunities, 1990; Garibaldi, 1992; Green & Wright, 1991; Holland, 1989, 1991; Hunter & Davis, 1992; Johnson, 1989; Leake & Leake, 1992; Schmidt, 1990; Taylor-Gibbs, 1988). In the education arena, many school boards, including Florida Dade County, New Orleans, Baltimore, and Milwaukee, formed committees to study the status of Black males (African-American Male Task Force, 1990; Committee to Study the Status of the Black Male, 1988; Simmons & Grady, 1990; Task Force to Address the Decline in Enrollment and Graduation of the Black Male, 1990; Wright, n.d). These committees recommended segregating male and female students, restructuring the curriculum, and increasing the presence of Black males as teachers and role models in the classroom. Detroit was part of this national movement.

In 1987, Detroit held a Black Child Placed in Crisis Conference. Almost 800 individuals attended the conference, with a focus on the education of Black children, particularly within Detroit (Robinson, 2008). The United Community Services of Metropolitan Detroit published a report in August 1989 documenting the educational problems of young Black males, their increasing criminal and drug activity, and their overrepresentation in jails, mental institutions, and military service. The *Detroit Free Press* also carried several articles discussing the plight of Black males (Bivins, 1990; Huskisson, 1991a; 1991b). On March 10, 1990, Ad Hoc Group of Concerned Educators from Detroit Public Schools Area B—including students, parents, staff, and community leaders—organized a conference. The topic was the education and socialization of inner-city males (*Memorandum of Law in opposition*, 1991, p. 2–3). Although the organizers anticipated approximately 75 to 100 participants, over 500 people attended. The keynote speakers were Dr. Jewelle Gibbs and Haki Madhubuti, authors of books on African-American males (Ad Hoc Group of Concerned Educators, 1990). The conference participants adopted a resolution charging Michigan's governor, Detroit-area representatives to the Michigan Legislature and the U.S. Congress, the Wayne County Board of Commissioners, and the Board to "convene hearings on the crisis of the African-American male."

In response to the conference, Dr. Clifford Watson, principal of Woodward School (a Detroit public school), developed a proposal entitled "Boys Developmental Academy." In July 1990, the proposal was forwarded to Dr. John W. Porter, Interim General Superintendent of Schools, who in turn authorized Dr. Arthur Carter, Interim Deputy Superintendent, to evaluate the feasibility of establishing a Male Academy. In October 1990, Dr. Carter formed a task force consisting of various educators and community leaders. The Task Force retained the legal services of Professor Robert Sedler, a law professor at Wayne State University. The Task Force met weekly for five months and gathered statistical data on educational performance, social delinquency, and disciplinary problems of males and females in the school system and in the community.

The Task Force prepared a December 7, 1990, report entitled *Male Academy Grades K-8: A Demonstration Program for At-Risk Males* [Task Force Report], and proposed the establishment of a Male Academy (Male academy grades K-8, 1991; Carter, 1991a). The report found the following related to the education performance of males: "The overall male drop-out rate was 54 percent, and for those two years behind in grade level, the drop-out rate was 80 percent. Two-thirds of the school suspensions were male. Of the 24,000 males who were enrolled in Detroit Public Schools at the time, fewer than 30 percent had cumulative grade point averages above 2.0" (Watson & Smitherman, 1996, p. 38). There were also findings of academic underachievement of males in reading and math, and low graduation rates. The Task Force also looked at unemployment rates and crime statistics. At the time of the report, Black male unemployment was 18.3 percent. Even more startling were the homicide and crime rate statistics, reflecting substantial increases for males 18 and younger, from 54 per 100,000 in 1980 to 292 per 100,000 in 1987. Ninety-seven percent of the drug offenders in Wayne County were Black males (Watson & Smitherman, 1996, p. 39). As a result of its findings, the Task Force recommended the implementation of a Male Academy.

The Male Academy proposal was discussed and unanimously approved by the Detroit School Board Community Confidence Committee (Male Academy to be discussed, 1991; Detroit School Board committee approves, 1991). On February 26, 1991, at a meeting attended by more than 200 people, the Board approved the proposal for the Male Academy (All-male school gets green light, 1991; Detroit oks school aimed at black males, 1991; Male Academy despite roadblocks, 1991; Vernon-Chesley, 1991). On April 26, 1991, the Board passed a resolution authorizing the creation of a Male Academy for the Fall 1991 term (Carter, 1991b). Although three Male Academies were authorized, they were often collectively referred to as the Male Academy. In May, Professor Sedler issued a legal opinion concluding that the Male Academy was constitutional (Sedler, 1991). The following month, principals were selected for each academy: Mr. Harvey Hambrick for the Marcus Garvey Academy, Dr. Clifford Watson for the Malcolm X Academy, and Mr. Ray Johnson for the Paul Robeson Academy. Each principal developed charters for their Male Academy (*Preliminary Statement*, 1991). All Academies were designed to serve boys from preschool to fifth grade. Grades six through eight were to be phased in later. The Academies were to offer a variety of unique programs including "Rites of Passage, an Afro-centric (Pluralistic) curriculum, futuristic lessons in preparation for 21st century careers, an emphasis on male responsibility, mentors, Saturday classes, individualized counseling, extended classroom hours, and student uniforms" (*Garrett*). The Board received over 1200 applications for 560 slots (Ray, 1991).

As early as February 1991, Elizabeth Geise, Chair of the Education Task Force of the Michigan National Organization for Women (NOW), wrote a letter to Superintendent Porter expressing her concern about the constitutionality of the Male Academy (Davis, 1991a; Porter, 1991). In March, the National Organization for Women Legal Defense Fund (NOWLDF) sent copies of its policy and legal analyses to the Superintendent and all Board members (Davis, 1991a). NOWLDF and the Detroit Chapter of NOW convened a public meeting to discuss the Academy. In July, Howard Simon, the Executive Director of the Michigan American Civil Liberties Union (ACLU), and NOWLDF members met with newly elected Superintendent Dr. Deborah McGriff. After failing to reach a compromise, NOWLDF and the ACLU resorted to legal intervention.

Concerned that gender, instead of individual achievement, was being used as a discriminatory label for determining access to the Male Academy, the ACLU and NOWLDF filed suit on behalf of several Black females: Shawn Garrett and her daughter and Nancy Doe (a pseudonym for a Black mother who chose to remain anonymous) and her three daughters (Parks, 1991). The district court judge issued a preliminary injunction on August 15, 1991, preventing the opening of the Male Academy. On August 26, a settlement was reached between the Board, NOWLDF, and the ACLU which, among other changes, allocated 136 seats, out of a total of 560, to girls. In response to the settlement agreement, the community launched a campaign urging parents not to send their girls to the school despite the legal ruling. There were articles in newspapers, interviews with key players, public rallies and protests urging defiance of the judge's ruling. As a result, the enrollment of girls was minimal and out of 453 students enrolled by the end of the semester, only 39 were girls (Moore & Associates, 1993).

This ending of the "master narrative" raises the question of what really happened with the *Garrett* case outside of the legal decision. Answering this question requires analyzing several other "hidden" narratives. This includes the narratives of the Black female plaintiffs, the organizations representing the plaintiffs, the Detroit School Board, and the Detroit community organizations and leaders supporting the Male Academy. Unfortunately, there is not an oral or written narrative of the Black female plaintiffs' story. There are only occasional statements in the media and legal discourse. Part of their story, however, can be pieced together from the discourse.

Shawn Garrett's story is probably representative of the story of other Black women in Detroit. In 1991, she was a 24-year-old Black single mother of a four-year-old daughter. She heard about the new schools with great teachers, uniforms, and a special curriculum that focused on African-Americans. She believed they would be wonderful for her daughter, but noticed that the school was just for Black males. She believed it was unfair for her daughter not to have the opportunity to go the new schools in Detroit, and thought something should be done to allow her daughter to go to one of the new schools (Davis, 1991b; Garrett, 1991a). After several friends suggested that she publicize her dismay with the unfairness of not admitting female students, she worked with two social justice organizations to address her concerns regarding the education system through the legal system (Wimberley, 1991). During the course of the proceeding, she was harassed by the Black community and withdrew from the case (Garrett, 1991b).

She was replaced as plaintiff by Nancy Doe (1991), a pseudonym for the other plaintiff, a 34 year-old Black female plaintiff and mother of three girls, ages 11, 6, and 5 (Jane, Judy, and Jessica Doe). Nancy Doe was ultimately successful in the legal case that still bears Garrett's name, but because Nancy Doe and her children are pseudonyms, we do not know who they are. We also do not know if Crystal Garrett or Jane, Judy, and Jessica Doe enrolled or attended the Male Academy.

What we do know is that their story is a familiar story, one about the struggle of Black women to actualize an educational opportunity based on their intersecting race, gender, and class status. It is a story that includes common themes in Black feminist literature: the challenge of gaining access to the legal system; the invisibility and marginalization of Black females in society, and the difficulty of partnering with social justice organizations for change, based on issues of race, class, and gender.

Another narrative can also be told, the story of the organizations who opposed the DMA initiative. These organizations were fulfilling their missions rooted in advocating for equity and non-discrimination: the American Civil Liberties Union and the National Organization for Women and their Legal Defense Fund. Their stance was that the legal system should play a critical role in ensuring that women and girls are not denied an educational opportunity on the basis of gender (ACLU, 1991). Because of the salience of race and gender in the DMA initiative, it is critical to know the race and gender of the key individuals and actors. NOWLDF was represented by Martha Davis, a White female lawyer, and Ruth Jones, a Black female lawyer. The Executive Director for NOW was Helen Neuborne, a White female. The law firm of Goodman, Eden, Millender, & Bedrosian, was also involved, through Richard Soble, a White male. The key representative of the ACLU was its Executive Director, Howard Simon, a White male. NOWLDF drafted most of the legal documents and served as lead attorney. The ACLU was primarily the local contact for the case, because NOWLDF was located in New York. In addition to the predominantly White organizations of NOW, NOWLDF, and ACLU, the Detroit Association of Black Organizations (DABO), led by Horace Sheffeld, a Black male, also opposed the Academy.

On the other hand, there were several individuals and entities that supported the Academies. The major supporter was the Detroit School Board and its predominantly Black leadership. The key spokespersons for the Board were the following individuals: the superintendent, Deborah McGriff, an African-American female; Lawrence Patrick, president of the Board, an African-American male; Frank Hayden, vice president, an African-American male; and Arthur Carter, Interim Deputy Superintendent for Community Confidence, an African-American male. Other key advocates for the Male Academy were the Male Academy school principals: Harvey Hambrick, Clifford Watson, and Ray Johnson, all African-American men. The law firm of Lewis, White, & Clay represented the Detroit School Board through the legal services of Eric Clay, an African-American male, Camille Stearns Miller, an African-American female, and Otis Smith, an African-American male.

There were also several community organizations that supported the DMA. These included the Citizens of Detroit, a coalition of community organizations, individuals, and educators; the Malcolm X Community Center, represented by Kwame Kenyatta, an African-American male; the Inner City Sub-Center, represented by executive director Paul Taylor, an African-American male; and the Coalition for All-Male and All-Female Academies, organized and led by Bernard Parker, a Wayne County Commissioner and an African-American male. The NAACP was ambivalent. The national organization opposed the academy in a resolution during the annual convention, but the local Detroit chapter opposed the resolution (Russell, August 21, 1991).

The other key player in the debate was the United States District Court, Eastern District of Michigan, Southern Division. The district court case was presided over by Judge George Woods, a White male. The judge issued a preliminary injunction against the Detroit School Board preventing the Male Academy from opening. (Appendix A contains a short synopsis of the key players.)

These key players created a multi-textured, multi-layered discourse. At one level, there was a legal case. A case in the field of law is the presentation of facts, the discussion of the relevant laws and statutes, and the judge's or court's decision. The discourse on the legal stage is structurally controlled, constrained, and limited by the requirement of precedent, rule-based analysis of case law, and rules of evidence, which control what information can be included and presented in court. Analyzing *Garrett v. Board of Education* (1991) from just a legal perspective fails to reveal the complexity of social issues and social problems underlying and influencing the case. It also excludes an examination of the outcome in society after the participants have moved from the courtroom to the community. Various legal scholars have analyzed *Garrett* from a critical race perspective (Brown, 1994; Caplice, 1994; Cummings, 1993; Gardenswartz, 1993; Gladden, 1992; Hill, 1993; Hsiao, 1993; Vergon, 1993; Weber, 1993; V. Williams, 2004). Though the critical race analysis of the legal case yields valuable insight on the operation of the law and the legal system, the articles do not include extensive discussion of the extralegal discourse outside of the legal case, largely documented by the media. This work represents the integration of legal and extralegal discourse through TASJ.

TASJ is a comprehensive and integrated approach to analyzing both the legal discourse and the media discourse. It contextualizes the legal case as a case study within a historical and social context of multiple narratives. It is the realization that the DMA initiative is a multi-layered, multi-textured, and multi-versioned narrative with multiple outcomes that requires using transdisciplinarity to analyze the narratives. These narratives are deconstructed through discourse analysis and reconstructed as a collective action frame. The collective action framework reveals that a social problem was defined, a cause attributed, a solution proposed, and an outcome achieved. More specifically, the problem was defined as the endangered social condition of Black boys, as evidenced by their overrepresentation in the criminal justice system and their poor academic performance in the education system. Their problems were magnified by the limitations of public education law in 1991. The social problem was evidenced by the absence of a patriarchal Black masculine hegemony within the home and school environment. The problems of Black males were attributed to three main causes: females as mother, teachers, and classmates; feminism and matriarchy; and White race and class privilege. The solution proposed was a Male Academy with male teachers, male principals, male classmates, a male rites of passage program, and an African-American centered curriculum. The outcome was a paradox.

On one hand, there was a legal decision and settlement agreement granting access to girls based on the role of the Black single mother plaintiffs and the advocacy organizations. At the same time, the outcome was essentially the denial of that same right of access through the actions of the Black community, community activists, and the Detroit School Board, which launched a public media campaign persuading the community not to send girls to the school. The outcome was, for all practical purposes, a Male Academy.

TASJ facilitates an analysis of outcomes to understand the complexity of social justice advocacy. TASJ requires using multiple lessons to analyze both oppression and activism. TASJ reveals that urban males were constructed as a social group based on their interwoven race, class, and gender status. They were portrayed as victims of policies and procedures in the education and legal system. They were also portrayed as being victimized in the interpersonal domain by women as mothers and teachers, and girls as students. Drawing on concepts of patriarchy, nationalism, racism, and sexism allowed the supporters to create a discourse through the media that garnered substantial community support. At the same time, the supporters were also able to use the community's antagonism toward feminism to substantiate the strategy of excluding girls.

The next chapter begins the deconstruction of the discourse and its reconstruction as a collective action social movement frame in order to undertake the challenge of understanding strategies for activism within structures of oppression.

PART II

SOCIAL JUSTICE IN ACTION: ANALYSIS AND APPLICATION

2

The Problem Defined

The Male Academy was a proposed solution to a specific social problem. Examining how the problem was defined through the dominant voices in the discourse reveals the powerful foundation for the collective action frame. A collective action frame includes the concepts of punctuation, attribution, and articulation. This chapter focuses on the element of punctuation and the definition of the social problem. The overall problem in the collective action frame was one involving the interaction among three entities: (1) a socially constructed group—the inner-city Black male, (2) a social structure—the education system, and (3) a political process—the legal adjudication of rights through a court proceeding. These are separate yet interlocking concepts, and it is the interlocking quality that creates the complex social problem. Deconstructing the discourse enables a succinct understanding of each concept and how the concepts intersect. Understanding the intersection is critical because it is at the point of intersection that additional themes of hegemony, patriarchy, and Black manhood emerge. By using TASJ and the academic disciplines of sociology, law, political science, and history we can understand how the social problem was defined in Detroit, ultimately influencing the outcome.

This chapter is divided into three sections. The first section examines the discourse about Black males in Detroit. A deconstruction of the discourse reveals the social construction of an intersecting race, class, and gender category of the "urban male." This was an economically disadvantaged and socially disenfranchised group with significant and crisis-level social and educational problems requiring immediate and drastic action. The social problem and the need for urgent action was demonstrated with five key discursive strategies: (1) using specific adjectives and phrases to describe Black males and their problems, (2) presenting the problems facing Black males as urgent, and impacting the Black race, (3) using legal terms to imply that Black males were victims of race, class, and gender discrimination, (4) minimizing the problems of Black female students in comparison to Black male students, and (5) claiming collective community responsibility for the status of Black males. This first section reveals that an analysis of social groups cannot be isolated from the social systems and political processes in which they exist.

The second section explores the structural and procedural constraints for social justice advocacy on behalf of Black boys. This section analyzes the legal interpretation of federal and state education and civil rights law. The Fourteenth Amendment of the Constitution, Title IX, the Michigan Equal Education Opportunities Act, and the Elliott-Larsen Act were legal obstacles that needed to be addressed. On their face, the laws limited the creative and innovative policy reform sought by the Detroit School Board. The legal arguments in the *Garrett v. Board of Education* case are analyzed to illustrate the obstacles that the political process presented for the Male Academy advocates.

The third section connects the first two sections. There was an underlying concept intermixed and embodied within the issues of the dire social status of Black boys, the inflexible structure of the education system, and the limits posed by legal interpretations of civil rights laws. At the point of intersection of individuals, structures, and process was the concept of power, authority, and control. In the Detroit Male Academy context, the discourse of the Male Academy supporters can be deconstructed to reveal the themes of hegemony, patriarchy, and Black manhood. These concepts, therefore, become the cement that binds together the building blocks of groups, structures, and process to create the solid, almost impenetrable foundation for the punctuation element of the collective action frame.

2.1 The Urban Male

Race, class, and gender are socially and culturally constructed categories influenced by historical contexts. They can also be seen as "social practice[s] situated within social structures of specific social relations and institutions" (Vojdik, 2002). These are practices that enforce and institutionalize domination and subordination. It is essential to deconstruct the discourse in the Male Academy debate to examine the construction of the categories of race, class, and gender, and the effect of these constructions on the outcome. In this particular case, race, gender, and class categories were intertwined to construct a socially identifiable, sympathetic, and helpless social group. This social group was defined as the "urban male." The "urban male" was created by the use of familiar adjectives.

The discourse reflects that a conscious decision was made by the Board to define the group as the "urban male" and to associate particular characteristics with this group. Rather than specifically using the phrase "Black male," the phrase "urban male" became a pseudonym for inner-city Black males, allowing the Board to highlight their intersecting gender, race, and class status, without explicitly referring to race or class. It is rare for males to be considered a disadvantaged group based solely on their gender identity (Note, 1991); rather, Black males are often considered a disadvantaged group based on their racial identity. But racial identity would also impact females, so the Board attempted to emphasize the intersecting race and gender identity of Black males, without specifically raising their racial identity as a basis for the disadvantaged status. For example, in the Board's Memorandum of Law the phrase "urban males" appears at least twenty-five times and the phrase "inner-city male" is used at least eleven times. In contrast, the phrase "African-American male" is only used three times, and the phrase "Black male" is used just once.

The Board's decision to use the adjective "urban" in reference to males was based on advice from its legal counsel, Prof. Robert Sedler. Sedler encouraged the Board to subordinate its discussion of race in light of concerns about racial segregation. On December 19, 1990, then-Superintendent Porter submitted the Male Academy Proposal to the Board. In his accompanying memo to Board President Frank Hayden, Porter (1990) noted that, "cabinet members also voiced concern about references to minorities and African-American males in the document. Members felt that these references alluded to segregation by race as well as gender." In response, Sedler (1991) noted that "public misperception about the nature of the Male Academy" as a race- and gender-segregated school may be due to statements by Board members and the Task Force referring to the Male Academy as an attempt to "save a generation of African-American males by special schools and special programs."

To correct the alleged "misperception" and, more importantly, to prevent a lawsuit by "NOW and other groups concerned about gender and racial equality," Sedler encouraged Board members and officials of the Detroit Public Schools to minimize the racial aspects of the Male Academy and to emphasize that the Academy was open to males of all races, even though the majority of the students would be African-American. Sedler (1991) stated

> [The Male Academy] is not a school for African-American males. Its student population will consist of inner-city males, without regard to race. Thus, any concern about racial discrimination in the operation of the Male Academy is inapposite. Since the student population of the Detroit Public Schools is approximately 90 percent Black in composition that racial composition is likely to be reflected in the Male Academy as well. Nonetheless, selection must be and is open to males of all races, and it may be assumed that Whites and Hispanics will comprise in the range of 10 percent...of the student population of the Male Academy.

Based on Sedler's advice, the rhetorical question and answer section of the Male Academy Brochure explicitly states

> Q: Is this a school just for African-American Males?
> A: No! Males from every nationality, race and/or religion will be welcomed.

The few specific references to race by the Board enabled it to minimize potential legal concerns about race discrimination, particularly in light of the Afro-centric curriculum and the predominantly Black school district. The use of the word "urban" allowed the Board to subtly refer to race without an explicit reference to race. Additionally, class issues that are often synonymous with urban, inner-city residents could be raised. Thus, the supporters created a basis for portraying the Black male as a victim and as a disadvantaged group based on his complex and intersecting identities.

The supporters accentuated the Black male victim status by repeatedly using a few simple, yet compelling, adjectives to describe the problems of urban males. The Board (Memorandum of law in opposition, p. 7, 43) described the needs and problems of urban males as "unique," "special," "different," and "complex." The Memorandum of Law (p. 28) described urban males as "socially deprived students with special needs" who require "additional footing...to competently compete with their counterparts." The Board (Memorandum of law in opposition, p. iii, 9, 15, 29, 30) often mentioned the "special needs of urban male students." The Cooper School Charter (Provisional Charter, 1991) referred to the "recognized needs of inner-city males." Porter's cover letter for the Task Force Report (Male academy grades K-8, 1991) made reference to the "critical multiple needs of African-American males," and the "unique needs of males." Superintendent McGriff (1991a) and Gardner (1991) (one of the Board's expert witnesses) both used the phrase the "special needs...of urban males." Smitherman (1991), in her expert affidavit, referred to the "unique language needs of boys." By using the words "unique," "different," "special," and "needs" in reference to urban boys, the discourse dramatized the problems of males and implied that these problems required a special, unique, and different solution, such as the Male Academy.

The Academy supporters also emphasized the crisis level of the problem with adjectives and phrases that highlighted the seriousness and urgency of the status of urban males based on the social environment. Jones (1991) claimed that "society has miserably failed the urban male" because "too many urban males are being blown away in the streets." The Task Force Report (Male academy grades K-8, 1991, p. 19) referred to the "vulnerability of urban males." The Report (p. 3, 7, 60) also contained the following phrases: the "urban environment, the obstacles, and the load males must carry just to survive"; the "declining status of the urban male"; the " 'crisis' relative to survival of urban males"; and the "precarious plight of young urban males." The "multitude of educational, social, health, and economic problems afflicting urban males today" was mentioned, as well as the "multiple, critical needs of a segment of students served by Detroit Schools" (Male academy grades K-8, 1991, p. 3, 7).

The problems were illustrated and accentuated by the supporters' frequent recitation of crime rate, incarceration, unemployment, and poor educational attainment statistics for urban males (Memorandum of law in opposition, p. iii, p. 1; McGriff, 1991a; Porter, 1991). The Detroit School Board's Male Academy brochure mentioned the "national crisis related to the employment, social and educational plight of males in urban areas" and cited statistics on male short-term suspensions, truancy, graduation and dropout rates. It mentioned the criminal justice system and the role of males in criminal activity and drug offenses. The unemployment rate was also included. Afrocentric scholar Asante (1991), in his affidavit, mentioned the statistics on urban males and commented on the "crisis nature of the problems facing young urban males," which "encourage social disintegration" and the "wholesale disruption of the lives of urban male children." Hale's affidavit (1991) stated that "statistics on the problems of African-American males are so well-known it seems pointless to repeat them." By including statistics about crime and employment, the discourse broadened the justification for the Male Academy beyond academic performance, creating the perception that the Academy could remedy all social ills.

The discourse reveals that the Male Academy supporters created a unique social group based on intersecting race, class, and gender status, then attributed special social problems to the group and defined the group and its problems as an unjust social condition. This was accomplished by using clichés and stereotypical images analogizing the condition of Black males to the extinction of animals. The supporters' discourse suggested that the Black male crisis indicated that the survival of the Black race was in jeopardy. This was done by the frequent use of the words "endangered" and "extinct" and the phrase "endangered species." The Board, in its Affirmative Defenses, called urban males an "endangered species" who would be "irreparably harmed" without the Male Academy. Bernard Parker, County Commissioner and Director of Operation Get Down, a local Detroit self-help group, said "This is a situation of the extermination of African-American males. We have to do something about it…we cannot wait for White people to tell us it's OK" (Gilchrist, August 19, 1991). A Detroit resident is quoted on *Nightline* (1991) as saying "What are you doing—it's Black boys that are the endangered species." William Raspberry (1991), a Black male nationally syndicated columnist, stated that "Black males are an endangered, and endangering, species." Kwame Kenyatta, director of the Malcolm X Center in Detroit, said on *Nightline* (1991) "Black males in this country is [sic] an endangered species, they have been targeted by this system for destruction and extermination and that has been historically the case." On *Crossfire* (1991), a Black man was quoted as saying "As long as the damage is Black boys, it's fine, OK…the system's set up to destroy Black boys." These phrases are consistent with Hare's research in 1985. Hare referred to Black males as the "endangered species" because of high dropout, suspension, and expulsion rates; high infant mortality rates; short life expectancy; and the likelihood of being unemployed, underemployed, or incarcerated (Irvine, 1990, p. 78). As a result of Hare's research (Irvine, 1990, p. 78) on Black fifth-grade boys, he concluded "black males are probably the most feared, least likely to be identified with, and least likely to be effectively taught."

The Male Academy supporters asserted that the Male Academy could prevent the extinction of the Black race. A September 16, 1991, *Detroit Free Press* letter to the editor (Singleton, 1991) stated "Our youths are our future. There is a dire need to seek solutions in preserving our race for the future. Young males are dying at a rate that will one day find us in the same position as the American Indians—here, but not there." These comments are supported by the comments of Susan Watson (1991a), a Black female columnist for the *Detroit Free Press*, who endorsed the Male Academy, saying "As it stands, the young African-American male is indeed an endangered species and when the African-American man's future is endangered, so is mine. And so is the future of every woman who chooses to build a life with an African-American man."

The supporters not only defined the Black male crisis as an unjust situation, they also created a moral and racial imperative. They implied that in order for the Black community to survive, the problems of Black boys were the most urgent and most important, deserving immediate attention. "I urge you not to let (women) into the male academies," said one father who planned to enroll his son in the program. "The greater need is within the Black man, we need to save the Black man" (Detroit Agrees, 1991). Helen Moore, a Black female Detroit community activist and supporter of the Male Academy, was quoted as saying "The pressing needs of Black males should take precedence over any other arguments" (Russell & Skwira, 1991). Board member Edna Bell, another Black female, is quoted as saying "The implementation of the male academy is important not only to our race, but also our nation" (Detroit School Board Committee, 1991). Dr. Spencer Holland (director of the Center for Education of African-American Males at Morgan State University and a staunch advocate for male academies) said "I am not anti-integration, and I am definitely not anti-female. But I have to be pro-Black boy because he's the one this educational system in America has failed most" (Gilchrist, September 3, 1991). Similarly, columnist Susan Watson (1991b) stated "As a woman who is first and foremost an African-American, I also believe that in this particular case, I cannot afford the luxury of waging a battle against sex-based discrimination when the future of Black men—a group that even the federal judge called an endangered species—is at stake."

The reference to the federal judge reflects the importance of analyzing not just the discourse describing the urban males and their problems within social structures in society, but also the discourse involving the political process and legal system. Legal terms associated with discrimination, such as "equal opportunity," "disparity," "inequity," "disparate impact," "remedial action," "affirmative action," and "limited participation," were used to suggest that males were the victims of discrimination and, as a result, deserved an exclusive and unique remedy. For example, the Task Force Report contains a section entitled "On the Matter of Gender and Equal Opportunity." This section discusses the need for equal opportunity for urban males to eliminate the "substantial inequities that exist in the community and the schools" resulting in "disparities in male and female performance" (Male academy grades K-8, p. 16; Memorandum of law in opposition, p. 1). The Board's brief argued that the Male Academy was necessary to "remedy present gender inequities in [the Board's] delivery of education to urban children" (Memorandum of law in opposition, p. 17), and to "alleviate the disparate impact of the current traditional education system on urban males" (p. 36).

In its analysis of Title IX and the Michigan School Code, the Board (Memorandum of law in opposition, p. 24) compared the purpose of the Male Academy—addressing the "limited participation of urban males in education programs"—with remedial and affirmative action programs. The Board admitted that there was no finding of gender discrimination, and conceded that the Male Academy was not an affirmative action program, (Memorandum of law in opposition, p. 24, 33–34) but nevertheless argued that the "[Male Academy] purpose is certainly consistent with those shared by recognized affirmative action programs," designed to address problems faced by "disadvantaged groups." Despite the Board's explicit denial of discrimination, its frequent references to discrimination created an implication that males were victims of discrimination and that females were the benefactors at the expense of males.

The discourse reveals that the Male Academy supporters attempted to restructure traditional views about the dominant status of males in society. This was done not only by applying terms typically associated with discrimination against females to Black males, but also by using a discursive strategy of contrast in which the problems of females were silenced, simplified, minimized, or categorized around the traditional gender context of pregnancy. The Board's discourse rarely mentions any statistics about the performance of females, thus creating the impression that only males were in crisis. The Board was not the only entity to ignore the concerns of females. Many newspaper articles about the Male Academy referred only to the problems of males and did not even mention female students. The City Council of Detroit adopted a resolution supporting the Male Academy, which did not mention females. The Council rejected the suggestion of its president and only female member to include Black females in the resolution and to urge solutions to deal with both genders. Instead, the resolution urged the Board to address the crisis of Black males and to "stand strong against any opposition that may arise" (Detroit City Council, 1991). When females were mentioned, "urban" was rarely used as an adjective to describe them. In the Board's Memorandum of Law, there are no references to "inner-city females," "black females," or "African-American females," and the phrase "urban females" appears only twice.

Conversely, the discourse also implied that the problems of girls were not critical, unique, different, and thus not deserving of special solutions. The Board (Memorandum of law in opposition, p. 15) asserted that the problems of males were "even more compelling" than those of females. The Task Force Report (Male academy grades K-8, p. 5) referred to "disturbing statistics that males lag behind their female counterparts at almost every grade level." The Board (Memorandum of law in opposition, p. 8) expressed the need to make its "educational programming...as effective for its male students as for its female students," noting that "the problems faced by inner-city males...differ in many respects from the problems faced by inner-city females." It was mentioned that "inner-city males [are] more at risk than females for delinquency, leaving school at an early age, drug addiction, becoming disciplinary problems, and other anti-social behavior" and that "male students in the Detroit School System were failing to succeed in greater numbers than female students within the school system" (p. 1–3). Smitherman (1991) attributed linguistic developmental differences between boys and girls to "the historical repression of males and society's more extensive exclusion of males than females from the linguistic mainstream." The "substantially lower achievement for males than females" was mentioned and it was asserted that "inner-city urban males are more 'at-risk' than other students within the system" (Memorandum of law in opposition, p. 1, 13). These assertions were made even though the female dropout rate was 45 percent, compared to 54 percent for males (Male academy grades K-8, p. 7). The Task Force Report also mentioned that California Achievement test scores for males and females in math and reading were comparable (p. 6).

The problems of females were not only minimized, when presented they were often stereotyped around pregnancy. "It has long been known that pregnancy and parenting duties constituted a significant cause for the drop-out rate for females" and "alternative programs housed in single-sex schools... specifically address the needs of these females" (Memorandum of law in opposition, p. 14). Similarly, according to the Task Force (Male academy grades K-8, p. 17), "females are not experiencing problems to the same severity and extent [as males]. When they do, pregnancy and parenting appear to be the primary cause." The Task Force (p. 18) indicated that schools (pregnancy-related Continuing Education Centers) were created to address the problems of females, but the needs of urban males remain unmet. Additionally, the Board did not mention that more than half of all females drop out for reasons unrelated to pregnancy (Memorandum of law in support, p. 25).

With the discourse effectively removing Black females as a meaningful factor in the equation of the social problem, the final discursive strategy could logically emerge. This strategy involved taking ownership of Black males. The discourse indicated that the Board and the supporters of the Male Academy claimed ownership of their "urban male" and asserted that the community had the right, the responsibility, and the moral obligation to address the male crisis. This declaration of proprietorship was accomplished through the frequent use of the word "our" and the phrase "our urban males." The February 26, 1991, Male Academy resolution (Detroit School Board, February 26, 1991) mentioned "the acute challenges facing our male students, and particular our African-American male students." Dr. Watson, in his *Nightline* (1991) interview repeatedly referred to "our African-American males."

The discourse, then, clearly reflects that the Black male and his current condition were defined as the social problem. This social group was renamed "urban male." Ownership and responsibility of the Black community to the urban male was claimed through the use of the possessive adjective "our" with urban males. References to females were infrequent and the problems of Black males were presented as much more severe that those of Black females. The social and environmental factors oppressing the urban male, including the criminal, employment, and education system were discussed, and the endangered status of the urban male was emphasized. Additionally, projections were made about the dire future for the Black race.

This presentation of Black males is consistent with Gibbs' finding: "Black males are portrayed...in a limited number of roles, most of them deviant, dangerous, and dysfunctional...Thus, young black males are stereotyped by the five "d's": dumb, deprived, dangerous, deviant, and disturbed" (quoted in Hopkins, 1997, p. 1). The work of Scott (1997) on damage imagery of African-Americans in the social sciences echoes this finding. His work examined social science images as subjective knowledge structures that are created by experts influenced by historical, social, personal, and ideological factors (Scott, 1997, p. xvi). Scott (p. 188) demonstrated that damage imagery has been used to call for social change and to justify social reform policies throughout history. In the Male Academy debate, Scott (p. 197) notes that damage imagery was used by Afrocentric scholars and supporters to promote the school. The use of damage imagery as a mechanism for social change is associated with the claim of "moral righteousness" (Scott, 1997, p. 136).

This relationship between damage image and morality is consistent with the concept of a collective action frame wherein the problem must be articulated in such a way as to garner moral support. The success of the collective action frame in defining the social problem was enhanced by the supporters' ability to create a connection between the social group and the social systems. The next section will reveal the way in which the education system and the legal system were woven into the definition of the problem.

2.2 Education Civil Rights Law

In addition to the social problem of the Black male crisis, there was another significant problem in this case study: the education system and civil rights law. In education law, research has played a significant role in the assessment of appropriate public policy and legislative rights. In 1991, neither existing case law nor existing research about single-sex schools strongly supported the position of the Detroit School Board and its justification for a Male Academy. To the contrary, there was a significant body of legal interpretation supporting gender equity in education for girls. Additionally, although there was some research on the benefits of single-sex schools for girls in the early 1990s (Salomone, 2003, p. 188–236), there was a paucity of research on the benefit of single-sex schools for boys, let alone Black boys in 1991 (Irvine, 1990, p. 76–79). This reality represented a significant challenge for those concerned with addressing the social problems of Black males through structural changes to the education system.

In light of the lawsuit by the ACLU and NOWLDF, the Male Academy supporters were faced with a problem involving the education system and the legal system. As part of the punctuation element of the collective action frame, not only does a social condition need to be defined, it must also be defined as unjust and immoral. The social condition needs to be connected to the concept of justice. Because the legal system is a forum for issues of justice and morality, the *Garrett v. Board of Education* case was an opportunity for the Male Academy supporters to portray the condition of Black boys as an unjust situation requiring judicial intervention in the education system. The Board's objective was to persuade the court that the Male Academy was constitutional, that it did not violate federal rules and regulations, and that it did not violate state laws. As basis for its proof, the Board relied on particular facts, existing legal cases, and novel interpretations of state and federal statutes.

The Board began its case by dramatizing the status of Black males with statistics of delinquency, drug addiction, academic performance, and "other anti-social behavior" (Memorandum of law in opposition, p. 2–3). The "status of the inner-city male" was detailed in the "Evidence of Need" section of the Task Force Report. The Board included the following statistical findings of the Task Force in its Memorandum of Law (p. 4):

> Research data indicate that the problems confronted by young males, particularly urban males, are highly complex and include specific attitudes, behaviors, and perceptions that appear interwoven. For instance, test data generated for Detroit students in grades 4, 7, and 10 indicate that a disproportionate number of males are underachievers in reading and math. For high school students who are in the correct age for their grade level (i.e., age 14 in the ninth grade) the dropout rate hovers around 25%. For students one year behind in grade (i.e., 15 years of age in the ninth grade) the dropout rate increases to 53%. When students lag two years behind in grade when compared to their age-mates, the dropout rate increases to 80%. Sadly, the district's most recent dropout study indicated that the male high school dropout rate is 45% over four years....
>
> The unemployment rate for urban males is often more than twice the state average. In Detroit, for example, the unemployment rate for all males, at the end of 1989, stood as 16.1% as opposed to 7.1% for rest of state. For African-American and Hispanic males the rate was especially high at 18.3% and 10.2% respectively....

> In Wayne County (the largest county in Michigan) the homicide rate for African-American males age 15–24 is 14 times higher than the national rate for all males. This homicide rate is almost twice the rate for African-American males in all of Michigan and 47 times the homicide rate for White males in Michigan. Of the 4100 youth admitted to the Wayne County Youth Home last year, 3500 were minority males. Sixty percent of the drug offenses in Wayne County were committed by 8th and 9th grade dropouts. In Wayne County alone, the number of young, minority men under the control of the criminal justice system is greater that the total number of minority men of all ages enrolled in college!...
>
> When males are compared to females on indices of achievement, attendance, graduation, expulsion, and school violations, at almost every grade level males lag behind their female counterparts, are least likely to attend school regularly, are more likely to be suspended, and are least likely to finish high school.

Against the background of these findings and statistics, the Board began its legal argument. Under the standard enunciated by the Supreme Court in *Mississippi University for Women School of Nursing v. Hogan* (1982), the Board was required to demonstrate that the gender-based classification of the Male Academy served an "important governmental objective and that the discriminatory means employed [were] substantially related to the achievement of those objectives." *Mississippi v. Hogan* involved a male student's denial of admission to Mississippi's all-female nursing school. The Board (Memorandum of law in opposition, p. iii, 11, 12, 37, 38) argued that the important governmental objective of the Male Academy was the creation of an environment for the "analysis and evaluation of various specialized and experimental curricula and guidance strategies aimed at improving the academic performance of urban males." The Board, by characterizing the Male Academy as an experiment, attempted to imply that the Male Academy could not be discriminatory because its intent was to gather data and not to exclude females. The Board also stated, as its justification for the "discriminatory means employed," that the exclusion of females was necessary because "co-educational programs have failed" (Memorandum of law in oppositon, p. 14, 29). By using the phrase "co-educational," the Board was able to imply that the presence of girls caused the failure of boys, without explicitly asserting that girls were the cause of the male crisis—a proposition for which it had no proof and which would appear to be discriminatory on the basis of gender in violation of the law.

Further, the Board claimed that the benefits of single-sex schooling were evidenced by the existence of many single-sex schools across the country and local, small-scale, experimental male programs initiated by two of the Male Academy principals. Ray Johnson, principal at Paul Robeson Academy, began a program for male students called "Man to Man" at Cooper School. Dr. Clifford Watson, principal at Malcolm X Academy, began a similar extra-curricular program at Woodward School involving male role models and teachers (R. Johnson, 1991; Memorandum of law in opposition, p. 9; C. Watson, 1991). The Board (Memorandum of law in opposition, p. 15) relied on assertions and claims in affidavits by its expert witnesses that a single-sex environment was necessary to address the unique problems of males, even though the claims and assertions were rarely substantiated by research. The Board (p. 15) stated that unlike *Hogan*, where the University of Mississippi failed to show that women lacked opportunities in nursing education, the Board's research indicated that male achievement was substantially lower than female achievement, justifying a "concentrated effort focused solely on boys."

The Board justified the Male Academy under *Califano v. Webster* (1977) and *Schlesinger v. Ballard* (1975), where the Supreme Court found evidence of "historic gender disparities" justifying the disproportionate benefits to women. *Califano v. Webster* was a program that provided women with higher monthly Social Security benefits than men with the same history of earnings. *Schlesinger v. Ballard* involved a statute that allowed female naval officers to serve thirteen years of commissioned service prior to mandatory discharge compared to nine years for males. Similarly, the Board (Memorandum of law in opposition, p. 17) asserted that the Male Academy would remedy "gender inequities" in the Detroit Schools. The Board thus attempted to place males in the same subordinated status on the gender hierarchy as females, suggesting that males had been victims of discrimination in the absence of programs geared specifically for their needs.

In order to effectively place males in the position of females, the Board attempted to minimize the impact of the Male Academy on females. The academic performance problems of boys were magnified by the absence of any references or statistics about the academic performance of girls. Although the 54 percent dropout rate for males was mentioned, the 45 percent dropout rate for girls was not. This was only a 9 percent difference (Male academy grades K-8, p. 7). There were also no substantial differences in male and female performance in reading and math on the California Achievement Test (p. 6).

The Board also attempted to emphasize the alleged "temporary" and "limited" nature of the Male Academy. It argued that females would only be minimally affected, as the duration of the program was only three years, and the total enrollment at the Male Academy was limited to 600. Although the Board claimed the Academy was only a temporary experiment, the Task Force Report provided for additional grades to be phased in later. This appeared to suggest that the intent of the Male Academy was long-term, rather than short-term.

The Board also attempted to minimize the potential benefits of the Male Academy for females. The Board (Memorandum of law in opposition, p. 14) maintained that the needs of females, which it asserted were primarily pregnancy and parenting related, were being specifically addressed by "alternative programs housed in single sex schools," referring to the Board's Continuing Education Centers. The Board of Education described its Continuing Education Centers (CEC) as follows:

> It is a comprehensive Detroit Public School-based and operated program into which pregnant students can transfer from their home school to continue their education for one or more semesters during pregnancy and after pregnancy. It includes students in grades 7 through 12. Students transfer back to their home school upon readiness to return. The students' programs are supplemented by classes in parenting, child development and care as well as by support services by nurses, counselors and homebound teachers. (M. Davis, 1991a)

The Board concluded that no material distinction existed between the purpose of the programs for pregnant girls and the proposed Male Academy. In making this conclusion, the Board, however, ignored an important distinction between the remedial nature of the CECs and the preventive nature of the Male Academy. Further, the Board did not acknowledge the distinction between the programs and services to be provided at the Male Academy—a specialized Afro-centric curriculum, specially trained staff, additional resources, Saturday classes, and career training for 21st century careers—and those at the CECs.

The Board also did not distinguish between the long-term nature of the Male Academy and the after-the-fact and short-term accommodation of the CECs. Additionally, two of the CECs only served low achievers. In contrast, the Male Academy was designed to serve a population consisting of an equal number of low, middle, and high achievers, as determined from several characteristics and attributes: achievement scores, citizenship grades, family status, attendance, grade point average, retention in grade, teacher assessment, potential for success, and letters of recommendation. The Board also inaccurately asserted that there were no programs to address the problems of males, neglecting to mention the role of the High School Development Center and the Middle School Development Center for boys with behavioral problems.

The Board also attempted to justify the Male Academy under federal law by using similar arguments based on the experimental nature of the Male Academy. Title IX of the Educational Amendment of 1972, 20 U.S.C. §1681(a) states, in part, "No person in the United States shall, on the basis of sex, be excluded from participating in, be denied the benefits of, or be subjected to discrimination under any education program or activity receiving federal financial assistance." Ignoring the policy concerns of remedying systemic gender discrimination against females underlying the purpose of Title IX, the Board asserted that the Male Academy was not prohibited by Title IX because Congress wanted to encourage innovative methods of education. Rather than focusing on the statute's explicit language prohibiting discrimination, the Board focused on the statute's exceptions for traditional and existing single-sex environments, such as military academies, social fraternities, youth service organizations, boy and girl conferences, father/son and mother/daughter activities, beauty pageants, religious organizations, and single-sex undergraduate public colleges. The Board, relying on the Third Circuit Court's analysis in *Vorchhiemer v. School District of Philadelphia* (1976), concluded that Congress did not intend to restrict or eliminate single-sex educational options such as the Male Academy. *Vorchheimer* involved a female student's denial of admission to an all-male public single-sex high school in Philadelphia. The Third Circuit found that because the school district had created an all-female public single-sex high school, the denial did not violate the Constitution. The Supreme Court, without an opinion, affirmed the decision by an equally divided court (4–4).

The Board also asserted that regulations promulgated by the Secretary of Education under Title IX allowed the Board to establish the Academy under the provisions addressing remedial action, affirmative action, and self-evaluation. In 1991, 34 CFR 106.3(a) stated "*Remedial Action.* If the Assistant Secretary finds that a recipient has discriminated against persons on the basis of sex in an education program or activity, such recipient shall take such remedial action as the Assistant Secretary deems necessary to overcome the effects of such discrimination." Likewise, 34 CFR 106.3(b) stated "*Affirmative Action*. In the absence of finding of discrimination on the basis of sex in an education program or activity, a recipient may take affirmative action to overcome the effects of conditions which resulted in limited participation therein by persons of a particular sex."

The Board argued that even though there was no specific finding of discrimination against urban males, the "limited participation of urban males in education programs and activities" provided justification for the Male Academy under Title IX (Memorandum of law in opposition, p. 24). The Board's suggestion and implication that males were victims of gender discrimination allowed it to place males in the gender-subordinated position of the females the statute was designed to protect. Though the Board had created a policy that on its face discriminated against females, it inverted the patriarchal reality and creatively argued that males, in fact, were entitled to Title IX's protection. This strategy was consistent with the Board's attempt to portray males as victims in need of unique remedies and females as beneficiaries of the education system at the expense of males.

The Board also argued that the Male Academy did not violate the Equal Education Opportunities Act (EEOA), 20 U.S.C. §1701 *et. seq.* 20 U.S.C. §1703, which says "No state shall deny equal educational opportunity to an individual on account or his or her race, color, sex, or national origin, by (c) the assignment . . . of a student to a school . . . if the assignment results in a greater degree of segregation of students on the basis of race, color, sex, or national origin." The Board noted that the floor debates on the bills in the House and Senate did not contain any reference to single-sex schools. It argued that the EEOA was not intended to prohibit a temporary single-sex school experiment such as the Male Academy. It distinguished the Male Academy from *United States v. Hinds* (1977) where sex-based assignments were permanent. The Board emphasized that participation in the Male Academy was voluntary, not mandatory, because students were not being "assigned" to any school in violation of the EEOA's prohibition on student assignment. As with Title IX, the Board ignored the policy concerns of race discrimination that motivated the development of the statute, focusing instead on a technical distinction between voluntary and mandatory enrollment.

The Board also addressed Michigan's Elliott-Larsen Act, which prohibited denying "full and equal" utilization of and benefit from education institutions based on sex (*Garrett v. Board of Education*, 1991). The Board argued that the "devastating statistics regarding urban males" established that the Male Academy served an important governmental interest (Memorandum in opposition, p. 29). The Board also argued that because "the current traditional co-ed program does not work," an experimental all-male Academy "is critical to expeditiously determine necessary curricula and training programs to keep urban males out of the City's morgues and prisons."

Finally, the Board addressed the alleged illegality of the Male Academy under the Michigan School Code (§380.1146), which prohibited the establishment of a "separate school on account of sex." The Board mentioned its "blind" selection process to support its argument that the Academy was not a single-sex school, contradicting the very name of the Academies, *Male* Academy. The Board's position under the Michigan School Code was inconsistent with its position under Title IX that the Male Academy, as a single-sex school, was allowed under the statute. The Board disingenuously (Memorandum of law in opposition, p. 35, n.7) used the provisional admittance of one female "conditioned only upon the resolution of this matter" to insist that there was no specific prohibition against female attendance, and that the Male Academy was not discriminatory. As a comparison, the Board maintained that although the programs for pregnant students and their children at the CECs did not specifically exclude males, the practical effect was an all-female program. Similarly, because the Male Academy did not specifically prohibit attendance by females, it, like the CECs, should not be considered illegal. The Board, therefore, denied that the Male Academy was a discriminatory single-sex program under the Michigan School Code. It (Memorandum of law in opposition, p. 36) asserted that it was merely a program for urban males to address "the legitimate and demonstrable needs of students at risk."

Thus, the Board, on one hand, denied that it discriminated against females, and on the other hand, justified their exclusion based on the crisis of males. Additionally, the Board used the phrase "students at risk" to include only males, reflecting its position that females were not at-risk and thus not in need of a special at-risk program such as the Male Academy. The Board, focusing on intent, created a subtle distinction between the purpose of the Male Academy and its effect on females. It insisted that because there was no overt attempt or intent to discriminate against females, the incidental consequence of excluding females should be subordinate to the need to obtain information about the "disproportionate academic failure of urban male students" (Memorandum of law in opposition, p. 31). Although the

Board specifically denied that the Male Academy was an affirmative action program, the Board suggested that because there were other "innovative alternative educational programs," including a minority-based cultural curriculum, programs for educationally handicapped students, programs for gifted and talented children, remedial programs, and programs for pregnant students (the CECs), the Code intended to allow the Board to address the problems of disadvantaged groups and unique populations, including urban males.

The Board concluded its argument by asserting that the harm to males from a preliminary injunction was greater than the harm to females without an injunction. The Board argued that females were not harmed because they would receive the same core curricula and were one of the intended beneficiaries of the Academy. The Board specifically mentioned its "Rites of Passage" Program, designed to "prepare boys to be men," as a program that could be modified to "prepare girls to be women," (Memorandum of law in opposition, p. 5, 8, 27, 31, 42) and frequently alluded to a Female Academy proposed for January 1992. These references reflected the Board's attempt to justify the Male Academy by its purported and undefined future benefits for females. The legal discourse reveals a strong advocacy for African-American males and a minimization of harm to females.

In conclusion, the Board's position essentially consisted of depicting the urgent nature of the Black male crisis and arguing that the crisis merited the unique single-sex solution of the Male Academy. The Board also argued that females were not as at-risk as males and that there were existing schools for the pregnancy-related challenges females faced. The Board even applied pro-female gender-related policy justifications in the legislative statutes to males. The Board's discourse, then, reveals a three-part social problem: (1) a social group, with interwoven socially constructed race, class, and gender identities, negatively affected and influenced by social systems as evidenced by high incarceration rates, high unemployment statistics, and high dropout rates; (2) a public education system that was failing Black males; and (3) federal and state rules and regulations that limited creative solutions to social problems. This definition of the problem incorporates the structural domain of power represented by the education system, the legal system, the labor markets, and the criminal justice system; the disciplinary domain of power represented by the laws and regulations governing the operation of the education and legal system; the hegemonic domain of stereotypes, ideologies, and beliefs; and the interpersonal domain evidenced by key players in the debate. The next section explores the operation of the domains in detail, with a particular focus on the role of the hegemonic domain.

2.3 Patriarchy and Black Masculinity

TASJ requires redefining the education crisis of Black boys in Detroit using sociological constructs of social groups, social structures, and domains of power. Black males must be seen as socially constructed groups based on their intersecting race, class, and gender identities. Their experiences unfolded in contested structures and systems, including the public education system, the federal legal system, and the inner-city of Detroit. The social problem, then, involved a socially constructed group attempting to restructure social relations within social systems. As reflected by the design of the Male Academy, the goal was to replace the existing and dominant matriarchal order in the school system with a Black patriarchal hierarchy reflecting Black masculinity through an African-centered curriculum, male role models, school names of Black male leaders, and a boys-only admission policy. The Academy would allow Black males as students, teachers, and administrators to implement their masculinity through a patriarchal hegemony within the Detroit public education system. This would, then, restore Black males to their "rightful" leadership roles in the school system, the Detroit community, and society.

Masculinity is a complex multi-layered concept and construct that includes hegemony, the privileging of men over women, and the dominance of masculinity over femininity (Kuzmic, 2000). Masculinity has been defined as "simultaneously a place in gender relations; the practices through which men and women engage that place in gender; and the effects of these practices in bodily experience, personality, and culture" (Vojdik, 2002). The concept of multiple masculinities recognizes the dynamic nature of masculinity, noting that hegemonic masculinity is a dominant form (Cohen, 2009). Masculinities should be seen as collective social practices, as "socially organized and meaningful actions in historical contexts" (Lesko, 2000, p. xvi). Masculinities "are constructed, performed, and revised" based on race, ethnicity, and sexuality (Lesko, 2000, p. xvii). The literature on Black masculinity (Dyson, 1993; Franklin, 1994; Haymes, 1995; Hunter and Davis, 1992; Lemelle, 1995; Mutua, 2006) demonstrates the complex interconnection between issues of race, class, gender, and culture in the construction and definition of the urban male. Black masculinity, as exemplified by the Black male, involves a complex and paradoxical construction. On one hand, the Black male is portrayed as an emasculated, vulnerable, and helpless victim, easily susceptible to oppressive social forces. On the other hand, he is the patriarch, leader, symbol, and future of the Black race (Murtadha-Watts, 2000; Irvine, 1990). Cole and Guy-Sheftall (2003, p. 132) recognize "black men's perception of their emasculated status," and "understand at a profound level the particular plight of Black men and the hostile world they inhabit." They disagree, however, with the assertion that "Black males have been the principal victims of the legacy of racial discrimination and prejudice in American society." Claiming the status as the "principal victim" enables Black men to demand change to move them from victim to victor and to the traditional gender role of a patriarch with privilege, power, and leadership authority in the Black community.

Discourse about Black masculinity, then, also includes discourse about patriarchy. Scott's (1997, p. 53) findings indicate that social scientists believed that "once black males were made men and patriarchs, black children, primarily black boys, would have positive role models and the black community would no longer be a tangle of pathology." Ransby and Matthews (1995, p. 527) note that calls for Black male role models are an attempt to "reclaim and redefine Black manhood." Black patriarchy, therefore, is essentially the implementation of the political, philosophical, and sociological concepts of Black masculinity within social institutions. The ideology of Black patriarchy, however, is radically inconsistent with the reality of single parent female households. It is also inconsistent with the leadership role that Black women have played and continue to play within the Black social, political, and economic structure. It does accord, however, with the widely held and accepted desire and expectation of many within the Black community that Black men should have a dominant leadership role and that Black women should be subservient and submissive to them.

Kuzmic (2000, p. 122) notes that "the power of patriarchy, as a system of socially constructed meanings about gender identity, lies in its ability to create the ideological conditions that support the institutionalization (social, cultural, political, educational, and familial) of a gender regime that privileges men." He (p. 123) further states that "schools in general, and the curriculum in particular, are a significant site in the politics of challenging and transforming the gender order power relations, and men's privilege." As such, reform initiatives around school policy, school curriculum, and school composition by gender must be conceptualized and recognized as powerful locations and opportunities either for change or the perpetuation of existing hegemonic structures.

A key concept, therefore, within Black masculinity and patriarchy is an almost one-to-one correlation between Black males and the Black community. The argument is often made that Black males are synonymous with the Black community, and that the status of the Black male is synonymous with the status of the Black community and American society. This is reflected by the justification of the National Urban League's Black Male Initiative. It was designed to "address the obstacles impeding the success of black men and boys—especially the poor and young who've fallen off the nation's radar screen" (2007a, p. 14). The Urban League (p. 15) notes that "ensuring the future of the black male is critical, not just for African-Americans, but for the prosperity, health, and well-being of the entire American family." Similarly, Detroit School Board member Edna Bell said, "The implementation of the male academy is important not only to our race, but also to our nation" (Detroit School Board committee approves, 1991).King (1992) indicates that "the experiences of Black men have become both definitive and representative of all African-Americans," ignoring the dynamic cultural, historical, political, and economic contexts of all African-Americans, and portraying an inaccurate picture of Black culture. As a result, there is "a very male-centered definition of the problems confronting the black community" (Ransby and Matthews, 1995, p. 526).

The consequences and implications for Black females of a patriarchal Black masculine hegemony are significant. Cole and Guy-Sheftall (2003, p. 217) note that "patriarchy, which is based on male superiority and supremacy...comes at the expense of women, children, and ultimately, other men." More specifically, they (p. 218) state that "the notion of the man as the one, true king of the house, head of the family, and leader in the community turns our homes and neighborhoods into hostile territories. It gives African-American men a false sense of power based on dominance and control." Collins (1991, p. 86) notes that many Black organizations and institutions—including community organizations, churches, schools, and the media—have been instrumental in subordinating the interests of Black women, for the "allegedly greater good of the larger African-American community," as symbolized by Black males. Collins (2006, p. 148) emphasizes that "when Black male leaders of churches and other community organizations remain so focused on saving Black manhood, they have difficulty seeing Black women as leaders and persist in viewing Black women primarily as supporters of Black men." She notes that "as a result of this focus on Black men, without a similar focus on Black women, Black men are perceived to be significantly more vulnerable and significantly more 'endangered' than Black women" (Collins, 2006, p. 148).

The hegemonic quality of patriarchy is evidenced by the fact that patriarchal ideas are also widely accepted by many Black women, who believe that gender issues must be subordinate to race advancement (Collins, 1991; King, 1992; Terrelonge-Stone, 1995). Black women have often encouraged and promoted a Black male patriarchy and Black male sexism at their own expense. Consequently, Black women have often undermined, overlooked, and sacrificed their own unique gender interests. hooks (1981, p. 182) states "Like Black men, many Black women believed Black liberation could only be achieved by the formation of a strong Black patriarchy" (Marable, 1983). Terrolonge (1995, p. 497) notes that Black women "were told in many different ways that the liberation of the black man was more important than was their own liberation."

A Black woman's statement to sociologist Kesho Scott (1991, p. 149) typifies this belief. The respondent states, "I guess I felt it was more important to get my rights as a Black than as a woman." Scott (p. 151) notes that many Black women have been willing to "be martyrs for the movement" and to take a "backseat to men's advancement." She claims that such willingness reinforces Black male sexism in the Black community by linking Black males with the future of the Black race and suggesting that Black males and Black females cannot simultaneously advance for their mutual gain. hooks speaks of the dual role of Black women as accomplices in the crimes perpetrated against women and the victims of those crimes "through their acceptance of an oppressive, patriarchal, sexist order" (hooks, 1981, p. 49). Paul (2003, p. 36) notes that "many of us tacitly accept the flawed truism that to privilege and validate the lives of black boys and men, we must underestimate and denigrate the experiences of black girls and women. In the process, we reinforce a pervasive and invariable sexism in the black community that is infrequently admitted and/or debated." Black women, then, often accept, support, and advocate for "pseudosolutions that further marginalize and denigrate black women" (Ransby & Matthews, 1995, p. 526).

This marginalization of Black women is consistently reflected in scholarly Black feminist work. Henry (1998, p. 153–154) refers to the invisibility of Black girls because of the dominant hegemonic discourse about Black males when she says "Black girls are invisible in social science theory and practice in qualitative ways. Interpretive studies on Black girls and schooling are meager...research on race, class, gender, and schooling rarely focus on the complexities that face young girls of African heritage but rather tend to perpetuate the popularized discourse of the 'endangered black male'." Paul (2003, p. 29) notes that Black girls are "a footnote in the discourse on the 'endangered black male'." Paul (2003, p. 31) recognizes the validity of concerns relating to Black boys and suicide rates, their overrepresentation in special education classes, their underrepresentation in gifted classes, the high diagnosis of attention deficit-hyperactivity disorder, and high incarceration rates, but also notes that "in this discussion of the endangered black male, some are unable or unwilling (except in the most cursory of fashions) to acknowledge that concerns about black girls and young women are consequential as well." She indicates that Black women represent the largest racial group in state prison, that Black girls struggle with low self-esteem, that there is an increase of violence and juvenile delinquency among girls, and that there is a significant health crisis, including HIV/AIDS, facing Black women. Cole and Guy-Sheftall (2003, p. 219) remark

> The reality that both Black men and Black women are willing to ignore or subordinate the concerns of Black girls for the larger and more pressing needs of Black males reflects the power of hegemony. We believe that it will be very difficult to dislodge the very deep and tenacious belief among many African-American men that they do not have any power to relinquish under a racist, capitalist system. They are likely to argue that more African-American women are educated and employed than African-American men. They will try to overpower our cries of sexism with references to the racism that oppresses all of us, but especially them. They will undoubtedly remind us of all the ways they are "an endangered species," as if we are not also "endangered"—not only from the greater society, but in many cases, because of them.

The hegemonic nature of discourse allows ideas, attitudes, and beliefs to be perpetuated, unquestioned, and unchallenged. More importantly, the power of hegemony is evidenced in its ability to perpetuate the "status quo by affecting the structures within which people think, so that they find it difficult or impossible to conceive of things in any other way" (Paechter, 1998, p. 3; Pascale, 2006).

In the Male Academy debate, the social problem was clearly defined to achieve consensus from the Black community. The discourse of the Black male social problem incorporated dominant social themes that were familiar to the Black community. Given the prevalence of perceptions about Black males, the strategy of using key words, such as "urban male," "our urban male," "endangered species," "crime rate," "incarceration rate," and "drop out rate," resonated within the Black community. Murtadha-Watts (2003, p. 55) has noted that "urban has become a metaphor for race... urban problems, such as poverty, homelessness, joblessness, crime, violence, single-parent households, and drugs, are seen as racial problems, the problems of blacks, and the primary problem of Black males." The reference to urban, then, was understood as a reference to race and gender, and specifically to Black males. Likewise, the endangered species metaphor was consistent with the commonly accepted view within the Black and White community that the inner city is a "jungle" with "potentially wild animals, violent destructive gangsters, or sexual deviants [lurking] in the young bodies of black males, who if left alone in their environments, would endanger the safety of American culture" (Murtadha-Watts, 2003, p. 54–55). The reference to "endangered species," then, was consistent with metaphors associated with Black males and the inner-city environment. The construction of Black males as victims, combined with the rhetoric of dropout rates and incarceration was also familiar to the community.

The power of hegemonic discourse, then, is reflected in its ability to affect and influence the behavior of a large and diverse audience. The discourse was designed to affect the audience of the Black community: community activists; Black single mothers who needed to be persuaded to send their sons to the Male Academy; and Black single mothers who needed to be persuaded to ignore the needs of their daughters. This discourse was designed not only to influence ideas, thoughts, and attitudes, but also to control and influence behavior. Using an exclusively Black male-focused perspective of the Black community created a logical connection and justification for instituting a patriarchal system in the Black community. One key strategy for resolving the problems and conditions of Black men was to change their status from powerless to powerful, from victims to victors, and from matriarchal controlled and emasculated men to patriarchal dominant leaders through the Detroit Male Academy initiative.

TASJ reveals the complex construction and deconstruction of a social problem. The social problem in the Detroit Male Academy initiative involved interwoven socially constructed individual and group identities, interlocking social systems and structures, and ideologies of power, privilege, entitlement, and domination. The urban male was the socially constructed race, class, and gender category. The interlocking social systems, structures, and institutions were the education system (including the Detroit Public School Board and the public schools), the legal system (including the federal court and the district judge), the Detroit community (including organizations and individuals supporting and opposing the Male Academy), and the media (including print and TV coverage). The ideology was one of Black masculinity and Black patriarchy.

In addition to these three components—individuals, institutions, and ideas—the social problem analysis clearly incorporates the four domains of power: interpersonal, hegemonic, disciplinary, and structural (Collins, 2009, p. 294). The hegemonic power domain is evidenced in the perpetuation and use of widely held and taken for granted perspectives about the endangered status of Black males, the expectation that women's needs should be subordinate to the needs of men, and the belief that Black men should be leaders. This domain involves ideology, culture, and consciousness and thus links "social institutions (structural domain), their organizational practices (disciplinary domain), and the level of everyday social interaction (interpersonal domain)" (Collins, 2009, p. 302). Much of the discourse that originates around the Male Academy debate is controlled by the individuals who have a strong affiliation with the Detroit School Board, and as such, have a keen interest in perpetuating the plans of the Male Academy. Thus, the education system at the macro-level and the individual Male Academy supporters at the micro-level serve to perpetuate a hegemonic perspective of the dominant ideology of male privilege, female subordination, education control, and Black male victimhood. Because the hegemonic domain of power operates within social structures, the school system, the legal system, and the media were key contested sites and opportunities for the operation and intersection of both the structural power domain and the hegemonic power domain. The disciplinary domain in the Male Academy was reflected in the policy initiative and the legal case. It was evidenced by the Board's attempt to change existing legal interpretations of rules, policies, and laws that affected, governed, and managed the public school system. The discussion about Title IX and its regulations, the Fourteenth Amendment and the Supreme Court's interpretation, the EEOA, the Elliott-Larsen Act, and the Michigan School Code evidence the role of the law in the education system. The domains of power provided a strong foundation for the discourse and debate about the social problem and the punctuation element of the collective action frame. They also provided a foundation on which the attribution element could be laid. The emergency nature of the Black male crisis had been documented, and the imperative of a Black male patriarchy had been justified.

In the definition of the problem, a hint of the cause is often alluded to in the silences and absences in the discourse. In this case, there is almost a complete absence of the perspectives, concerns, and problems of females. The punctuation element foreshadows the anti-female rhetoric in the Academy supporters' attribution elements. Excluding the problems of females from the definition of the crisis created a logical transition to the attribution element, where the cause for the crisis was placed on females as mothers, teachers, and students, as well as on feminism and matriarchy.

3

The Cause Attributed

Chapter 2 discussed the punctuation element of the collective action frame—defining a social problem as unjust and requiring immediate and drastic attention. This chapter explores the second element of the collective action frame: attribution. Attribution is identifying individuals, groups, or structures on which a "sense of blame or causality" can be placed (Snow & Benford, 1992). The discourse reflects that causality, in part, was attributed to females: mothers as parents, girls as classmates, and women as teachers. Within the classroom and outside the classroom, women, based primarily on their gender status alone, were portrayed as responsible in varying aspects for the social and education failure of Black males. Causality was also attributed to ideologies associated with the female gender: matriarchy and feminism. Finally, the racial dynamic emerged in the discourse based on the organizational and institutional presence of the predominantly White political organizations of NOWLDF and the ACLU. These institutions were portrayed as symbols of race and class power and privilege. The oppositional nature of the DMA debate is evidenced in the dichotomy between the issues in the punctuation element and those in the attribution element. The punctuation element involved males, masculinity, and patriarchy. The attribution element involves females, feminism, and matriarchy.

The groups, individuals, and social structures accused of being responsible for the problem were essentially either female or White. They were accused of perpetuating gender, racial, and economic privilege at the expense of inner-city Black males. This chapter explores the issues of gender and femaleness at the macro and micro levels in the debate. First, the role of the students, teachers, and mothers is examined, followed by a look at matriarchy and feminism. The chapter concludes with the third section's discussion of White race and class privilege.

3.1 Females

Females were identified as one of the major causes of the Black male crisis. The primary argument was that Black boys did not have a good home or school environment because there were few Black male role models in the home as fathers and in the classrooms as teachers. More specifically, the cause of the Black male crisis was the presence of girls in the classrooms; the presence of women as teachers; and the role of mothers as parents.

The responsibility attributed to females as students and teachers can be seen by the frequent use of the word "environment" by the Board and Male Academy supporters. For example, the Board's Memorandum of Law (Memorandum of law in opposition, p. 60) indicated that the Male Academy would provide the "kind of environment and experiences that ensure that target, at-risk youth succeed." Similarly, the Board (p. 15) asserted that, according to its experts, a single-sex environment provided an "environment most conducive" to addressing the goal of the Male Academy. Hale (1991), one of the Board's expert witnesses, referred to the Male Academy as a "homogeneous setting" providing "an environment responsive to their [urban males] needs."Smitherman (1991), another of the Board's expert witnesses, refers to a "single-sex environment" providing a "healthy, positive setting."

References to the "environment" often included references to "co-education." One key element of the proposed "environment" was the absence of female students. References to "co-education" are often synonymous with the presence of female students (Paechter, 1998, p. 11), thus negative references to co-education were used to imply that the presence of female students was correlated with the failure of male students. In its Memorandum of Law, the Board (Memorandum of law in opposition, p. 14) asserted that the exclusion of females was substantially related to the important governmental interest of addressing the academic and social failure of Black males because "co-educational programs aimed at improving male performance have failed." Smitherman (1991) indicated that a "single-sex educational environment" rather than a "coeducational setting" is necessary for boys "to practice and develop their social language skills in a healthy, positive setting with strong male linguistic role models." Dr. Watson

(1991), principal of the proposed Malcolm X Academy, stated that the "traditional coed setting has not provided the environment that is necessary for males to succeed and/or survive within the current system." Expert witness Gardner (1991) also mentioned the "socially competitive and attention diverting aspects of co-educating," asserting that the Male Academy would eliminate this problem.

In addition to the use of the words "environment" and "co-education," the Board's discourse and the discourse of proponents of the Male Academy illustrated that females as students were considered a distraction to Black males in the classroom. Dr. Watson (*Crossfire*, 1991) stated, "Isn't there a possibility that taking six-year-old and seven-year-old Black boys, moving them away from the distraction of girls so that they can study and maybe not just do well academically but save their lives is worth trying when you're losing half of them?" Asante (1991), in his affidavit, referred to the Male Academy as a "school environment...in which high expectations can be encouraged without the distraction of young males vying for the attention of young women." According to Jones (1991), another expert witness for the Board, "there is too much 'macho competition' in school between boys when girls are the 'prize'." The discourse surrounding the justification for a Male Academy illustrates that girls were accused of getting male students in trouble and were often blamed for teachers' decisions, thus "making females responsible for bad conduct by males" (Sundberg, 1991a). Below are several examples from NOWLDF documents and newspaper articles illustrating how supporters of the all-male environment, including young male students, attributed blame to girls.

1. A Detroit male teacher of an all-male elementary school class in Detroit states that girls are "often showing the boys up in class....That can lead to bad behavior, and just turning off to learning." A third grader in this classroom is quoted as saying "You do it better because there aren't no girls around to make you act silly" (NOWLDF, p. 24).
2. A male student in a Baltimore school that has implemented single-sex elementary school classes says: "It feels wonderful to be in here...girls get you in trouble because every time the girl will do something, the teacher gets on your case" (NOWLDF, p. 24).
3. A ten-year-old fifth grade boy is quoted as saying: "They're [girls] always messing with you. They won't let you do your work" (Kelly, 1992).
4. A ten-year-old male student at Marcus Garvey Academy is quoted as saying "It should have been all boys. Girls get you in trouble" (Gilchrist, August 29, 1991).

5. A nine-year-old boy at Matthew Henson School, Baltimore's single-sex classroom experiment is quoted as saying "[girls] disturb you when you're working and they get their work finished and you don't" (Cooper, 1990).
6. A Detroit male teacher says that "boys feel stifled in a classroom with girls." He states that sex-segregated classes provide a greater benefit for males because "they are less prone to rivalries over the opposite sex and less inhibited in their approach to learning" (Russell, August 27, 1991).
7. Annette Polly Williams, a Black Wisconsin state legislator, is quoted as saying "young girls...completely subvert what's needed in these schools to help Black males" (Innerst, 1991).

Although these references refer only to "girls" in general, it is important to realize that because inner-city school districts are predominantly Black, these comments primarily refer to Black girls. These comments further suggest that young Black male students and Black male educational leadership equate the need for a single-sex environment with a negative attitude toward Black female students. The comments conflict with research documenting the passivity of females, their traditional silence in the classroom environment, and male domination of space and time (AAUW, 1992; Grant, 1984; Paechter, 1998; Sadker & Sadker, 1994).

Not only were female students implicated as a cause, the predominantly female teaching staff was also implicated. Malveaux (n.d.) noted that the criticism of students and teachers "sends boys the message that something is so wrong with girls and women that they are incapable of learning in their presence." The discourse about the need for Black male teachers, Black male role models, and Black male mentors implied that one of the factors impeding the progress of urban male students was the presence of female teachers (Male academy grades K-8, p. 25; Memorandum of law in opposition, p. 3). Dr. Holland asserted that African-American male students need to be taught by male teachers, either Black or White, because "females cannot teach boys how to become men" (NOWLDF, p. 22). In fact, the December 5, 1990, *Washington Post* referred to a Black male teacher as a "father figure" who "reinforces his students' sense of maleness" (Cooper, 1990). Dr. Watson (1991) stated, "When the male students arrive at school, for the most part, they interact with predominantly female staff. As a result, they have few male role models. Male role models are needed to interact with the male students to better assess their social and educational needs." He further asserted that "the lack of sufficient role models and the lack of specific attention to particular needs of the males has indeed crippled the existence of the male success rate within the Detroit Public Schools." In a particularly harsh statement in his August 16, 1991, *Crossfire* interview, Dr. Watson said to Ruth Jones, the Black female attorney on NOWLDF's legal staff, "Do you have any brothers? Have you seen the movie *Boyz N the Hood*? Ms. Jones, are you a man? Ms. Jones, you're not capable in my estimation, as I'm not capable in my estimation [of] being a complete role model for females."

The discourse also refers to the insensitivity of female teachers and the need to train female teachers "to effectively educate inner-city males" (Carter, 1991). Although Jones (1991) did not propose the exclusion of female teachers, she does refer to the benefit of "the adult role model offered by male teachers and female teachers gender-sensitive to the special needs of urban male students." Dr. Watson (1991) noted that

> when problems develop between the two sexes, a teacher (often female) will tend to listen and accept a complaint from a female student more readily and may treat the male student unfairly. In many instances the males may be suspended or expelled for what has been deemed to be inappropriate behavior.

These perceptions provided a justification for Prof. Sedler's comments sanctioning hiring preferences for male teachers for the Male Academy. In his legal opinion, he (1991) suggested

> In the experimental setting of the Male Academy, it is certainly legitimate to give preference to male teachers. Indeed, in my opinion, again because of the experimental setting, it would be legitimate and legally permissible to treat maleness as a bona fide occupational qualification for service at the Male Academy.

Treating "maleness as a bona fide occupational qualification," however, suggests that "femaleness" is not a bona fide occupational qualification and presumes that based solely on their gender, females are not qualified to instruct males. The statement also assumes that all males, just because they are male, are more qualified to instruct males, regardless of their teaching skills and experience. Despite the sexism inherent in these comments, they created a justification for excluding female teachers from the Male Academy.

Although a majority of the comments only referred to the gender of female teachers, there were comments that referred to race, revealing the intersectionality of race and gender. Malveaux (n.d.) noted that since "black women teachers have historically been the backbone of urban school systems", there is a belief that "black women cannot teach black men." Kunjufu, justifying the need for male role models, is also quoted as saying, "Black boys' behavior is often judged (largely by White female teachers) against a female model, leading teachers to suspend African-American boys and place them in special education classes" (Ray, 1991). Because White females have such a dominant presence in the classroom, the criticism of female teachers was often a way to implicate White racism and the systems of domination and oppression of Black men inherent within that structure.

Thus, based on references to the environment, to co-education, and to male role models, the discourse illustrates that causality for the Black male crisis was attributed in part to female students and female teachers. Because the social problem involved the educational performance of Black males, the causes needed to be relevant to the educational experience. As such, the attribution of causality to students and teachers created a logical connection to the classroom. The references evidence an "anti-female ideology," implicating the mere presence of females as the source of Black male social ills, "rather than poor economic and social conditions founded on race and sex discrimination" (Sundberg, 1991a). They also minimize the role of other dynamics, besides gender, that affect the educational experience of students in the classroom and influenced the design of the Male Academy, including teacher training, additional resources, and curriculum changes.

In addition to female students and teachers, causality was also attributed to mothers. The overall argument was essentially parallel to the two-prong argument for students and teachers: that female students created a bad classroom environment for males and that female teachers were not appropriate role models in the classroom for Black males. Similarly, the argument against mothers was that mothers were problems as parents in the home environment and were not appropriate role models for Black males. Like the discourse about the school environment, concerns were raised through references to the home environment. Several comments specifically addressed mothers and their role in raising children.

The visibility of single mothers in the debate was highlighted by the Black women plaintiffs in the *Garrett vs.Board of Education* lawsuit. Two Black single mothers and their daughters were plaintiffs.

Paragraphs 7 and 8 of the Preliminary Statement of the Complaint filed by NOWLDF and the ACLU described the plaintiffs.

> Plaintiff SHAWN GARRETT, a twenty-five year old African-American woman, is a resident of Detroit and a product of the Detroit Public Schools. Her four-year-old daughter, CRYSTAL GARRETT, will be in pre-school this Fall, 1991. Because of her own experiences in the Detroit Public School system, Shawn Garrett is very concerned about the educational experiences that her daughter will have in that school system. Shawn Garrett wants her daughter to have every opportunity to complete her education, pursue her goals in life and avoid the traps of pregnancy, drug abuse and other problems that often cause urban girls to drop out of school. If the Male Academies had been open to girls, Shawn Garrett would have applied to have her daughter Crystal attend one of the Academies. Plaintiff Garrett proceeds individually and as next friend to her daughter, Crystal Garrett, who is a minor.

As will be discussed in Chapter 5, Shawn and Crystal Garrett withdrew from the case prior to the court's decision. The other plaintiffs were given pseudonyms to protect their identity:

> NANCY DOE, an African American woman, is a thirty year old resident of Detroit and a product of the Detroit Public School system. Nancy Doe's daughters, Jane Doe, Judy Doe and Jessica Doe, ages 11, 6, and 5, respectively, will attend the Detroit Public Schools this Fall, 1991. Because of her own experiences in the Detroit Public School system and as a teen mother, Nancy Doe is very concerned about the educational experiences that her daughters will have in that school system. Nancy Doe wants her daughters to have every opportunity to complete their education, pursue their goals in life and avoid the traps of pregnancy, drug abuse and other problems that often cause urban girls to drop out of school. If the Male Academies had been open to girls, Nancy Doe would have applied to have her daughters attend one of the Academies. Plaintiff Doe proceeds individually and as next friend to her daughters, Jane Doe, Judy Doe and Jessica Doe, minors. Nancy Doe and her daughters proceed pseudonymously and will, upon the Court's request, file copies of their original affidavits under seal.

The plaintiffs, then, were Black single mothers and their daughters. Shawn Garrett was employed as an insurance clerk (Gilchrist, August 6, 1991) and Nancy Doe was receiving public assistance. Doe's affidavit says "I am a single mother who receives no assistance in raising my daughters from their fathers. I am the recipient of public benefits to help me keep a satisfactory home for my family. I became pregnant in high school, and understand the burdens of teenage pregnancy."

There is no reference in the discourse to Crystal Garrett's father or Shawn Garrett's husband or partner. The fathers of the daughters were not a party to the lawsuit. The dynamics of the case may have been very different had the fathers of these girls brought suit, along with their mothers. In fact, the absence of fathers was symbolic of the state of Black males and the problems in the Black community. The absence of Black males lent further credence to criticism of single parent female-headed households. Seventy percent of all male students for the Woodward Elementary School in Detroit came from single homes headed by a female member of the family (C. Watson, 1991), so the rhetoric reflects the reality that a majority of students in Detroit were from single-family homes.

There were repeated references in the discourse to the words "female-headed households," "family structure," "single-mother," and "role model." Often the references also included an implication that Black single women were responsible for the condition of Black males. One of the most vocal proponents of single-sex schools for Black males, Dr. Spencer Holland (NOWLDF, p. 19), wrote that "the single parent, female-headed households in this nation's urban communities deny the young Black male child a major vehicle necessary in the socialization process of all boys, an adult male." This statement implies that single Black mothers are responsible for the absence of fathers and male role models for their Black male child. Smitherman (1991) specifically linked linguistic skill differences between males and females to "the disproportionate number of males being reared in female-headed households, the decline in intact family structures, and the absence of positive male influence." Baltimore's Matthew Henson principal Leah Hasty stated that she formed the single-sex class so that a Black male teacher could serve as "a positive role model for Black boys who come from female-headed households" (Cooper, 1990). Asante (1991), noting that "many young male African-American children are from single-mother families" and that "role models are particularly important for male African-American children," remarked that the "home environment of such families cannot give structured information of a historical, cultural, and moral nature to make an impact on such children or change the quality of the society overall." He further commented that one of the purposes of the Male Academy was to "project humanistic and pluralistic values to interdict serious problems occurring in society which have their roots in the deterioration of family structure in an urban environment." Similarly, Gardner (1991) stated that an "all male educational environment would likely foster the adoption of more socially valuable and appropriate sex-role responsibilities and functions." James Q. Wilson, professor at UCLA, was quoted as saying that boarding schools enable inner-city males to be "inculcated with the moral, political, religious or ethnocentric instruction lacking in families without fathers" (Katz, 1991). He further stated that "neighborhood standards may be set by mothers but they are enforced by fathers, or at least adult males."

These statements refer not just to the presence of females as mothers, but also to role models, values, and morals. The language clearly suggests that Black females cannot provide a quality moral environment for Black boys. Rather than placing blame on Black males as fathers and husbands, blame was placed solely on females within two social environments: the classroom and the home. Through TASJ, the home and school can be viewed as interlocking social structures within the structural domain. Within these structural domains, day-to-day interactions between males and females occur in the interpersonal domain. These interactions in the interpersonal domain between children and parents, as well as students and teachers, were used by the Male Academy supporters to justify the DMA initiative. The argument was that the DMA would allow the classroom dynamics to be restructured through the disciplinary domain with different classroom rules and procedures to accommodate males, masculinity, and patriarchy. The need to implement a masculine patriarchal order implicated the existing matriarchal feminist order and the hegemonic domain. The next section explores the issues of matriarchy and feminism as they were manifested in the debate.

3.2 Matriarchy and Feminism

The discourse of the Male Academy debate reflects the way in which the social problem and social cause were intertwined within commonly accepted hegemonic ideas and attitudes. The collective action framework reveals a tight, logistical, and simplistic structure. The Black male problem was due to females. As a result, Black girls needed to be removed as students, females needed to be removed as teachers, and Black mothers needed to be removed as the heads of households. The classroom environment with male role models would address both the school environment and the home environment. Black male role models in an all-Black school would provide Black boys with a proper moral curriculum, in a good environment—one without female students or teachers—where they could be trained to be leaders and patriarchs for their race and could assume their rightful place in the home and community. Ransby and Matthews (1995, p. 527) note that the cry for Black male role models reflects an underlying assumption that Black patriarchs are needed to "give moral direction to the floundering female-headed households that have destabilized the black community." Often the increased value placed on Black manhood is associated with a simultaneous devaluation of Black womanhood and the perpetuation of stereotypes about Black women (hooks, 1981).

In light of the role of Black women as mothers and teachers in transmitting values to children, many stereotypes about Black women have developed around their relationships with children (Collins, 1991; Joseph & Lewis, 1981). Black women have been portrayed as "failing to discipline their children, of emasculating their sons, of defeminizing their daughters, and of retarding their children's academic achievement" (Collins, 1991, p. 74). Portrayed as stereotypical "matriarchs" and "welfare queens" (Collins, 1991, p. 115), Black women are often accused of being responsible for the intergenerational transmission of poverty and poor values, as well as the deteriorating Black family structure as evidenced by the high rates of Black, female-headed households.

This portrayal and causality is consistent with Scott's (1997) damage imagery thesis. He notes that although leading experts sometimes differ on the precise causes of pathologies in the Black community, "virtually everyone agreed that 'matriarchy' had adverse consequences for the personalities of black people, and most experts had no qualms about exploring them" (p. 74). Scott documents leading social scientists' references to role models, discipline, the socialization of Black men, and the attribution of responsibility for the emasculation of Black men to Black women as matriarchs. hooks (1981, p. 75) points out that the portrayal of Black women as matriarchs and welfare mothers is often associated with the presentation of Black men as "weak, effeminate and castrated" due to the dominance of Black women. Black women have often been criticized for de-masculinizing Black men and succeeding at their expense. "[T]he matriarchy myth suggested that once again Black women had been granted privileges denied Black men," implying that Black women had a power, which in reality they do not (hooks, 1981). Paul (2003, p. 16) notes that "we [Black women] continue to assume blame for abandoning and emasculating black men, as well as compelling them to abandon us." She said that the success of Black women in some spheres in society has been used against them by juxtaposing their accomplishments with the failures of Black men. Wallace (1995, p. 221; Staples, 1979) remembers that she and other Black women during the Civil Rights Movement were often accused of "destroying the Black man's masculinity, castrating him, working when he didn't, making money when he made none, spending time at church praying to a jive white boy named Jesus while he collapsed into alcoholism, drug addiction, and various forms of despair."

Cole and Guy-Sheftall (2003, p. 82–83) discuss the twin myths of Black emasculation and Black matriarchy:

> It was widely accepted that racism had emasculated black men, prevented their legitimate claims to manhood, and compelled them to demand their rightful place as men (even patriarchs) in a white male-dominated society that had rendered them powerless. Secondly, Black women, more privileged by the racial social order because they are less threatening, are powerful matriarchs who need to step back and support Black men's long overdue quest for manhood.

This perspective is consistent with the black nationalist approach where "strong African-American women in Black families and Black civil society were labeled deviant" (Collins, 1991, p. 107). As a result, in order to effect change, Black women were expected to be subservient supporters of the grander cause of Black manhood and patriarchy. Toni Cade recognized this dynamic when she said "There is a dangerous trend...to program Sapphire out of her 'evil' ways into a cover-up, shut-up, lay-back-and-be-cool obedience role" (Cole & Guy-Sheftall, 2003, p. 94). Thus, Black women have been depicted as "damaging" Black males through their portrayal as "Saffire, the domineering woman who emasculated her man" (Scott, 1997, p. 78).

The matriarch and Saffire stereotypes perpetuate the belief that Black women, rather than institutionalized racism, are responsible for the state of Black men. By "blaming the victim" (Ryan, 1971), such comments ignore the role of complex racial and economic factors that influence and affect inner-city neighborhoods, including economic restructuring, joblessness, unemployment, and poverty (Wilson, 1987, 1996). They also fail to attribute any responsibility to males and their role in creating female-headed households through the fathering of children and their subsequent absence. Notably, blame is rarely attached to Black males or Black fathers for being absent from their homes. The role and importance of Black fathers in the lives of Black girls is almost never mentioned.

Thus, Black male victimization by Black female dominance and incompetence has become a common justification for perpetuating the ideology of Black male privilege, Black female subordination, and the primacy of race over gender. In Detroit, a sympathetic character of the Black male was created without attributing any responsibility to Black boys or Black males for their own conduct. At the same time, blame was easily attributed to commonly accepted negative and stereotypical images of Black women as domineering matriarchs in single-female-headed households, and Saffires who attempted to control and emasculate men. Likewise, Black girls in the classroom were portrayed as little Saffires and little matriarchs, trying to control and dominate the classroom.

Consistent with the matriarchy concept and running parallel with it in the discourse was the concept of feminism. The Black female plaintiffs were represented in the legal proceedings by three organizations: the ACLU, NOWLDF, and the law firm of Goodman, Eden, Millender, & Bedrosian. NOWLDF drafted most of the legal documents and served as lead counsel. The key attorneys from NOWLDF were Ruth Jones, an African-American female, and Martha Davis, a White female. Even though Ruth Jones was an African-American female lawyer for NOWLDF, the organization as a whole was generally seen as female and White. As a result of NOWLDF's leadership role in the lawsuit, the organization, its attorneys, and their values were an easy target of the Male Academy supporters. The criticism of the organization was often based on its mission to advocate for gender equality. Additionally, as a predominantly White feminist organization focused on equal rights for women, the organization was perceived as anti-Black and anti-male.

The feminist status of NOWDLF provided additional ammunition for the Male Academy supporters. In fact, the word "feminist" was often used to derogatorily refer to NOWLDF and its members (Russell, August 5, 1991a, 1991b; All-girl schools, 1991). Patrick Buchanan on *Crossfire* (1991) suggested that Ruth Jones, the NOWLDF attorney, was "willing to sacrifice Dr. Watson's kids on the altar of [her] feminism and [her] ideology." NOWLDF represented and symbolized a female matriarchy. It supported and advocated for the presence of girls in the classroom and the presence of female teachers in schools. It also protected the matriarchy of Black single mothers by bringing a lawsuit on their behalf—a lawsuit grounded in feminist rhetoric.

The Complaint filed against the Detroit School Board is an allegation of discrimination based on gender and sexism. NOWLDF challenged the Board's primary justification that the crisis merited the exclusion of girls. The Complaint represented the legal arguments of the plaintiffs in opposition to the Male Academy. In light of the short time frame involved with the planned opening of the Male Academy, NOWLDF was asking the Court to issue a preliminary injunction. (A preliminary injunction is a legal ruling issued by a Court to temporarily stop a particular action until a more comprehensive review of the legal rights can be determined). Four elements must be proven for a court to grant a preliminary injunction. On behalf of the Black mothers and daughters, NOWLDF attempted to prove the following four elements: (1) that the plaintiffs were likely to prevail on the merits of their constitutional and statutory claims, (2) that the plaintiffs would suffer irreparable harm without the injunction, (3) that the harm caused to others by granting the injunction was minimal; and (4) that the public interest required the injunction.

From a legal perspective, the plaintiffs needed to prove that the exclusion of girls from the Male Academy was discriminatory on the basis of gender. The central legal position was that under *Mississippi University for Women School of Nursing v. Hogan* (1982), gender could not be used to deny children in the public school system equal benefits, services, and educational opportunities. In *Hogan*, the Supreme Court held that Mississippi's policy of excluding men from the School of Nursing lacked an "exceedingly persuasive justification" and perpetuated gender stereotypes. The Court stated that a gender-based classification must serve an "important governmental objective" and that the discriminatory means must be "substantially related to achieving that objective." The plaintiffs argued that the Board could not justify its gender-based classification under the standard in *Hogan*. They asserted that the Board could not prove that excluding girls was "substantially related to achieving...the worthy and important objective of improving the lives of urban boys and men" (Memorandum of law in support, p. 12). Conversely, the attorneys emphasized that there was no evidence that the presence of girls in the classroom was substantially related to the difficulties facing urban males. Noting that in *Hogan* the Court expressed concerns about the "inaccurate assumptions about the proper roles of men and women," NOWLDF argued that the position of the Board was based on gender stereotypes. It also stated that the Board's use of gender, rather than educational performance, as the basis for Male Academy eligibility implied that girls were not at risk (Memorandum of law in support, p. 14). In other words, NOWLDF challenged the Board's use of "at-risk" and the Board's strategy of only using that term in reference to Black males.

The plaintiffs relied on affidavits from its expert witnesses to prove that many girls in the Detroit School System were in fact at risk and that the urban crisis was not exclusively male (Memorandum of law in support, p. 7; Preliminary statement, p. 13). They argued that the female dropout rate of 45 percent also reflected a lack of opportunities and low self-esteem for girls (Preliminary statement, p. 13). Specifically, they noted that "urban girls also drop out in significant numbers, suffer loss of self-esteem, become parents at an early age, get involved in criminal activity and suffer from high poverty rates" (Memorandum of law in support, p. 14). It was noted that the problems of girls were not limited to pregnancy because only 40 percent of the girls who dropped out did so for reasons related to pregnancy or parenting. NOWLDF also used the Male Academy resolution, which stated that the progress of males was the same as their female peers in the preschool and primary years, to suggest that the Board itself recognized that both boys and girls were in need of significant assistance. By using the Board's own documents, NOWLDF attempted to undermine the Board's claim that the problems of girls were primarily pregnancy-related and that the crisis was much more devastating for males than females.

Further, the plaintiffs' attorneys mentioned that not all males served by the Academy were at risk. They noted that the Male Academy did not exclusively target at-risk males, but rather all males from a "mix" of backgrounds. These backgrounds included high, average, and below average achievement, a range of social classes, and other factors such as citizenship and attendance. In addition, the attorneys suggested that in light of the required parental involvement, many at-risk boys would be excluded from the Male Academy. They argued that parents of the most at-risk boys would be least likely to attend school functions and participate in the Academy's programs. In its Reply Brief, NOWLDF also challenged the Board's attempt to argue that the Male Academy was not a sex-segregated school in violation of the Elliott-Larsen Act, but rather a special program allowed under Michigan law to serve the needs of students at risk. NOWLDF (Reply brief, p. 8) emphasized that "designating all boys as 'students at risk'...would permit racial segregation by merely defining Black children as 'students at risk'." By challenging the Board's circular reasoning that at risk was synonymous with Black males, NOWLDF illustrated the logical weaknesses in the Board's arguments.

In addition to criticizing the Board's use of gender rather than achievement as a basis for determining need, NOWLDF argued that the Board's Rites of Passage program perpetuated the myth that boys and girls have different roles in society. They noted that the Male Academy brochure and the Task Force Report described the Rites program as a "program that prepares boys to be men." The curriculum involved ten rites of passage: personal, spiritual, economic, emotional, physical, mental, political, social, historical, and cultural. Despite the gender-specific language describing each rite, NOWLDF (Memorandum of law in support, p. 6, 14; PS, p. 6, 9, 11) noted that the rites addressed problems confronting both boys and girls, and therefore, did not require a "uniquely male atmosphere." The attorneys emphasized that all aspects of the curriculum would be beneficial to both boys and girls, including the Afrocentric (Pluralistic) curriculum, futuristic lessons in preparation for twenty-first century careers, an emphasis on spirituality and civic responsibility, mentors, Saturday classes, individualized counseling, extended day-extended hours, student uniforms, foreign language classes, competitive sports, and a highly trained and motivated teaching staff. The attorneys also expressed concern that the success of the Academy could be erroneously attributed to the exclusion of girls, rather than to the unique curriculum, the trained teachers, the increased per capita spending, and other special resources.

NOWLDF also responded to the Board's justification for the Male Academy based on its allegedly experimental and voluntary nature. Disagreeing with the Board, NOWLDF argued that the voluntary, as opposed to mandatory, assignment of boys to the Academy did not remedy the Male Academy's constitutional weaknesses because females were still excluded based on their gender. NOWLDF further argued that the Male Academy should not be considered experimental because there were three Academies, rather than one, and no control group was included to evaluate their effectiveness.

NOWLDF (Memorandum of law in support, p. 17) used racial analogies to emphasize the discriminatory nature of the Board's argument, suggesting that if experimentation were allowed, there would be "no bar to special, experimental academies offering educational programs designed for white males, or segregated academies for the disabled or separate schools for ethnic minorities." The attorneys (Reply brief, p. 14) also stated that "treating girls unequally as part of an experiment to help boys is no different than treating Blacks unequally as an experiment to see whether the races learn better when they are segregated." Similarly, NOWLDF (Memorandum of law in support, p. 18) argued that the Male Academy should not be considered an affirmative action program since it was not narrowly tailored to remedy specific sex discrimination. They (Memorandum of law in support, p. 19; Reply brief, p. 9) noted that there was no justification for the Board's "contemporary reverse-discrimination" in the absence of evidence that the presence of girls in the classroom was related to the Black male crisis.

NOWLDF supplemented its constitutional arguments with statutory ones, arguing that the Board's actions violated Title IX. NOWLDF (Memorandum of law in support, p. 20–21) claimed that the Board, through the Male Academy, was illegally extending "different aid, benefits, and services" to boys and "refusing participation of girls" on the basis of sex. NOWLDF noted that the Office of Civil Rights of the Department of Education in August 1988 and April 1990 (in response to inquiries from the Superintendent of Dade County Schools and the Wisconsin Department of Public Instruction) stated that in the absence of safety or privacy concerns, sex-segregated classes violated Title IX (see Memorandum of law in support, p. 22–23, Exhibit G and H to Complaint). Additionally, the attorneys relied on a Michigan Department of Education letter to the General Superintendent of Detroit dated February 7, 1990, indicating that single-sex schools violated Title IX (see Memorandum of law in support, p. 23; Exhibit F to Complaint).

The plaintiffs' attorneys also responded to the suggestion in the Task Force Report that the Continuing Education Centers (CECs) for girls justified the Male Academy for boys. They noted that Title IX, viewing pregnancy as a "temporary disability," contained a specific exception for single-sex classes for pregnant girls. NOWLDF emphasized the disparity in the educational environment between the Male Academy and the CECs. They asserted that unlike the Male Academy, the CECs did not offer an enriched educational environment, were not preventive, did not serve the same age group as the Male Academy (preschool through fifth grade); and had a different purpose from the Male Academies. They stated that there were no comparable schools to the Male Academies for girls in grades preschool through eight. The attorneys (Memoradum of law in support, p. 25; Preliminary statement, 13; Male academy grades K-8, 15-17) emphasized that a very small number of at-risk girls were served by the CECs and that pregnant and parenting girls comprised less than half of the female dropouts.

In addition to Title IX arguments, NOWLDF also argued that the Academy violated Michigan's Equal Educational Opportunities Act (EEOA) and the Elliott-Larsen Act. EEOA prohibited the assignment of students to schools, such as the Male Academy, that increased racial or gender segregation. They also noted that the Board's publications indicated a "preference, limitation, specification, or discrimination based on... sex" in violation of the Michigan State Elliott-Larsen Act. The attorneys (Preliminary statement, p. 11; Memorandum of law in support, p. 6) argued that the Board implicitly assigned male students to the Academy by discouraging girls from applying. They referred to the publicity and advertising that called the schools "*Male* Academies." Further, the Male Academy brochure and one of the school's charters, prepared by the Superintendent, specifically stated that "*males* are welcomed." In response to the Board's attempt to use the admission of one female out of 600 students to imply that the schools were not discriminatory, NOWLDF (Reply brief, 8) stated

> the suggestion that an institution labeled as a Male Academy and held out to the public as a school for boys can avoid the legal consequences of gender discrimination by admitting a single-girl raises tokenism to an art form. Not even George Wallace attempted such a blatantly transparent ploy to shield segregated schools from legal redress.

This approach was consistent with NOWLDF's use of blatant racial segregation examples as a comparison for gender discrimination, analogizing race and gender discrimination. Although effective as a tool for legal arguments, it ignored the effects of the intersecting race and gender oppression on Black females.

In addition to arguing that they were likely to succeed on the merits of their position, the plaintiffs' attorneys also discussed the balance of equities—the harm to each party. They asserted that if the court allowed the Male Academy to open without girls, the plaintiffs would be denied important educational opportunities. They emphasized that any delay or harm to the male students or teachers because of the injunction should not be attributed to females. They also implied that because the Board decided to institute the Male Academy despite knowledge of its possible illegality and the disapproval by the General Superintendent's Cabinet, the Board should not prevail (see Preliminary statement, p. 6; Exhibit E to Complaint).

Thus, the plaintiff's attorneys used many different strategies and legal arguments to advocate for the legal rights of females to attend the Academies. In requesting that the federal court issue an injunction to prevent the opening of the Male Academies, NOWLDF focused on the four required elements. They argued that the plaintiffs were likely to prevail on the merits of the constitutional and statutory claims, that the plaintiffs would suffer irreparable harm without the injunction, that the harm caused to others by granting the injunction was minimal, and that the public interest required the injunction. More specifically, the argument was that the Academies were unconstitutional and discriminatory based on gender; that girls would be harmed; that the harm to boys without the Academy was minimal; and that the public interest of gender equity required the injunction.

The legal representation of the Black female plaintiffs by the ACLU and NOWLDF allowed the issue of racial betrayal of Black women against Black males to surface in the discourse. Lending support to this argument was one particularly vivid photograph on the front page of the *Detroit Free Press*, a headshot of the Black female plaintiff, Shawn Garrett, standing next to the ACLU Executive Director Howard Simon, a White man. The article mentions the lawsuit and states that Garrett spoke at the news conference "flanked by an attorney from the ACLU and officials from NOWLDF" (Gilchrist, August 6, 1991). According to hooks (1981, p. 69), this alliance between White males and Black females is often viewed by Black men as the equivalent of a Black women "allying herself with a racist oppressor."

Likewise, the alliance with NOWLDF by Black females was also viewed as betrayal. An exchange on *Crossfire* (1991) between Dr. Watson and Ruth Jones, the African-American lawyer with NOWLDF, illustrates this point.

Watson: As a Black woman, I think you have a duty and I wished I could have pulled you aside in the courtroom—you have a duty to our community. I wonder what are you first, are you a female first or are you an African-American male person [sic]?

Jones: I'm a Black woman first.

Watson: What you're doing to destroy Black boys in the city of Detroit clearly means that you're a woman first, working not for our interests but working for the interests of women, in this case White women.

Jones: I wish I could have taken you aside because I firmly believe the fight is not against us. I know you're looking at us like we're the enemy. You're looking at me like I'm some Uncle Tom.

Watson: You're clearly the enemy.

These comments, by the principal of the proposed Malcolm X Male Academy, criticizing Ruth Jones, individually, as a Black woman, and as a symbol of feminist ideology through her membership in NOWLDF, reflect the antagonism of supporters to any position opposed to Black males. As a Black woman, Ruth Jones' position was viewed as both anti-Black and anti-male:

> The harsh reality is that Black women are often victimized by the sexism of Black men who may be compensating for the ways in which racism disempowers them and makes them feel unmanly. Rather than striking out at those who may be responsible for their oppression, some Black men lash out at Black women because they are accessible and vulnerable targets who lack the power to protect themselves or to retaliate. (Cole and Guy-Sheftall, 2003, p. 203)

Historically there have been unfortunate consequences for Black women who fought for gender equality and against sexism within the Black community. Often "debates became an ideological ploy to heighten guilt in Black women over their supposed collusion with whites in the oppression of Black men" (King, 1988, p. 302). Based on the attitude that to advocate for feminism was to advocate against Black liberation, it was politically difficult for Black women to actively fight against sexism, at least within the context of the women's movement and the Black liberation struggle. Barbara Smith (1995, p. 254) notes that "so many black people who are threatened by feminism have argued that by being a black feminist...you have left the race, are no longer a part of the black community." As a result of this polarization of identity, Black women have been put in the uncomfortable and awkward position in racial and gender debates of choosing to support movements that fail to adequately address their status. During the Clarence Thomas-Anita Hill Supreme Court hearings, Hill was brutally reprimanded because her testimony challenged the prevailing attitudes that racial loyalty must always supersede gender issues for African-American women (Cole & Guy-Sheftall, 2003, p. 72). Sociologist Kesho Yvonne Scott (1991, p. 148) notes that many Black women hide their feminism for fear of being associated with disliking men or having "some special loyalty to white women." Many Black women are hesitant to openly advocate for gender equity for fear of doing so at the expense of racial unity and accusations of racial betrayal. The difficulty associated with advocating for gender equity in the context of racial oppression has led to silence and fear being the dominant response by many Black women. Speaking of Black women, hooks (1981: 195–196) says:

> They fear feminism....They are afraid to openly confront white feminists with their racism or black males with their sexism, not to mention confronting white men with their racism and sexism. I have sat in many a kitchen and heard black women express a belief in feminism and eloquently critique the women's movement explaining their refusal to participate. I have witnessed their refusal to express these same views in a public setting. I know their fear exists because they have seen us trampled upon, raped, abused, slaughtered, ridiculed and mocked.

In light of the dichotomy inherent in the "race-versus-sex argument," many Black women choose race and racial unity over feminism. "Many blacks regard the role of uniting all blacks to be the primary duty of the black woman, one that should supersede all other roles that she might want to perform, and certainly one that is essentially incompatible with her own individual liberation" (Collins, 2006, p. 143). Consistent with the rhetoric during the sixties with the rise of both Black nationalism and feminism, "accusations of disloyalty to the race on the part of Black women would become more widespread and hostile" (Cole & Guy-Sheftall, 2003, p. 94). Cole and Guy-Sheftall (p. 84) note

> There was an explicit message in Black nationalist discourse about the destructive aspects of feminism and Black women's quest for liberation. It was very simple. Feminism is a white middle-class movement that retards racial unity and draws Black women from their more urgent work—eradicating racial oppression. Affirming Moynihan's thesis about the negative consequences of a Black matriarchy, the Black Power movement was in large part dedicated to the restoration of Black manhood.

Because many Black females reject feminism as "white," it has been difficult for Black females to comfortably attach themselves to a strategy to address their unique intersecting racial and gender status. The reality, however, is that "more than thirty years after the feminist movement encountered charges of racism and elitism, the executive directors of women's organizations and the senior staff are still overwhelmingly White" (Collins, 2006, p. 174). As Sharpley-Whiting (2007, p. 154) states,

> At the bottom, feminism is not widely understood as a movement to end sexism, racism, and/or male privilege, but as predominantly and unalterably white and as a move to unseat aspiring black men. For many feminism is the equivalent of kicking a black man while he is down, kneeing him in the groin to make him holler "Uncle," when we know full well that that groin will more than likely be consumed by prostate cancer because of unequal access to health care.

Stereotypes about feminism as "reject the penis" and "a militant-no-men-type" movement have contributed to the reluctance of Black women to embrace feminism and feminist ideology or gender affirmation (Sharpley-Whiting, 2007, p. 151).

TASJ reveals the power of the hegemonic domain. Attitudes and stereotypes about girls, mothers, and female teachers provided a strong justification for decisions related to the DMA. Matriarchy and feminism were viewed as an oppositional consciousness to patriarchy and masculinity. The challenge for those opposing the Male Academy was not only the general antipathy of the Black community toward feminism, but also the community's perception of feminism as White, the presence of predominantly White organizations as legal counsel, and the role of the "White" judicial system. Additionally, the connection between race and class emerged because single-sex schools are generally private and seen as an option for Whites and those with higher income levels. The race and class dynamics are discussed in the next section.

3.3 Racism and Class Privilege

Any position not supportive of the Male Academy and Black males was an oppositional, antagonistic position. It was viewed as either racist or classist, as the "Black position" became synonymous with supporting the Male Academy and Black males. African-American columnist Clarence Page (1991a) noted that even mild criticism of the Male Academy "invites the charge that you are hostile to young Black males." The NAACP also came under attack. Joann Watson, Executive Director of the Detroit NAACP chapter, expressed her "distress that some Black leaders in Detroit are urging a protest of the NAACP because the organization adopted a resolution opposing the schools" (Gilchrist, Richardson, Trimer-Hartley, & Brum, 1991). Using inflammatory and accusatory language, Detroit community school activist Helen Moore said "We think they have sold out [referring to the Board's decision to settle the lawsuit] (Russell, November 7, 1991). Spencer Holland, referring to those who opposed the Male Academy based on racial segregation concerns, said "that kind of thinking is for all of those middle-class Black folks—those Ebony-magazine reading Black folks" (Gilchrist, September 3, 1991). The editorial staff of the *Detroit Free Press* (Male Academies court reversal, 1991) expressed concern that "some may try to prevail by turning this debate into a political, even racial conflict." One parent commented, "I don't think White society really wants to see Black males make a turn for the better. They could fill up a county jail...and nobody says anything about that. But when they come up with something positive, they start talking about constitutional rights...it's racial and political" (Stewart, 1991). The debate, however, was always political; race and class were always critical factors.

Much of the Male Academy debate unfolded within the structural domain and the disciplinary domains. The structural domain involved the federal judicial system and the federal court and the disciplinary domain involved the adjudication process in which legal principles were presented and arguments set forth. The legal context of the DMA case created an opportunity for supporters to raise the issue of race, as the court system is generally seen by minorities as a racist structure that is used to perpetuate oppression. Although this case was a civil case, the experiences of minorities within the criminal court system have influenced their ideas, attitudes, and perceptions about the legal system. In fact, a *Los Angeles Times* article referred to Judge Woods' decision as the "racist federal court ruling" (Harmon, 1991). The legal representation of the plaintiffs by NOWLDF and the ACLU enabled the Male Academy supporters to further attribute blame to White individuals, White institutions, White organizations, and White race and class privilege. The Board, as an affirmative defense in its legal arguments, alleged that the ACLU and NOWLDF were the real parties in interest, and not the Black female plaintiffs, Nancy, Jessica, Judy, and Jane Doe. The Board, in effect, argued that it was the White organizations, and not the Black female plaintiffs, who were challenging the Male Academy.

The interpersonal domain of key individuals included the attorneys, their organizations, and the judge. There was substantial antagonism toward the ACLU, NOWLDF, and in particular, Judge George Woods. Referring to NOW and the ACLU as the "unelected social engineers," the "pious plaintiffs," and "special interest groups," a *Washington Times* editorial (Trashing Detroit's initiative, 1991) stated that "Detroit's predominantly Black students have problems enough with high dropout rates, drugs and crime. To that list of woes, now add the ACLU, NOW and the U.S. District Judge George Woods." Bernard Parker, Wayne County Commissioner and organizer of the Coalition for All-Male and All-Female Academies, was quoted as saying "We are against the ACLU, NOW, and Judge Woods for what they have done" (Gilchrist, August 27, 1991). The Detroit News editorial criticized the decision, stating "NOWLD[E]F and ACLU fund have used the coercive power of courts to impose a form of pedagogy they prefer" (The Male Academy Compromise, 1991). Board member April Coleman accused the ACLU and NOW of using "Satanic influences to conspire against Black males" (Detroit agrees, 1991). According to columnist Jim Fitzgerald (1991), Coleman also accused them of a "conspiracy to bring doom and destruction upon African-American males." An editorial in the *Atlanta Constitution* (All-Male schools: change laws, 1991) referred to the ACLU and NOW as "discrimination alarmists."

Judge Woods was particularly targeted. One Black male marching in opposition to the Judge's ruling said "For the first time there was an organized plan to take over our destiny as Black people, and it came down to a decision by a White man." A Black female marcher said "I feel (Judge Woods) didn't have a right to choose what is best for my son" (C. Williams, 1991). Dr. Clifford Watson was quoted as saying "Clearly, this is an example of a White federal judge making a decision for the African-American community which he does not live in and which he does not understand" (Gilchrist, August 16, 1991). The antagonism and "disaffection" toward Judge Woods in the media was so strong that fellow Detroit district judge Avern Cohn defended Judge Woods' decision and criticized the *Detroit News'* coverage of Judge Woods (Cohn, n.d.). As Watson's comment reflects, racial issues were closely connected with class and residency.

The judge, the ACLU, and NOW became symbols of not only racism, but also class privilege, school choice, and local control over school decisions. One mother whose son was to attend the school said "the Judge has the economic power to send his child to an all-male or an all-female (private) school" (Russell, August 16, 1991). School Board members were particularly vocal in their anger and frustration toward the ACLU, NOW, and NOWLDF. Board vice-president Frank Hayden referred to the decision to settle as a "surrender to the

ACLU and NOW and to those who would deprive Detroit parents of the right to choose a single-sex environment for their child in a public school" (Russell, November 7, 1991). He said it was "the same right wealthy suburbanites enjoy in a private or parochial school" (Hayden, 1991; n.d.). Hayden (September 9, 1991) continued,

> Much of the debate over the male academy has been inappropriately centered on the relative merit of same-sex and coeducational schools. Rather, the question raised by this controversy is: Who shall have the right to choose between same-sex and coeducational schools? The Board of Education decided that parents have the right to choose the educational environment they deem best suited for their children. The leadership of the American Civil Liberties Union and the National Organization of Women, most of who are not residents of the city of Detroit, have concluded that the choice should reside with them and the federal courts, rather than with Detroit parents....As this issue continues to be addressed, it might be wise to reflect on the relative ease with which self-appointed do-gooders such as the ACLU and NOW, supported by an oppressive federal judiciary, are able to undermine, to the detriment of the children, the legal and prudent decisions of elected officials and parents.

Superintendent McGriff's (DPS Chief comments, 1991) comments were similar.

> I deeply regret the action of the ACLU and NOW in filing suit.... The fundamental question raised by this controversy is: Who shall be empowered to make decisions affecting the education of Detroit's children? Will it be the leadership of the ACLU and NOW, most of whom reside outside the city of Detroit? Or will Detroit's parents and voters retain the right to expend their tax money as they see fit on behalf of their children....Parents of children attending religious and private schools have always enjoyed the right to select all-male or all-female school environments for their children.

Lawrence Patrick, Jr., president of the Detroit Board of Education in an October 29, 1991, *Free Press* article, stated that "It is simply a fact that most of the leadership of the ACLU and NOW who have instigated this controversy do not reside in the city of Detroit. Were they Detroit taxpayers and parents, their views, however, misguided, would properly have been accorded greater weight." Patrick (Detroit Board of Education President vows, 1991) further stated "the right of Detroit's parents and voters to [expend] their tax money as they desire on behalf of their children's education has been grievously diminished." The Board's remarks were criticized by the *Detroit Free Press* and by a reader of the *Free Press* as "divisive," "inflammatory," "suburban-bashing," "demagoguery," "ill-advised," and a "thinly veiled exploitation of racial tensions" (All-male Schools: McGriff's inflammatory remarks, August 15, 1991; Tanay, 1991). The Board's sentiments, however, were echoed by others. A *Detroit News* article stated tha: "Marchers, who demonstrated on behalf of the Coalition for Male Academies said White suburbanites involved with NOW and the ACLU are meddling in Detroit affairs" (C. Williams, August 22, 1991). Paul Taylor, executive director of the Inner-City Sub-Center, said "They [ACLU and NOW] really have no vested interest in the city. For them to have a determination of what we do with our school money is crazy" (C. Williams, August 22, 1991). The fact that according to Karen Sundberg, (1991b) Vice President for Membership of the Detroit NOW Chapter, "overwhelmingly, the vast majority of Detroit NOW Board members and chapter members reside in the City" was irrelevant. For the Detroit community, the ACLU, NOW, and the federal court system had become the visible symbol and representation of the intangible concepts, race and class oppression, the school choice debate, school funding, and school quality.

The Board contrasted the educational opportunities available to White, upper-class/suburban parents (such as private single-sex schools and better-quality public schools) with those available to Black, inner-city poor parents. The issue of school choice was raised as a class-based dynamic. Superintendent McGriff said, "I only want to be able to give parents (in Detroit) the same options that other parents have who are middle class" (Ilka, August 14, 1991). McGriff was further quoted as saying "We are providing parents with the same option they have in the private sector" (Moss, August 13, 1991). Lawrence Patrick, president of the Board, stated "Parents who could afford to send their children to single-sex schools had a choice, while poor parents sending their children to public schools did not" (J. Wilson, 1992). A *Los Angeles Times* article indicated that parents believed that Judge Woods' decision discriminated on the basis of race and income, quoting one as saying "If you have money, you can go to whatever kind of school you want. But the average Black guy can't go to special schools" (Harmon, 1991). Harvey Hambrick, principal of Marcus Garvey, was quoted as saying "We are a public school with a private school flair" referring to the mostly male academy (Eng, 1991). These statements reveal the level of antagonism that existed toward the White organizations, the federal judge, and the school funding system. The Black community largely believed that it was a victim of racism and class privilege. The legal system was viewed as a site of racial oppression, with the ACLU, NOWLDF, and Judge Woods symbolizing White racism through their opposition to the Male Academy. These three also came to represent the school choice debate and issues of class.

This chapter has discussed the multi-layered attribution element and the themes of matriarchy, feminism, racism, and class privilege as dominant discourses in the attribution element. In the attribution element, the education system, the legal system, and the family were contested sites in the structural domain. The power of hegemonic domain was clearly revealed by the prevalence of several commonly accepted ideas, beliefs, and attitudes in the Black community, including stereotypes about Black women as Saffires, matriarchs, and welfare mothers. Many members of the Black community believed that there was a Black male crisis and that it could be attributed to issues related to women and girls. Thus, at the micro-level interpersonal domain of power, the everyday interactions between male and female students, between students and teachers, and between mothers and sons were criticized. The argument was made that Black female students were a distraction to the learning environment necessary for Black males to achieve. Female teachers contributed to the problems of Black males by their femaleness and associated inability to teach, sympathize, and appropriately masculinize or be a role model for Black boys. The curriculum in the school system and the teaching practices were criticized as being feminine and consequently inappropriate for Black boys. Finally, mothers were criticized in their role as matriarch in the homes and portrayed as being ineffective in raising boys.

The interpersonal domain also included the White judge, the White and feminist organizations, and the Black female plaintiffs. Their roles caused them to be attacked as symbols of racism, classism, and feminism. By linking these concepts to individuals, organizations, and structures through explicit and implicit discourse, the Male Academy supporters created a strong and cohesive collective action framework with the punctuation and attribution frames clearly and logically linked together. The third component, articulation, will be discussed in the next chapter where the solutions to the problems based on the causes are analyzed.

4

The Solution Proposed

The third component of a collective action frame is articulation, meaningfully interconnecting diverse events and experiences to encourage social action. Articulation must connect the punctuation and attribution elements. The objective is to create a solution to the problems based on the causes. In the Male Academy debate, the discourse reflects that two key solutions emerged: one legal and one socio-political. The legal solution was a result of the district judge's decision preventing the Male Academy from opening as initially proposed by the Detroit School Board. As a result of the preliminary injunction, there was a settlement agreement between the Detroit School Board and the Black female plaintiffs, negotiated by NOWLDF and the ACLU. The settlement agreement was part of the operation of the disciplinary domain within the structural domain of the legal system. The settlement negotiations involved determining the practices and policies for admitting girls. The settlement was seen as undermining the objective of the Male Academy—an all-male environment based on masculinity and patriarchy. As a result, the supporters felt that it was important to engage in collective action to undermine the objective of the settlement agreement. This collective action formed the basis for the second solution.

The second solution was a media campaign to persuade the community not to support the settlement agreement and to support the Male Academy as initially conceived. The media campaign was a battle about the hegemonic domain and which ideology would be dominant: matriarchy and feminism or patriarchy and masculinity. The absence of Black girls would reflect a victory for patriarchy, whereas their presence would be viewed as a victory for matriarchy. Because the campaign had to influence ideas and attitudes, a familiar and well-known theme was needed. Black nationalism became the theme and strategy. The first section examines the settlement agreement and legal outcome. The second section examines the socio-political outcome and the community's response through a media campaign. The final section demonstrates the articulation element of the collective action frame with a discussion of Black nationalism.

4.1 The Settlement Agreement

The legal case was debated and decided in federal district court in Detroit. The district court was presided over by Judge George Woods. On August 15, 1991, the court granted the plaintiffs' request for a preliminary injunction to prevent the Male Academy from opening. The court found that the plaintiffs were likely to succeed on the merits of their claim under the Fourteenth Amendment, Title IX, and Michigan law. The court did agree with the Board, however, that the objective of the Male Academy was important in light of the "compelling need" illustrated by the statistics about Black male academic and social performance. In fact, the court (*Garrett*, 1991, p. 1014) specifically "acknowledged the status of urban males as an 'endangered species'." Nevertheless, the court noted that the Board failed to sustain its burden of proving a substantial relationship between the male crisis and the presence of girls in the classroom. The court (p. 1007) stated

> Although co-educational programs have failed, there is no showing that it is the co-educational factor that results in failure. Even more dangerous is the prospect that should the Male Academy proceed and succeed, success would be equated with the absence of girls rather than any of the educational factors that more probably caused the outcome.

The court further noted that the educational system also failed females. Additionally, the court found that the plaintiffs could suffer serious, irreparable, and immediate harm in the form of lost opportunities to learn, gain self esteem, and be trained for a successful future.

In its oral opinion from the bench, the court suggested that the parties meet and stated parenthetically

> Indeed there has been a cry for help within this community. It is possible, the Court sees it as possible, that the exclusion of some can be

> rectified to the benefit of all, including the young, black male, who is indeed an endangered species. Perhaps it may be that implementation here is premature. There are windows of opportunity here for the defendants in this Court's considered judgment. However, this Court is not co-counsel for one side or the other, nor is it an amicus from which either party could draw inferences from.

With the judge's preliminary injunction coming just days before the start of the school semester, the Detroit School Board needed to make a decision. It could either accept the result of the preliminary injunction and prepare for a full trial, or it could negotiate a compromise with the plaintiffs' attorneys to see if some form of the Male Academies could go forward for the beginning of the school year. The Board decided to settle the case with NOWLDF and the ACLU.

After intense negotiation from August 23 to August 26, the parties agreed on a temporary settlement (Stipulation and Agreement, 1991). The agreement provided that 136 seats out of the 560 seats would be set aside solely for girls at the re-named Afro-centric Academies. Boys would begin attending the Academy on August 28, 1991. On the same day, applications for girls would be available at specific locations in Detroit. The plaintiffs would be granted the right to review the Board's materials about the Academy and the Board would widely distribute brochures and applications about the Academy and publicize the opportunities for girls through public service announcements. The selection process for females would be completed by September 6th. On the 9th of September, girls would begin attending the Academies. Seats vacated by boys during the year would be reserved for girls, and none of the 136 seats set aside for girls would be filled by boys. The Board was required to use its best efforts to fill the 136 seats. The agreement specifically stated what the best efforts should include, as follows:

> The efforts shall include, but are not limited to, notice to each principal in the school system, notice to Local School Community Organizations (which includes P.T.A.s) at each school, notice to the City-wide School Community Organization, a mailing to approximately 1,000 community organizations, an announcement in "The Reporter" (the Detroit Public Schools letter to the community), and public announcements to be run on WDTR-FM (90.9) radio to its listening audience to advise the public that vacancies continue to exist in the current Academies and that female students are welcome to apply. (Stipulation and Agreement, p. 3)

The settlement agreement also allowed each party to continue to pursue litigation options. After initial trial preparation by both sides, a final settlement agreement with substantially the same terms as the temporary agreement was submitted to the court on November 7, 1991. The final settlement, however, further provided for male- and female-focused classes, with the requirement that the classes be comparable and provide equal benefits and services. Teacher assignments were not to be made based on gender. All publications of the Board were required to emphasize that the Academies were nondiscriminatory and that both genders were welcome. The Board was prohibited from discouraging students of one gender from applying. The plaintiffs' attorneys were also entitled to visit the Academies, and monitor and inspect for compliance.

The terms of the settlement substantially benefitted the Male Academy supporters. Less than 25 percent of the seats were set aside for females. Boys were able to begin attending school earlier than girls. The leadership, structure, and curriculum were essentially the same. There would just be a few girls enrolled in each grade within the three schools, which would not substantially impact the culture of the school. Although the settlement largely resulted in a plan that maintained the predominantly Male Academy, the Detroit School Board and Male Academy supporters were not satisfied. The perspective of many Male Academy supporters was that the settlement was a victory for the plaintiffs—the "pushy little girls" (Page, 1991b). More specifically, it looked like a victory for the black female "matriarch" plaintiffs, the NOWLDF feminists, the little matriarch Black female students, and the "white racist" ACLU organization. Thus, the settlement agreement and the legal solution did not address one of the alleged major causes of the social problem—females in the classroom. The settlement, to supporters, appeared to reinforce a matriarchal, feminist hierarchy. As a result, a media campaign was waged by Male Academy supporters to address the way in which they believed the legal decision and the settlement agreement undermined key objectives of the Male Academy. They wanted an all-male environment with no girls. The next section analyzes this media campaign.

4.2 "For Black Boys Only"

Sharpley-Whiting, Collins, Cole, and Guy-Sheftall all acknowledge the power of mass media and its role as the forum for "negotiating Black gender politics" (Cole & Guy-Sheftall, 2003, p. 182; Collins, 2006, p. 151; Sharpley-Whiting, 2007). In the case of the Male Academy, the real debate unfolded in the media, where short, politically charged phrases could be used that would resonate with the Black community. It was in this forum that the thoughts and attitudes of the community became apparent. The goal of the Male Academy supporters was to encourage social action to implement the Male Academy. This meant having parents not send their daughters to the schools. More specifically, with a majority of Detroit Public School parents being single mothers, Black women, in particular, needed to be persuaded not to enroll their daughters and to not take advantage of the legal right that had been created by the settlement agreement and the judge's decision. The supporters' strategy was rooted in race loyalty. The absence of girls from the Male Academy was necessary to actualize and affirm the discourse of the supporters about the causes of the problems—females, matriarchy, feminism, and racism. On the other hand, the presence of Black girls in the classrooms would represent the success of the White and female forces of opposition (the ACLU, NOWLDF, and the federal court), as well as the ideologies associated with matriarchy and feminism. It was a strategy that recognized the power of the structural domain of the media. The media is interconnected with communities. The relationship between these two structural domains facilitated the supporters' attempt to influence social action to change the education system through the Male Academy.

The discourse documents the strategy. It was a strategy that specifically targeted the court's decision. Dr. Watson, principal of Malcolm X, in his documentary about the Malcolm X Academy, stated

> The Detroit community did not accept Judge Wood's ruling.... The Detroit community had picketed and protested against NOW's lawsuit throughout the preliminary hearing that resulted in the granting of an injunction against the District. Community groups and community coalitions were formed and met on a regular basis to mount their protest campaign and to organize a city-wide effort to effectively "defeat" NOW's legal "victory." (Watson & Smitherman, 1996, p. 50)

The coalitions that formed were "encouraging," "telling," and "urging" parents not to send their daughters (Deal Reportedly Reached, 1991; Gilchrist, August 29, 1991; Gilcrhist, August 19, 1991; Gilchrist, September 10, 1991; Russell & Skwira, 1991; Russell & Hamada, August 25, 1991; Walters, 1991). One coalition in support of the Male Academy was called the Citizens of Detroit. Spokesmen for the coalition indicated that the coalition would "collect money for a campaign encouraging parents not to send their daughter to the schools" (Gilchrist & Musial, August 28, 1991). Another group was called Coalition for Male and Female Academies. They said, "The judge can mandate but the people have spoken loud and clear." The group planned a conference to "urge parents who submitted the 27 new applications not to enroll their daughters" (Russell, September 5, 1991). There was also a group of over 100 called the Coalition to Save the Detroit Academy (Briscoe, 1991). Additionally, the Citizens of Detroit was another group that formed as a coalition of community organizations, individuals, public officials, and educators. They encouraged the community to reject the court's decision (Male academies' support group to defy court order, 1991). Rallies were held with over 300 people (Harmon, 1991) and many protesters were female parents (We will have, 1991). Even female columnists for the *Detroit News* (DeRamus, 1991) and the *Michigan Chronicle* (Worth, 1991) were supporters of the Academy.

The culminating rally cry, therefore, became "Don't send your girls,"; "Keep your girls at home"; and "Don't enroll them" (Walters, 1991). The principal of Malcolm X, Dr. Watson, stated, "Right now, our community is saying keep your girls at home. Don't enroll them." The mindset of the advocates was so strong against the presence of Black girls, that not only were Black mothers told not to send their girls to the Male Academy, they were told to stay home. To stay home? To not even attend school? This rhetoric is consistent with the attitudes of many Black men that Black women belong in the home, and not on the political battlefield.

Not only did the "community" encourage and almost demand that girls stay home, the School Board also actively opposed including females in the Male Academy experience both before and after the court's ruling (Detroit Academies: any plan to accept girls, 1991). The statements of Board members and the Board's literature indicated that the Board's attitude toward females was one of exclusion and marginalization. Although there was no explicit prohibition against female enrollment, the court and plaintiffs' attorneys noted that the name for the Academy (*Male* Academy), as well as the Board's literature about the Academy, "clearly excludes females from real participation in the program" (*Garrett*, p. 1012; Transcript, p. 40–44). The plaintiff's attorneys emphasized to the court that the Board's resolutions, the Male Academy proposal, the Male Academy's charters, and the brochures indicated that girls need not apply: "every statement, every action, [made] sure girls knew they weren't welcome. What in effect we have here is the Board doing everything except hammering up a sign on a door that says, "For boys only. Girls need not apply" (Transcript: 10–11). Garrett stated, by affidavit, that she did not apply on behalf of her daughter because

> Everything I've heard and read has referred to the academies as all-male. I've never heard or read anything that suggested that females were welcome to apply to the Male Academy. In fact, it was clear to me that females were not eligible for the benefits being offered at the Academies. (Reply brief, Exhibit A)

The Board's attitude did not change after the ruling. It did not encourage female enrollment with the same enthusiasm and spirit as the initial male enrollment. For example, the Male Academy brochure specifically stated that "males are welcomed" and were "encouraged" to apply. On the other hand, Board comments indicated that females were being "permitted" and "allowed" to apply (Gilchrist & Musial, August 28, 1991; Russell & Hamada, August 25, 1991). The Board agreed to "*let* female students attend, but vowed to continue to fight the ruling" (Detroit Agrees to Let, August 27, 1991). Superintendent McGriff stated: "I do know of single-gender institutions which have a clear mission of catering to the needs of one gender, but still *allow* the other gender to attend" (Russell, August 15, 1991). Even NOWLDF expressed its concern about proposals to create schools and programs that would emphasize the needs of African-American males, though "allowing" girls to be part of the student body" (NOWLDF, 1991, p. 26). In light of the traditional invisibility and silence of Black girls in the classroom environment (Grant, 1984), the Board's comments suggested that girls would be even more excluded in an environment designed for males that, out of necessity, admitted females. Though the Board pledged to use its best efforts to advertise the vacancies for girls, the discourse reflects that the Board did not want to and did not encourage the attendance and enrollment of girls.

Many Board members publicly expressed their disappointment, their reluctance to admit girls, and their desire to continue to fight the court's decision (Patrick, 1991b). Dr. McGriff (1991b) stated that she "was not pleased" with the settlement outcome and would continue to pursue legal avenues "on behalf of the right of Detroit parents to guarantee their right to choice." Board vice-president Frank

Hayden in a September 9, 1991 editorial in the *Detroit Free Press* stated "We have, with regret, authorized the superintendent to create a plan to admit females in the male academies. There is no question that the program we had hoped to provide will be seriously weakened as a result of the necessity of compliance." Board president Patrick was quoted as saying "I deeply regret the action of the court preventing the male academy from opening as scheduled" (Detroit Board of Education President vows, 1991). Even after the settlement was final, the Board indicated that it would agree to the settlement only with "reluctance" (Detroit Board of Education President Speaks, 1991).

The reluctance of the Board to admit students was discussed in a letter from a community member to the Interim Deputy Superintendent, Dr. Arthur Carter. The significant references from the letter are included below.

> To encourage equal-gender enrollment at its newest academies, the Detroit Public Schools should be airing public service announcements on its own radio station, WDTR-90.9 FM. Currently, when WDTR personalities speak about the new academies, they seem to discourage female enrollment. This is not surprising since some of those same persons are organizers and spokespersons of groups that aggressively support gender-specific education. Listeners to WDTR could easily conclude that the Detroit Public Schools urges opposition to what has been alleged on the air as a racist conspiracy perpetrated in part by a so-called "zionist front" organization. Furthermore, some WDTR personalities have accused African-American parents who consider enrolling their daughters in the academies as being disloyal to their own race.... To enroll their young girls into a controversial setting, parents need encouragement and reassurance from respected educators. To demonstrate the sincerity of the Detroit Public Schools, public service announcements should be recorded by those Board members and DPS administrators closely identified with the development of the new academies... (Trey, personal communication, September 19, 1991)

The Board further attempted to discourage females from attending the Male Academy by a last minute proposal for a separate Female Academy. The female academy proposal did not arise, as did the Male Academy, after the formation of a committee, months of careful study, and the presentation of a detailed written proposal. Despite acknowledging in February 1991, the "equally urgent and unique crisis" facing female students, the resolution of clarification mentioning the Female Academy was not passed by the Board until August 13, 1991, after the lawsuit was filed (Transcript, 1991, p. 38; Memorandum of law in opposition, 1991). Though three Male Academies were created, only one female academy was proposed, which would open January 1992, at the earliest (Gilchrist, August 16, 1991). In light of the timing of the proposed female academy, the ACLU stated that the proposal was "obviously" a response to the lawsuit (Kelly, 1991). It appears, therefore, that the Female Academy was mentioned in an attempt to keep the Male Academy all-male and to prevent the desegregation of the Male Academy, rather than a genuine desire to focus on the problems of females.

There were, then, three strategies at work: a legal settlement maintaining the essential qualities of the Male Academy, a media campaign persuading females not to access even the limited legal rights that were granted by the settlement, and the potential development of a separate Female Academy. All three strategies included the absence of girls from the Male Academies, which would be a victory for the Male Academy supporters. Thus, Black girls became the sole symbol of matriarchy, feminism, class privilege, and White racial privilege. Black girls, through their role as plaintiffs, through their representation by the ACLU and NOWLDF, and through their victory from the district judge, became a symbol and image that needed to be replaced by Black males. Black males, on the other hand, in a Black Male Academy would represent Black patriarchy and affirm Black masculinity. They would also symbolize a victory over White race and class privilege, and the subjugation of Black matriarchy and White feminism. These strategies were complemented by another strategy—Black nationalism. Black nationalism is discussed in the next section.

4.3 Black Nationalism

Black nationalism can be described as having three core themes. "Despite considerable variability in how African-Americans understand and articulate Black nationalist ideology, I suggest that Black nationalism's main ideas of self-definition, self-determination, and self-reliance resonate with the experiences of large numbers of African-Americans and with important cultural norms of American society" (Collins, 2006, p. 75). Black nationalism within the context of inner-city Detroit and the DMA created the opportunity to mobilize African-Americans as a collective group in support of Black male patriarchy, which meant in opposition to class privilege reflected in economic and residential segregation; and against matriarchy and feminism (Collins, 2006). The Detroit School System was primarily Black as a result of the *Milliken v. Bradley* decision, which did not require busing for the suburbs (Mirel, 1993, 1998; Wolf, 1981). The context of segregated Detroit provided the perfect scenario for an ideology of Black nationalism.

The discourse simultaneously promoted Black nationalism and a pro-Black male political consciousness, as well as an anti-feminist, anti-White, anti-upper class political consciousness. The supporters first defined the Black male as an endangered species and implied that the future of the Black race was at stake. They also asserted that females as students, teachers, mothers, and feminists were the primary cause of the Black male crisis. The supporters promoted a patriarchal and an anti-matriarchal theme by emphasizing the need for Black male leadership by Black male teachers and Black father-figures. The Male Academy curriculum and programs, including an Afrocentric curriculum and a male-dominated Rites of Passage program, served to facilitate their goals. They also used the presence of the predominantly White political organizations to raise issues of race and class through the question of who should decide the policy issues affecting inner-city Black school systems. The legal system was also implicated as a racist system that perpetuated injustice. By restructuring and recharacterizing the Male Academy debate as one involving racism, classism, and gender privilege for women, the supporters laid the foundation for the theme of Black nationalism.

Black nationalist overtones emerged in the context of discussion about the curriculum of the Male Academy, and the Board's ability to determine the content of its curriculum, including the Afrocentric emphasis, approved by the Board in a February 26, 1991, resolution. Prof. Sedler (1991) noted that because the school population was 90 percent Black, such a curriculum was appropriate.

> It is fully permissible for the Detroit Public Schools, with a 90 percent Black enrollment, to have an Afrocentric curriculum, not only in the Male Academy, but throughout the system, just as it is permissible for other school systems to have a Eurocentric curriculum, as virtually all other school systems in Michigan do.... [T]he Detroit Public Schools can conclude that an Afrocentric curriculum—for the Male Academy or for all the schools in the system—will best meet the educational needs of the student population that the Detroit Public School serves.

These statements caused the ACLU (Denenfeld, 1991) to express concern that the "Afrocentric emphasis" could indirectly discourage students of other races and cultures in violation of federal and state law prohibiting discrimination on the basis of race. The ACLU Statement on all-male academy, issued on May 29, 1991, stated that the ACLU was concerned about the Male Academy "fostering racial and sexual segregation" (ACLU directors oppose all-male academy, 1991). Similarly, discourse in the media reflects concerns about the Afrocentric curriculum. A letter to the editor in the *Detroit Free Press* stated "I do not agree with the ACLU and NOW that the academy is sexist; I believe it is racist," because the proposed "Afro-American emphasis" is not appropriate in a public school setting" (Shandor, August 28, 1991). Another letter to the editor stated "I hope that the curriculum for the Black academies is not as racist as it appears" (Barrett, September 16, 1991).

The themes of Black nationalism and self-determination were captured in the press release by the Citizens of Detroit (CD), a coalition of community organizations and individuals, public officials, and educators, who "encouraged parents not to register their daughters" at the Male Academy.

> It is the position of CD that African-American males are endangered due to the long-standing social and economic crisis conditions in the community, produced by a racist system which has bred hopelessness and inward community violence. Believing conditions worsen if the academies do not open, CD feels others not of the African-American community have no understanding of its unique problems and therefore are unqualified to determine what is in the best interest of African-American youth. CD feels the creation of the male academies is simply a matter of Black survival, an immediate positive alternative and responsibility falling solely on the shoulders of the African-American community. For outsiders to attempt to set policy counter to African-American control of their communities is nothing less than raw and aggressive racism. The decision of the court and the suit sponsors are a direct challenge to the right of African-Americans to determine their destiny. (Male academies' support group to defy court order, 1991)

The comments on *Nightline* (1991) of Kwame Kenyatta, director of the Malcolm X Community Center, demonstrate the coalescing of several disparate issues into a common theme of Black nationalism, self-determination, and self-reliance.

> So we think that NOW and the ACLU are outsiders and it's really a question of self-determination. Detroit is 90 percent Black, and as a Black community we have a right to decide what the educational system

> will be in our community.... Integration has never worked.... Nobody questioned these various different military schools where you send the White boys off to learn how to be little boys and great mercenary soldier, nobody questions that. But when it comes time for African men to decide for themselves and the African community to decide for itself, then there's a question.... It's not about sex; it is about Black men and Black people accenting their right to self-determination.

Kenyatta's statement that "it's not about sex; it is about Black men and Black people accenting their right to self-determination" succinctly summarizes what the Male Academy represented for many Black residents of Detroit.

His statement connects the gendered discourse about manhood with the racial discourse about Black nationalism and Black power (A. Davis, 1981; Giddings, 1984; hooks, 1981, 1990; Marable, 1983). hooks (1990, p. 58) notes that "oppressed Black men and women have rarely challenged the use of gendered metaphors to describe the impact of racist domination and/or Black liberation struggle," which equates freedom with manhood. She argues that this association of Black liberation with manhood reflects the continued "sexualization of Black liberation in ways that support and perpetuate sexism, phallocentrism, and male domination" (hooks, 1990, p. 60; hooks, 1981, p. 182–183).

The nationalist movements of the 1920s, 1930s, 1950s, and 1960s, publicly led by those such as Marcus Garvey, Elijah Muhammad, Malcolm X, Martin Luther King, Stokely Carmichael, and Amiri Baraka, often promoted and encouraged associating Black power with Black manhood and male dominance (Collins, 1991, p. 86; Higginbotham, 1992; hooks, 1981; Hunter & Davis, 1992; Marable, 1983, p. 101; Murray, 1975; Radford-Hill, 1986). Although the public face of Black nationalism was associated with men, many women worked behind the scenes in influential positions. The centrality of Black nationalism in *Garrett* is evidenced not only by the explicit discourse of the Board and its supporters, but also by names for the Male Academy: Marcus Garvey, Paul Robeson, and Malcolm X. Commenting on the choice of the name Malcolm X, Dr. Watson (Watson & Smitherman, 1996, p. 44) remarked that "from the outset Superintendent Porter and other Black conservative forces in the administrative hierarchy of the District thought the name... was too radical." It, however, was selected by a school-community group who hoped that the name would "inspire its Black male students not only to transform themselves but also to position themselves as community and world leaders" (Watson & Smitherman, 1996, p. 46). A key element in Black cultural nationalism is racial solidarity, in which Black women and men submerge "their individual needs, goals, and concerns to those of the Black community as a collectivity. Theoretically, all make sacrifices so that racial solidarity can be maintained. But in actual everyday life, African-American women typically sacrifice more" (Collins, 2006, p. 111). There is an assumption within Black nationalism and its accompanying view of Black solidarity that all other differences and specific interests related to, for example, feminism, or LGBT, must be suppressed and "submerged for the alleged good of the group" (Collins, 2006, p. 19). In Detroit, for example, Black women were expected to wait for the one proposed Female Academy (Russell, August 5, 1991; August 7, 1991).

The theme of Black nationalism, then, became the cement connecting the ideologies associated with the punctuation and attribution elements. The ideology of Black masculinity and patriarchy was reflected in the justification for the Male Academy. The emasculated state of Black males in the school and home environment required immediate attention. Additionally, the legal and education systems were inflexible social structures over which Black males had little authority or control. These problems were alleged to be caused by White race privilege, female gender privilege, and upper-class privilege. These ideologies were symbolized by Black female plaintiffs, the NOWLDF feminist organization, the White class-privileged ACLU organization, and the White federal judge. These symbols and their associated ideologies needed to be replaced by another symbol and its accompanying ideology. The symbol would be Black males and the ideology would be Black nationalism.

Black nationalism would be a political and governmental structure with power to control individuals, organizations, social systems, laws, and regulations. Essentially, Black nationalism would control all the domains of power: structural, disciplinary, interpersonal, and hegemonic. Black nationalism was about implementing a counter-oppositional hegemony of patriarchy (hegemonic domain), which would be used to justify the operation of the patriarchal-based policies and practices (disciplinary domain) in schools and communities (structural domain) through Black male leadership (interpersonal domain).

The three components of Black nationalism were present in the discourse of the Male Academy supporters: self-definition to define the needs of the Black race as synonymous with those of Black males, self-determination to determine and decide appropriate laws and policies, and self-reliance to depend on the race to implement the policies and procedures. The right of self-determination and the emphasis on self-reliance could only be actualized by defying the court order and the power of racism, feminism, and classism it represented. The absence of girls at the Male Academy would accomplish this objective. The next chapter documents the initial outcome of the collective action frame in 1992 and then looks at almost 20 years of changes in the law, in the education system, and in Detroit.

5

The Outcome Achieved

The collective action frame is designed to encourage social action. Its goal is outcome-oriented. Frame alignment assesses the success of the frame in achieving the desired outcome. The outcome is an essential component for understanding the effect of the frame and assessing the efficacy of the social justice strategy. In 1991, the outcome of the Male Academy debate revealed the success of the collective action frame. Very few Black girls enrolled and the Academies were essentially Male Academies. Over the past almost 20 years, there has been a great deal of social justice activism at the national, state, and local levels, including changes in laws and increased research on single-sex schools. This chapter explores the initial outcome, changes in federal and state laws involving education, research on single-sex schools, and the effect of the changes on Black girls, especially those in Detroit.

5.1 The Academies

The Academies were created to be all male. Of the 560 students initially admitted, there was only one girl (Gilchrist, August 27, 1991, p. 1A). The court transcript indicated that President Patrick of the Board of Education said that the girl "got in through a glitch in the system" (Transcript, 1991, p. 43). When the three Academies opened in August 1991, three girls began with approximately 549 boys. About 24 girls, who applied during the one-week application period for girls, began the following week (Bruni, September 5, 1991; Gilchrist, September 10, 1991, p. 8A; Lack of female students, 1991). At the Paul Robeson Academy, only 14 out of 160 students were female (Tetzeli, August 10, 1992, p. 78). The cover page of the September 10, 1991, *Detroit Free Press* depicts a physical education class with China

Randle as the only Black girl in a third-grade class of eight Black boys, one of a total of four females at the Marcus Garvey School (Gilchrist, September 10, 1991, pg. 1A). She is shown standing on the far right by herself, with eight boys next to her. The same article depicts another Black girl, leaning against a wall as four Black boys walk by her. The caption says: "Third-grader Danielle Hall, 8, takes a breather Monday at the Marcus Garvey Academy in Detroit. It had been planned as an all-male school." One class at Malcolm X had 27 boys and one girl and out of seven teachers, five were male. Despite the settlement agreement and the allocation of 136 seats out of 560 to girls, as of the end of the semester, only 39 girls were enrolled (Moore & Associates, 1993). With less than 7 percent of the enrolled students being female, the male-focused classrooms would clearly benefit the majority of the students at the Academy who were male. The images of Black girls who attended were ones of isolation and marginalization in a predominantly male setting.

ACLU director Simon attributed the limited enrollment of females to several factors, including "pressure from community groups to urge parents of females to keep their daughters away" (Wolffe, September 4, 1991). In response to the limited enrollment, Bernard Parker, a Wayne County Commissioner who organized and led the Coalition for All-Male and All-Female Academies (New solution or segregation, 1992) stated, "In essence, we've been able to get around the judge's decision and give power to the people." Likewise, Ray Johnson, principal of Marcus Garvey Academy, stated that the 146 males out of 160 students demonstrated the "will and the power of the community" (Tetzeli, 1992). The Academy population was 98 percent Black, with the remaining 2 percent Arabic or Caucasian (Moore & Associates, 1993). When the re-named African-centered Academies opened in September 1991, there was only one white child enrolled. His mother said that it didn't matter "if they stick him in with 1,000 colored kids, as long as he learns" (Dozier, 1991).

The academies, then, in August of 1991, were essentially predominantly Black, male schools. Although NOWLDF was successful in obtaining a preliminary injunction preventing the Male Academy from legally excluding females, in actuality the Academies largely excluded girls and the legal rights of Black females were essentially not protected. The settlement agreement only reserved one-quarter of the admission slots for females, and protected males who had been admitted, virtually sanctioning the Male Academy and the biased selection process. It did not provide that an equal number of females as males be admitted. It allowed the males to begin one week earlier than the females, giving them a head-start at the Academy. It created a one-week application period for females (though subsequently extended) in contrast to the three-week application period for males. It did not require that the names of the Academy be changed to include female leaders, but allowed all of them to retain the names of Black male leaders. This is significant because the Academy that opened in January was called the Mae Jemison Academy and though not explicitly a Female Academy, it was initially predominantly female. Thus, the names of the Academy corresponded to the gender of the students enrolling. The settlement agreement, by its very terms, did not create an equal opportunity for females.

The settlement agreement created and condoned an environment in which female students would be marginalized and excluded by a male-centered administration, a male-focused classroom environment, male-focused charters, and a predominantly male student body. By failing, at minimum, to require that an equal number of female students as males be enrolled before the opening of the Academy, both the court and the plaintiff's lawyers, in effect, conceded the battle they had won by the preliminary injunction and sacrificed the opportunities gained by the injunction in the settlement agreement. The court's sanctioning of the settlement agreement, in effect, reversed its initial ruling and allowed the School Board and its supporters to achieve their objective. The terms of the settlement agreement and the limited enrollment of females at the Male Academy illustrate the success of the supporters' collective action frame.

The collective action frame was a powerful and cohesive force mobilizing and pressuring the Black community to defy a court order and to actualize its will against forces of opposition. The Board and its supporters presented the Black male as a sympathetic, vulnerable character, victimized by a variety of forces because of his Blackness, maleness, and poverty. By simultaneously framing the Black male as a victim of Whites and women (Black and White), and as the future of the Black race, the Board and its supporters created a strong foundation for the nationalistic discourse in support of the educational objectives of the Male Academy. The Board's frame resonated within the predominantly Black, inner-city, urban, and poor community. Against this powerful and cohesive frame, the plaintiffs—the Black mothers and their daughters—were faced with overcoming an insurmountable oppositional consciousness that incorporated maleness, male supremacy, and Black nationalism.

So effective was the frame that the supporters were able to silence the Black female plaintiffs and virtually eliminate any opposition. Shawn Garrett withdrew from the lawsuit before the August 15, 1991, hearing. The following is her statement of withdrawal:

> Today I have voluntarily withdrawn from my lawsuit against the Detroit Board of Education over the issue of the all-male Academies offering special benefits and programs only to young men, and not to young women such as my 4-year-old-daughter Crystal. When this lawsuit was filed, I never could have imagined the emotional responses that it would arouse, and the personal harassment and hostility aimed towards me and my daughter. The last 10 days have been more difficult that any other time in my life. I have been harassed and criticized by people who are closest to me, as well as by perfect strangers. I can no longer subject myself or my daughter to continued harassment and threats. I am truly disappointed that in 1991, a person who stands up for her rights and the rights of her young daughter would have to go through what Crystal and I have endured. I still believe that this is an important lawsuit, and that the Male Academies must be opened to students of both sexes. I still believe that segregation in any form is wrong. I still believe that people who feel discriminated against should stand up for their rights. I only hope that others who stand up for rights and [sic] not be subjected to similar harassment, and will not be afraid to ask the Courts to vindicate their rights. (Garrett, 1991b)

At oral argument, her attorney stated "Shawn Garrett has been subjected in the last few days to enormous pressure, both public and otherwise in this case, and has been forced in order to protect her daughter's interest, to withdraw" (Transcript). Though Garrett refers to her withdrawal as voluntary, her statement and her attorney's statement suggest that her withdrawal was involuntary, a result of the harassment and antagonism of the community and the inability of her lawyers and their organizations to encourage her to persevere in spite of the difficulty. The suit was able to be heard only because of the anonymous plaintiff, Nancy Doe. Whereas Garrett's voice was silenced, Doe's presence was never seen, her voice was never heard, and her identity never openly revealed.

The attacks on Garrett, her subsequent withdrawal, the anonymity of Doe, the minimal participation of Black girls at the Academies, and the absence of effective legal and political representation epitomize the exclusion, marginalization, invisibility, and ultimately, the political powerlessness of Black females. Dr. Watson (Watson & Smitherman,

1996, p. 48) noted that "interestingly, but not surprisingly, NOW had difficulty finding a Detroit parent to lend her name to the lawsuit." There were no Black women's political advocacy organizations that could represent the Black mothers and daughters. As a result, Doe's and Garrett's legal concerns were represented by the ACLU and NOWLDF and these organizations became their voices and their faces. Although NOWLDF had a female African-American lawyer intimately involved in the *Garrett* case, the President of NOWLDF and the lead attorney were White women. The ACLU attorneys, the Executive Director, and the President were White men. Thus, the Black female plaintiffs were overshadowed by their predominantly White organizational representation. This allowed the Male Academy supporters to racialize an initially gender-based issue. Despite their ability to advance persuasive legal arguments on gender discrimination, these organizations lacked the political power in the community to overcome the supporters' powerful collective frame. Likewise, the NAACP and the Detroit Association of Black Organizations, though opposed to the Male Academy, were not strong voices for Black girls.

One explanation for this failure of representation by these organizations on behalf of Black females is that these organizations were not created to respond to the unique and interwoven race, class, and gender concerns of Black females. The political organizations' primary political agendas were not rooted in the complexity and intersectionality of Black women's interests. Gender equity was the focus for NOWLDF, civil rights for the ACLU, and racial equality for the NAACP and the Detroit Association of Black Organizations (DABO). Though the interests of the Black females are encompassed by these organizations, as political organizations with political philosophies and political agendas, their interest in the Male Academy debate was limited to their narrow organizational mission and furthering their political and ideological agenda. Their focus was not the unique, intertwined race, class, and gender concerns of Black females. Lacking the voice to address the multi-dimensional interest of Black females, much of their discourse was uni-dimensional. It revolved around race and used racial examples as analogies for gender and rarely even mentioned Black females.

For example, the NAACP's Resolution (1991b) on the Male Academy reflected its organizational concern about race segregation and race discrimination. The resolution stated that "the NAACP, while cognizant of the complex problems of the African-American male, must reaffirm its historical opposition to school segregation of any kind, and call upon all persons concerned to find workable alternatives to the proposed segregated education for African-American males" (NAACP, 1991b). The NAACP resolved that "all units of the NAACP be encouraged to develop various projects that can be targeted to the needs of African-American males." The NAACP expressed its concern about the policy implications of segregation, noting that de jure segregation has been used to oppress Blacks. The NAACP Legal Defense Fund submitted a position statement with the Plaintiff's Reply Brief. The statement emphasized that the return to any policy of segregation "legitimizes the very mechanism that was used effectively to hinder and disadvantage generations of African-Americans" (NAACP Statement on Proposals, 1991b, p. 3).

The national organization said that race and gender segregation may make it more difficult to address other contentious issues involving race, such as the Afrocentric curriculum, affirmative action, minority status, male teacher hiring, and the overrepresentation of Black male students in special education classes and disciplinary programs. Thus, the primary focus for the NAACP was the racial segregation implications of the Male Academy and its preference to address the problems of Black males without segregation of any kind. Its policy statement only tangentially and marginally addressed gender issues affecting Black females and did not address the joint effects of both racism and sexism on Black females. Its resolution on the All African-American Male Schools did not even mention females at all. Its national position, however, was undermined by the local Detroit chapter, which opposed the resolution during the national convention. Executive Director Joann Watson of the Detroit branch viewed the schools as "a level of redress and a response to discrimination" (Russell, August 21, 1991).

Similarly, although the Detroit Association of Black Organizations (DABO) opposed the Male Academy, neither its April 16, 1991, letter to the Detroit School Board, nor its August 26, 1991, letter specifically mentioned Black females. The April 16 letter encouraged the Board to reconsider and revisit its Male Academy resolution. The August 26 letter encouraged the Board not to appeal Judge Woods' ruling. Although they do refer to the poor academic achievement of both males and females, both letters indicated that DABO continued its "unqualified support" of the Board's resolve to "improve the academic and behavioral performance of African-American males" under the resolution dated February 26, 1991. Though opposing the

Male Academy and commending the Black mother and her daughter, as well as the ACLU and NOWLDF, for bringing the suit, DABO did not address the challenges facing Black females or the sexism of many supporters of the Male Academy.

Likewise, many of the arguments of the ACLU and NOWLDF used racial segregation analogies and focused on opposition to any type of segregation, rather than specific concerns about the social advancement of Black females (Statement of the Metropolitan Branch ACLU, 1991). Their legal briefs also contained many analogies to race. ACLU Executive Director of the Detroit chapter, Howard Simon, noted that there would be concern if a board decided "the education of white children and black students will improve" if they were separated (Detroit News Staff and Wires, September 10, 1991, pg. 3A; Gilchrist, Richardson, Trimer-Hartley, & Brum, September 10, 1991, p. 1A). NOWLDF Executive Director Helen Neuborne, on *ABC's Nightline*, suggested that the Board's self-determination argument could logically lead to the following conclusion: "if in the 50s, South Carolina parents decided they didn't want to integrate the schools, that would be okay and outsiders couldn't come in and say Black children have a right to be at those schools with white children." Thus race segregation and race discrimination were used to accentuate the inappropriateness and illegality of gender segregation and gender discrimination.

Although effective for purposes of the legal argument, these analogies were ineffective in securing support for the Black women plaintiffs. These arguments also failed to address the impact of gender segregation on Black females, even as the organizations tried to counter the Board's claims of gender discrimination against Black males. The tendency of the women's movement to use racial analogies and to equate White women's gender status with the racial status of Blacks has alienated Black women primarily because it ignores their multiple and interlocking subordination in both the class and gender systems (Giddings, 1984, p. 308). Additionally, comparing gender segregation to race segregation was not an effective strategy because the Detroit school system was already racially segregated. In its 1974 *Milliken v. Bradley* decision, the Supreme Court held that Detroit's mostly White suburbs could not be compelled to integrate with the city as a means to racially integrate the Detroit school system, as the segregation was the result of de facto, rather than de jure segregation. As a result of white-flight, the inner-city Detroit school system was 90 percent Black and 2 percent white, with a small percentage of Arabs and Hispanics.

The ACLU's and NOWLDF's use of race can be contrasted to the Board's use of race. Whereas the Board used race to highlight the complexity of the status of urban males and the factors affecting them, the ACLU and NOWLDF used race to provide a comparison for issues of gender. Race functioned as an integral element in the Board's arguments, and was integrated into its characterization of urban males and its defense of the Male Academy. The material conditions of an already racially segregated school district created a powerful justification for the Board's racially grounded arguments of self-determination and nationalism.

Deconstructing the legal and popular discourse and restructuring the discourse as a collective action frame reveals the reasons for the Male Academy supporters' initial success. In its punctuation element, the Board redefined a specific social group—the urban male—as victimized, oppressed, emasculated, and powerless based on his intersecting race, class, and gender status. The inner-city, poor, Black male was portrayed as endangered and endangering, needing the exclusive attention and resources of the Black community. The supporters created a moral imperative for the Male Academy by linking the Black male crisis to the future of the Black race, suggesting that the status of the race was in jeopardy. The supporters urged Black women, in particular, to sacrifice their gender interests and concerns for the "good of the race." In light of this call for unity, it became politically difficult and unpopular for Black women to oppose the Male Academy.

The presence of the ACLU and NOWLDF only heightened the vulnerability of those who opposed the Academy, subjecting them to accusations of race betrayal and feminist loyalty. The supporters relied on well-known stereotypes about feminism as a lesbian-oriented, White women's movement, with an anti-male agenda. They essentially equated feminism with racism toward Black males. The supporters also relied on widely accepted stereotypes about females, and Black females in particular, to strengthen their position regarding the Male Academy. By portraying Black girls as distractions in the classroom and female teachers as unqualified to instruct Black males solely because of their gender, the supporters created a logical—albeit discriminatory and sexist—relationship between the Male Academy and the exclusion of female students and female teachers. In addition, they portrayed Black single mothers as inadequate and responsible for the male crisis based solely on their intersecting race, class, and gender status, rather than a combination of social and economic factors. Supporters, then, not only attributed the cause of the crisis to females, they were also able to perpetuate an anti-matriarchy, anti-female political consciousness. The anti-female consciousness was combined with a Black nationalist ideology. The Black nationalist discourse about self-determination and the rights of parents to create educational opportunities for their children—specifically Black sons—enabled the supporters to link the Male Academy with a Black male patriarchy.

The discourse illustrates that categories of race, gender, and class were constructed in ways that perpetuated dichotomies and polarized identities. For example, "male" came to symbolize Black pride, nationalism, Black unity, and power (hooks, 1981; Hunter & Davis 1992). Through the role of the ACLU and NOWLDF in their advocacy of females, "female" became associated with White, the upper-class, racism and radical feminism (Collins, 1991; hooks, 1981; Joseph and Lewis, 1981). Whereas Black boys symbolized potential and opportunity, Black girls symbolized hindrance or obstacles. This polarization of mutually interdependent categories of race and gender successfully coerced and persuaded many Black men and Black women to adopt their racial identity as their primary identity and to suppress their concerns about gender inequality and sexism in the Black community. This either/or characterization in discussions of race and gender is typical of dominant group discourse, which precludes addressing the and/both status of Black women (Collins, 1986; Crenshaw, 1989; Feldman, 1995; Giddings, 1984; Scales-Trent, 1989). As a result of this polarization of identity and exclusion of Black women, Black women have been put in the uncomfortable and awkward position in racial and gender debates of choosing to support movements that fail to adequately address their status (Collins, 1988; hooks, 1984). The dichotomization of race and gender identity inhibits and prevents Blacks and Whites, and in particular Black women, from openly advocating the end to multiple oppressions in society. The *Garrett* case illustrates the power of oppressive discourse to silence and quiet opposition and to perpetuate oppression (Deitch, 1993; Gregory, 1993). By adopting the slogans "Don't send your girls" and "Keep your girls at home" as their rallying cry, the supporters created a succinct, coherent, logical, and practical action designed to accomplish their goal of a Male Academy (Walters, 1991). The power of the slogans was that they integrated the punctuation and attribution elements into an articulation element that simultaneously accomplished multiple political objectives. It affirmed the supremacy of Black males and a Black male patriarchy. It acknowledged the subordinate traditional role of women and girls in the home. It also attacked feminism and feminists. The slogans reaffirmed and reasserted the Black community's power of self-determination and denied the power of the "White" legal system to control decisions and outcomes in the Black community.

Although the ACLU and NOWLDF were successful in obtaining a preliminary injunction from the federal court prohibiting the exclusion of girls, their discourse did not have the authority or power to counter that of the Male Academy supporters. The organizations also lacked the political power to persuade Garrett not to withdraw, to persuade Nancy Doe not to be anonymous, to negotiate a fair and equitable settlement protecting the rights of females, and to encourage parents to send their daughters to the Male Academy even in the face of strong opposition. There was little resistance to the Academy supporters' powerful frame and certainly no extralegal collective action in response to that frame. Unlike the supporters' discourse, which defined the crisis and attributed blame to females and ideologies of privilege, the opposition's discourse did not fit into a collective action frame. There was no punctuation, attribution, or articulation element by which to garner support for their position. Moreover, the mere presence of White organizations and a feminist organization served to heighten antagonism toward the group whose interests the organization sought to represent—Black girls and their mothers. The *Michigan Chronicle* (We will have, August 21–27, 1991) noted that most of the protesters supporting the Male Academy were female parents, even though NOW "blasted the academies as discriminatory to women." The antagonism of Black women toward NOW increased the vulnerability of Garrett and Doe as the Black women plaintiffs, making them susceptible to accusations of racism and racist betrayal through their alliance with the ACLU and NOWLDF.

This case study demonstrates that the constructions and definitions of race, class, and gender categories for Black males, Black females, White males, and White females in Detroit influenced the outcome of the educational policy debate. The racialized gender, class, and nationalistic discourse created an outcome that perpetuated existing structures of hegemony and domination. Black women were criticized, marginalized, victimized, and ultimately excluded from an important educational opportunity and legal right. As a result of the inadequate legal and social representation, Black women, in effect, were silenced and excluded in the discourse, and ultimately, in the Academy. Further, the dissension within the NAACP between the national chapter and the local chapter prevented any strong advocacy by the NAACP, particularly in light of that organization's concerns about racial discrimination (Russell, August 21, 1991). The predominantly Black Detroit School Board was able to use the presence of the ACLU and NOWLDF to garner support for the Male Academy based on race, and to ignore the issues of gender equity. The Male Academy case illustrated the ability of the Male Academy supporters to challenge race and class hierarchies while simultaneously reinforcing the gender hierarchy of patriarchy. The discourse of the Male Academy supporters reflected that race, class, and gender categories were defined and constructed in a manner that ensured the success of the initiative. As a result, in 1991, the Detroit Black community and the Detroit School Board were essentially able to implement the three male Academies. Figure 2 demonstrates this outcome.

FRAME	KEY CONCEPT	SYMBOL
A. PUNCTUATION: Define the problem	Blackness, Maleness, Poverty	Black Boys

1. Define the endangered urban male as a crisis and unjust situation
2. Demonstrate the injustice of the legal system and education system
3. Incorporate an ideological approach of masculinity and patriarchy

FRAME	KEY CONCEPT	SYMBOL
B. ATTRIBUTION: Attribute blame	Whiteness, Femaleness, and Wealth	Black Girls

1. Blame females as mothers, teachers, and students
2. Blame institutions and organizations: legal system, NOWLDF, ACLU
3. Blame ideologies of feminism, matriarchy, racism, class privilege

FRAME	KEY CONCEPT	SYMBOL
C. ARTICULATION: Propose a solution	Black Nationalism	Black Male Academy

1. Implement a media campaign: For boys-only; Don't send your girls
2. Negotiate a settlement agreement to address legal and education system
3. Promote Black nationalism

D. OUTCOME: Predominantly Black Male Academy

1. Male student dominance: Only 39 girls
2. Patriarchy and masculinity affirmed
3. Exclusion, silencing, and marginalization of Black women

Figure 2 Detroit Male Academy Collective Action Frame

Figure 2 reflects the power of the collective action frame. It also represents the manner in which race, class, and gender were constructed and symbolized to represent ideologies. The supporters, by incorporating interwoven identities, interlocking social structures, and ideologies into a collective action frame, were essentially able to achieve their desired outcome in 1991—three predominantly Male Academies.

What has happened since 1991? The *Garrett* case began in 1990 when a small group of educators decided to convene a forum on the Black male crisis in Detroit. Since then, there have been transformative changes in both the legal system and the education system, and scholars have engaged in extensive research, which has received a lot of publicity in the media. There have been significant legal developments at the federal and state levels. The legal activity has in turn influenced and affected the education system, particularly in Detroit.

At the federal level, the developments involved all three levels of government: the judicial branch, the legislative branch, and the executive branch. At the state level in Michigan, there were amendments to state laws and to the Michigan Constitution through a ballot initiative. This legal activity proceeded in tandem with publicity about educational research on gender differences and the benefits and challenges presented by single-sex education. As a result of federal, state, and local developments, the Detroit Public Schools were able to implement two single-sex academies—one for males and one for females. The next section reviews key historical developments in the single-sex school debate since *Garrett*. The chapter concludes with a reflection about Black girls and Black feminism.

5.2 Single-Sex Schools

Five years after *Garrett*, on June 26, 1996, the Supreme Court issued a ruling on the constitutionality of single-sex public universities in *United States v. Virginia* (1996). The case involved the Virginia Military Institute's (VMI) admission policy of excluding women on the basis of gender. In 1990, an anonymous woman complained to the Justice Department about the all-male admission policy (Schriver, 2003). In response, the Department of Justice (DOJ) brought suit against VMI and the State of Virginia, alleging that the school's admission policy violated the Fourteenth Amendment. A lower court agreed and suggested three remedies to the State of Virginia: admit women, create a "comparable alternative" for women, or stop accepting state funds. In response, the State of Virginia chose to create a "comparable alternative" called the Virginia Women's Institute for Leadership (VMIL) at Mary Baldwin, a private all-girls college (*U.S. v. Virginia*, 1996).

During the court proceedings for VMI, there were similar proceedings involving the Citadel University, South Carolina's all-male military academy. Prior to the Supreme Court's decision, Shannon Faulkner became the first women to attend the Citadel in 1995 (Janofsky, 1996). She, however, had to drop out after one week due to the harassment and mental abuse (Schriver, 2003). Like VMI, the Citadel had also tried to establish a "comparable program" at Converse College—a private all-women's institution—to avoid desegregating the Citadel (Citadel gets a way out, May, 1995). The Supreme Court's decision would impact both of these institutions.

In *Virginia*, the Court (1996) ruled that the exclusion of women did violate the Fourteenth Amendment because VMI failed to meet the "intermediate" scrutiny standard, that is showing that the gender classification served an "important governmental interest" and that the means employed was "substantially related" to achieving the objective. The Court emphasized that the justification for single-sex schools could not rely on overly broad generalizations about differences in talents, capacities, preferences, or tendencies of males and females. The Court also found that the VMIL alternative was not "substantially equal," which was the standard of analysis, rather than the lower court standard of "substantive comparability." Influencing the court's decision was the fact that women had been part of the United States Military, Navy, and Air Force academies since 1976 (Tuchman, 1996). In 1980, 214 women graduated from West Point, Annapolis, and the Air Force Academy (Academies graduate first women, 1980). This integration undermined many of VMI's arguments.

In light of the Supreme Court decision in 1996, the Citadel admitted its first class of four women, and two of those women graduated in 1999 and 2000. In 1997, VMI admitted its first class of fourteen women, who graduated in 2001 (Kahn, 2001). In 2002, the Citadel graduated its first class of seven Black female cadets (B. Smith, 2002). There were 100 women in the 2002–2003 academic class (Schriver, 2003).

The transition for women into these institutions was not easy (Coed Citadel still a work in progress, 2006; de Vise, 2009). Nancy Mace (2001) detailed the challenges of breaking the gender barrier at the Citadel in 1996. Two of the four females admitted they left after a hazing incident when their sweatsuits were set on fire "just below their breasts" (Schriver, 2003). This incident was part of an "intolerable environment" of harassment and abuse. The culture at the academies, as evidenced by the language and discourse, reflected a "culture of violent hypermasculinity," grounded in a belief about the inferiority of women (Vojdik, 2002). The use of terms such as "faggot, queer, female, pussy, cunt, whore, butch, fucking little girl," was common, as were references to menstruation, abortions, and rape. These references were used to describe men who failed to meet expectations of masculinity and manhood (Vojdik, 2002). It was into this culture that women were admitted and expected to assimilate. Though women were admitted and graduated, the experiences of women at these institutions revealed "reports of misogyny, sexism, sexual violence, and hyperbolic maleness" (Schriver, 2003).

These experiences were consistent with those faced by women integrating the United States military. Project Athena was a longitudinal research project by the United States military in 1975 to assess the integration of women into West Point (Adams, 1979). When the class of 1980 graduated, it appeared as if the integration of women was complete (Academies graduate first women, 1980). However, the Tailhook scandal in 1991 and the Aberdeen scandal in 1996 involving the rape and sexual assault of women indicated "the deeply rooted nature of sexism, misogyny, sexual misconduct, and discrimination in the military" (O'Neill, 1998). The vice-chair of the Senior Review Panel on Sexual Harassment commissioned by the Secretary of the Army in 1996 concluded that "it will take 40 years to change the culture" (Grossman, 2001). Even as recently as 2010, Navy policy prohibited women from serving aboard submarines (Jerven, 2010). This policy was seen as "one of the last bastions of gender segregation" (Jerven, 2010). Sixteen years after the repeal of the combat exclusion law, the final obstacle for full integration of women into the Navy was removed allowing women to serve on submarines (Navy welcomes women to serve in submarines, April 30, 2010).

The continuing challenge of integration is further reflected by an ongoing investigation of VMI in 2009 by the Department of Education's Office of Civil Rights for sex discrimination with respect to "tenure and promotion policies; handling of student and employee complaints; and the school's marriage and parenthood policy" (Lindsey, 2009). It is also important to note that the "comparable alternative" VWIL is still in existence as the nation's only all-female cadet corps with a strong enrollment (MBC celebrates, 2004; Women Flock to VWIL, 2001).

The challenges of dismantling all-male institutions reflects the complexity of social justice activism. The *VMI*, *Citadel*, and *Garrett* cases opened a door of opportunity and also a door of challenge. *VMI* and the *Citadel* cases created an education opportunity for women within powerful male institutions. VMI and the Citadel had a 150-year-old history—a history grounded in ideologies of power, privilege, masculinity, and manhood. The longevity of the institutions evidenced the power and strength of interlocking and intersupported structural, disciplinary, interpersonal, and hegemonic domains.

TASJ provides an approach for understanding the relationship between oppression and activism. VMI and the Citadel, as both military and education institutions, represent the structural domain of interlocking social systems. Within these systems, male leadership and authority controlled the interpersonal domain of day-to-day interactions. They also administered the policies, procedures, and practices in the disciplinary domain. This is evidenced by acknowledgement of the 1997 Citadel president that "unwritten and unsanctioned traditions" had become rituals at the Citadel (Vojdik, 2002, ftnt. 250). The operation of the disciplinary domain was guided by a long-standing history and ideology of male privilege as evidenced by the hegemonic domain.

Understanding the domains is critical to implementing an effective advocacy strategy. Dismantling this powerful military and educational structure required judicial intervention, particularly in light of the strong community opposition to integration and proposals for alternative, separate, and unequal programs. Access to these institutions for women could only come through a combination of legal action and individual activism. Legal intervention, alone, was not sufficient. There were also courageous individuals who were willing to exercise the rights and willing to suffer and sacrifice for the privilege and right of equal opportunity and non-discrimination. Shannon Faulkner, Nancy Mace, the seven Black women graduates (Jamey McCloud, Renee Hypolite, Natosha Mitchell, Adrienne Watson, Sha Peterson, Geneive Hardney, and Toshika Hudson), and others were the women who marched forward through the door that had been opened by judicial activism. The woman who opens the door is often unable to take advantange of the opportunity. Just as Shawn Garrett was pressured and harassed into withdrawing from the lawsuit because of community opposition, Shannon Faulkner also was forced to withdraw from the Citadel. Just as Nancy Doe, an anonymous woman, invisible and unknown, had to be the ultimate plaintiff in the *Garrett* case, an anonymous, invisible, and unknown plaintiff was required for VMI to go forward.

Although the legal action initially created access for women to the institutions within the structural domain, it did not substantially address the other domains—interpersonal, hegemonic, and disciplinary. As a result, activism continues to address the other domains to ensure that women's experiences at predominantly male institutions are free of sexism and discrimination. This activism must be informed by research, consistent with the intent of Project Athena. Its goal was to "provide decision makers at the United States Military Academy with multiple measures of the problems studied so that recommendations and subsequent decisions will be made based upon sound, scholarly research" (Adams, 1979). The objective was to be proactive and preventive, rather than reactive and remedial. That objective must continue as long-stranding traditions and ideologies are challenged by women.

The *VMI* and *Citadel* cases involved activism on the judicial level on the issue of single-sex schools. The option of single-sex education environments was not precluded by the Supreme Court's decision. Though finding that VMI's single-gender admission policy was unconstitutional, the Court's ruling did not prohibit single-sex institutions. The Court did, however, find that if there were single-sex institutions, they must be equal. Although this Supreme Court decision in 1996 involved higher education, it provided a foundation for subsequent legislative and executive activity involving gender and the education system, particularly in the elementary and secondary school context a few years later.

On January 8, 2002, President Bush signed the No Child Left Behind Act of 2001 (20 U.S.C. 7201). Section 5131(a)(23) of Title V, "Promoting Informed Parent Choice and Innovative Programs," provides that "funds made available to local educational agencies under section 5112 shall be used for innovative assistance programs, which may include...programs to provide same-gender schools and classrooms (consistent with applicable law)." Section 5131(b) required that the innovative programs meet three requirements: promote challenging academic achievement standards, improve student academic achievement; and support an overall education reform strategy. The Act required the Secretary of Education to issue guidelines for school districts under the Act.

The need for guidelines from the Department of Education arose because the provisions of NCLB created uncertainty under Title IX regulations and the clarification was needed to ensure that the two legislative acts were not inconsistent. Because No Child Left Behind provided for same-gender schools and classrooms, "consistent with applicable law," guidelines were needed to ensure that the creation of same-gender schools was not in conflict with existing law. In particular, the conditions under which gender-based admissions decisions, including single-sex classes or schools, could be made without being discriminatory on the basis of sex under Title IX needed to be addressed. Although Title IX prohibits discrimination on the basis of sex, there are many exceptions. With respect to admission decisions to educational institutions, the statute only applies to institutions of vocational education, professional education, graduate higher education, and to public institutions of undergraduate higher education. (§1681(a)(1)). There are also exceptions for certain religious organizations, education institutions training individuals for military services or merchant marine, public educational institutions with traditional and continuing admissions policy of admitting only one gender, Boy or Girl conferences, father-son or mother-daughter activities, scholarship awards in beauty pageants, and social fraternities or sororities and youth organizations, such as the Boy Scouts, Girl Scouts, YWCA, and YMCA (§1681(a)(3–9)).

Although the statute did not address elementary and secondary schools, the regulations did. The Title IX regulations in 2002 allowed elementary and secondary schools to have single-sex classes or activities for physical education, human sexuality, and chorus or vocal classes (34 CFR 106.34(c, e, f)). The regulations also allowed students to be separated for remedial or affirmative action objectives (34 CFR 106.3). Additionally, the regulations addressed admission decisions involving non-vocational schools, stating "A recipient which is a local educational agency shall not, on the basis of sex, exclude any person from admission...unless such recipient otherwise makes available to such person, pursuant to the same policies and criteria of admission, courses, services, and facilities comparable to each course, service, and facility offered in or through such schools" (Sec. 106.35(b)).

The Guidelines (United States Dept. of Education, 2002), then, attempted to address the difference between the exclusion of coverage for admissions decisions at non-vocational schools in the Title IX statute and the inclusion of provisions with respect to admissions decisions at non-vocational institutions in the regulations. The Guidelines (2002) explain that a district

> cannot use a single-sex admissions policy—which is not itself subject to Title IXs prohibition—as the predicate for otherwise causing students, on the basis of sex, to be excluded from participation in, be denied the benefits of, or be subjected to discrimination under any education program or activity receiving Federal financial assistance. For example, school districts may not establish a single-sex school for one sex that provides the districts only performing arts curriculum. Students of the other sex also must have access to a comparable school with that curriculum. It has been our longstanding interpretation, policy, and practice to require that the comparable school must also be single-sex.

Essentially, then, the Guidelines acknowledged that non-vocational single-sex schools would be allowed if each sex had a comparable single-sex school. The Guidelines also recognized the tenuousness of the legal foundation, noting that although there was a statutory exemption in Title IX for single-sex public schools, the schools could be challenged on constitutional grounds. To provide more guidance, particularly with the No Child Left Behind law, the Office of Civil Rights in May 2002 issued its "Notice of Intent to Regulate regarding Single Sex Classes and School." Four years later, after almost 6000 comments, final rules were published on October 25, 2006, effective as of November 24, 2006. Although 96 percent of the comments opposed the changes, the regulations were implemented (NWLC, October 24, 2006).

The new regulations address both single-sex classes and single-sex schools. Section 106.34(a) sets forth the general standard for single-sex classes, providing that a recipient of federal funds "shall not provide or otherwise carry out any of its educational programs or activities separately on the basis of sex, or require or refuse participation therein by any of its students on the basis of sex." The exceptions in subsection (a)(1–4) under the prior regulations for single-sex classes or activities remained substantially the same: physical education classes, human sexuality classes, and vocal range for choruses (106.34(a)(1) through (4)). The new provisions, however, in subsection (b) provide four conditions under which nonvocational single-sex classes or extracurricular activities can be offered (106.34(b)). First, there must be a substantial relationship between the single-sex component and an important educational objective. The important objective can be to improve students' educational achievement under a policy of providing "diverse educational opportunities" or addressing a "particular, identified educational need for students." Second, the implementation of the objective must be evenhanded. Third, the enrollment must be voluntary. Finally, the students of the excluded sex must be provided a "substantially equal" co-educational class or activity in the same subject or activity. The factors relevant to determining whether the activity or class is "substantially equal" include "policies and criteria of admission; the educational benefits provided, including the quality, range, and content of curriculum and other services; the quality and availability of books, instructional materials, and technology; the qualifications of faculty and staff; geographic accessibility; the quality, accessibility, and availability of facilities and resources provided to the classes; and intangible features, such as reputation of faculty." The Guidelines also require that the class or activity be evaluated every two years to ensure that the justification is genuine and not based on "overly broad generalizations about the different talents, capacities, or preferences of either sex" and that there is a substantial relationship between the single-sex nature and the achievement of the important objective (Section 106.34(b)(4)).

Section 106(c)(1) addresses single-sex schools. It provides that if a district creates a single-sex public nonvocational elementary or secondary school, it must also operate a "substantially equal single-sex school or coeducational school" for the excluded sex. There is an exception if the school is a single-sex charter school under state law. The substantially equal factors remain the same as those for single-sex classes or extracurricular activities. Additionally, the regulations prohibit making admission decisions on the basis of sex for vocational programs. These new regulations in 2006 substantially changed the landscape for many school districts across the country. Through federal legislative, executive, and judicial activity, the same theme has been communicated in the past ten years: Single-sex schools are acceptable if there is a "substantially equal" (coed or single-sex) school experience for the excluded sex and the justification for the single-sex status is substantially related to an important educational objective.

Although many school districts were able to immediately take advantage of the flexibility and opportunity provided by the federal activism, several school districts, including the Detroit School District, needed to wait for state-level activism. Michigan, like Florida, Wisconsin, Delaware, and Massachusetts, had state laws that prohibited single-sex schools (National Coalition for Women and Girls in Education,

2008; Silva, 2008; Give single-sex schools a try, 2008; Wisconsin Department of Public Instruction, 2006; Vaznis, 2008, 2009). These laws were a barrier in 1991 and were still a barrier in 2004 when the Detroit Public Schools announced plans to open two single-gender academies. According to the Detroit Public School Board, the announcement was "wildly applauded by many Detroit residents who appreciate the value of single-sex schools" (District halts plans, 2005). This excitement was tempered, once again, by a familiar pattern. The Detroit ACLU "immediately attacked the concept, deriding it as sexist and threatening to take the District to court, citing a little used state law that prevents public school systems from...running single gender schools" (District halts plans, 2005). The School Board CEO, William Coleman, said, "I regret the fact that the leaders of the ACLU don't believe in parental choice and feel they know what's best for Detroit parents" (District halts plans, 2005). Thus, in August 2005, the school district said that it would make the Douglass Preparatory Academy for Young Men and the International Academy for Young Women co-ed schools. The Detroit School Board indicated that they would work with state legislators to change the law (Detroit tosses plan for same-sex schools, 2005; District halts plans to open, 2005).

Coleman, who was appointed as CEO in July 2005, became the General Superintendent of Detroit Public Schools in January 2006. He worked and partnered with the legislature to change the statutes (Dillon, 2006). Sen. Buzz Thomas (D-Detroit), who proposed the legislation, said the return to single-gender classes would maximize the opportunities for some students to succeed because studies show that male and female brain development occurs at a different pace. He noted in particular, the need for "young boys, who often have greater difficulties in school than girls" (Gongwer News Service, 2006b; Thomas, 2006). Another male senator said that in high school 90 percent of his "attention was focused on a tall, blonde girl," and that if he "had put more effort into his studies he may have gone further in life" (Gongwer News Service, 2006b).

Based on the legislative support, three bills were enacted to address existing state laws prohibiting single-sex classrooms, programs, or schools (Gandy, 2006b; Gongwer News Service, 2006a, 2006b). The Michigan Revised School Code and the Elliott-Larsen Act, as interpreted in *Garrett*, prohibited the operation of single-sex schools. The Revised Code stated that "a separate school or department shall not be kept for a person on account of race, color, or sex." The Elliott-Larsen Act prohibited discrimination by a school against a person on the basis of "religion, race, color, national origin, or sex." Two bills addressed the Revised Code and one addressed the Elliott-Larsen Act (Michigan Senate Fiscal Agency, 2006a; 2006b; 2006c).

Senate Bill No. 1296 (Public Act 303 of 2006) amended Section 1146 of the Revised School Code to provide that a school district "may establish and maintain a school, class, or program...in which enrollment is limited to pupils of a single gender if the school district.... makes available to pupils a substantially equal coeducational school...or substantially equal school for pupils of the other gender." Additionally, the amendment provided that participation by students in a single-gender school had to be "wholly voluntary" and that their participation would not be considered voluntary unless there was a "substantially equal coeducational school ..." House Bill No. 4264 (Public Act No. 347, 2006) was also enacted specifically to provide that "the board of a first class school district" could implement single-sex schools if participation was voluntary and if there was also a "substantially equal coeducational school" and "a substantially equal" single-sex school for the other gender. This legislation only applied to Detroit because Detroit was the only "first class" school district in Michigan with an enrollment of at least 100,000 students (Michigan House Fiscal Agency, 2006).

The third bill was House Bill No. 6247 (Public Act 348), which amended Section 4 of the Elliott-Larsen Civil Rights Act. The new amendment provided that a school district could establish and maintain single-gender schools under the terms and conditions of the Revised School Code. These laws, effective as of September 2006 (Michigan Information and Research Service, 2006), collectively seemed to remove any state law barriers to the implementation by the Detroit Public Schools of the federal Department of Education regulations permitting single-sex schools. In December 13, 2006, the Superintendent's Newsletter stated "Obtained legislative approval of single gender schools by lobbying for amendments to the school code and the Elliot-Larsen Civil Rights Act. This approval permits us to expand enrollment at two defacto single gender high schools: Frederick Douglass and the Detroit International Academy. Frederick Douglass High School increased its enrollment from 195 students to 261 students. The Detroit International Academy increased its enrollment from 90 to 264 students" (Coleman, 2006, 2007).

Even in the midst of these legislative and educational changes related to gender in Detroit and Michigan, other legal issues continued to arise. In December 2006, a ballot initiative resulted in an amendment to the Michigan Constitution (T. Martin, 2006). In response to the Supreme Court decisions in *Grutter v. Bollinger* (2003) and *Gratz v. Bollinger* (2003) on affirmative action at the University of Michigan, a conservative group promoted a ballot initiative to prevent the use of affirmative action in Michigan. The Amendment provides that universities, colleges, and school districts cannot "discriminate against, or grant preferential treatment to, any individual or group on the basis of race, sex, color, ethnicity, or national origin in the operation of public employment, public education, or public contracting." The Michigan NOW chapter (2007) suggested that this constitutional action negated the state law amendments providing for single-sex programs or at a minimum, caused the state law provisions to be inconsistent with the constitution because the state law amendments provided for preferential treatment based on gender (Pollock, 2006). This is still an unresolved issue.

The issue that remains to be addressed and clarified is whether there is a constitutional challenge resulting from the inconsistency between the revised Title IX regulations and the Equal Protection Clauses of the Fourteenth Amendment of the United States Constitution and the Michigan Constitution. The Fourteenth Amendment prohibits discrimination on the basis of protected categories, including race and gender. Under the Fourteenth Amendment, the Supreme Court determined in *Brown v. Board of Education* (1954), that separate could not be equal. The key question, then, is whether separate but equal on the basis of gender in the elementary and secondary school context is constitutional (Calce, 2009; ACLU, 2006). The primary difference between race and gender in constitutional analysis is the standard of review that is applied to the justification. Race-based or national origin classifications are subject to a strict scrutiny analysis and require that the use of the classification is narrowly tailored to achieve a compelling governmental interest. On the other hand, gender-based classifications are subject to an intermediate scrutiny analysis, wherein the classification must be "substantially related" to an important governmental interest.

In the Supreme Court's most recent race-based analysis, the Court has been reviewing challenges from non-minorities to the use of affirmative action as a tool for addressing and remediating past discrimination against minorities (*Grutter v. Bollinger*, 2003; *Gratz v. Bollinger*, 2003; *Ricci v. DeStefano*, 2009). In analyzing the use of race in admission decisions, the court in *Grutter* ruled that a narrowly tailored use of race is permitted under the Fourteenth Amendment to further a "compelling interest in obtaining the educational benefits that flow from a diverse student body." Yet, the finding also cautioned that in 25 years, the justification for racial preferences to promote diversity would probably not be appropriate. In 2007, the Supreme Court ruled that race-based school assignments in Seattle, Washington, and Jefferson, County, Kentucky, were discriminatory, because they failed to justify the use of race to achieve a compelling governmental interest and did not exhaust other possible race-neutral approaches (*Parents Involved v. Seattle School District*, 2007). These Supreme Court rulings reflect the increased sensitivity and scrutiny applied to justifications for advantage and opportunities based on race. Race-based decisions have a higher standard than those based on gender, based on a perception that there are legitimate reasons for gender-based classifications based on "real" differences between genders (Kiselewich, 2008). The question, though, is what are the differences and how much weight should these differences be granted in assessing the appropriateness of gender-based separation, particularly in the education context. In fact, NOW (2004) noted that the compelling interest of diversity supported in *Grutter* is inconsistent with a single-gender environment. The decision of the Court also seems to reflect a growing dissatisfaction with preferences based on physical characteristics (Reverse discrimination suits flourish, 2009).

Understanding the role of race and gender in education is critical for social justice advocacy. Their role influences the definition of the problem, the perceived cause of the problem, and proposed solutions. There has been a great deal of debate since *Garrett* on single-sex schools. Much of the debate has involved the definition of the problem. Is there a boy crisis within and outside of education? Is there an achievement gap for boys? Are schools shortchanging girls? Are girls excelling in schools at the expense of boys? Which boys and girls are we really talking about? Is it White boys? Black boys? White girls? Black girls? Latinas? Latinos? Poor kids? Rich kids? The fundamental issue that first must be clarified is the definition of the problem, because it influences the justification for the solution.

The Black male crisis was the justification for Detroit's male academy proposal in 1991. In 2010, almost 20 years later, that crisis continues. Websites such as *blackboysincrisis.com* (Clay, n.d.) and *blackboysreport.org* of the Schott Foundation site focus on the challenges of Black males. Black males continue to have high dropout rates, high rates of imprisonment, high rates of drug abuse, low college enrollment rates, and high special education placement rates (Schott,

2008; Graves, 2006). The condition is documented and evidenced by the following articles, book, and report titles: "Black Males Left Behind (Mincy, 2006); "The Portrait of the Black Male" (National Urban League, 2007a; 2007b; Morial, 2007), and "Plight Deepens for Black Men, Studies Warn" (Eckholm, 2006).

The Black Male crisis continues—not only at the national level, but also at the local level in Detroit. According to Schott (2008), "Black male students in Michigan had a 33 percent graduation rate, compared to a 74 percent for white males. In Detroit, the graduation rate was 20 percent for Black males." The Black male crisis in Detroit remains a critical challenge with high dropout rates and low graduation rates (Bouffard, 2008; Dybis, 2009; Editorial Projects in Education Research Center, 2008, 2009; Hawke, 2007; Hulett, 2009; Satyanarayana, 2009). At a Boys to Men Education Forum in Detroit in 2009, "one in three of the 225 teens...said they had to sell drugs to survive. Many boys ages 13–17,...said they needed drug money for bus passes, food and other basic needs for them and their families" (Gerritt, 2009). The article further noted that "asked why their peers stayed away from school, these teenage boys gave answers that might seem remote to people living just 20 miles to the north, but they are real. Some couldn't afford to eat. Others had absent or incarcerated parents, or lived in homes that couldn't afford to pay for a bus ticket or electric bill. Others cited violence, drugs, gangs and negative peer pressure." Secretary of Education Arne Duncan said in 2009, "Detroit's troubled public schools are ground zero for education" (Detroit schools "ground zero," 2009). Detroit leads the nation with the school to prison pipeline (Gerritt, 2009; Black male dropouts lead nation in incarceration, 2009). The crisis has been long-standing, deeply rooted, and well documented. The crisis is not new and is often not news. What is new or news is the "boy crisis."

In the past decade, the "boy crisis" has emerged as a critical social problem. This "boy crisis" is said to be generally evidenced by the decreasing enrollment of males in colleges and universities, lower academic performance by males, and a general disengagement of males from school and life (Sax, 2007; Gender matters: boys will be boys, 2006; Sommers, 2000). Page (2008) describes the crisis, stating "Stories and statistics describe unmotivated, easily distractible boys who are falling behind in test scores, forgetting their homework or, when they finish it, forgetting to turn it in or are unable to find it in their disorganized backpacks. When their grades slip and their adolescent concepts of manhood are crushed, they would retreat to video games or even less productive escapes, rather than ask for help."

This crisis has been attributed to changes in teaching methods, ADHD medications, the increased use of video games, the absence of a competitive element in the academic educational experience, environmental and physiological factors, and an absence of an intentional focus on managing the transition from childhood/boyhood to adulthood/manhood (Sax, 2007). The crisis has been chronicled by Sax (2007, 2006) in books titled *Boys Adrift* and *Why Gender Matters*, and by Gurian (2007; 2009). There is even a website called "Why Boys Fail," discussing the boy crisis (Whitmire, n.d.). Sax and Gurian, two of the most vocal proponents of single-sex schools, believe there are fundamental "real" differences between boys and girls—differences that can be best addressed in a single-gender environment. According to Sax, "single-sex education allows the school to create an alternative culture in which it's cool to study, in which team competition for academics is the most natural format imaginable, and in which restoring Kenntnis (experiential learning) to its rightful place is likely to yield immediate positive results" (Sax, 2007, p. 187). Sax, a medical doctor with a doctorate in psychology, focuses on different development stages between boys and girls. Gurian, a family therapist, has published numerous books on differences and founded the Gurian Institute to promote teacher training on gender differences. This "boys industry" includes researchers, advocates, and psychologists (Mead, 2006, p. 17).

Although the race of boys is rarely mentioned, the level of attention to the "boy crisis" suggests that the dominant group must be "white, middle-class boys" (Weil, 2008). Because the Black male crisis has been documented and discussed with little progress for the last 20 years, the "new" focus and extensive media coverage of the "crisis" reflects a concern that "historically privileged boys could be at risk" (Mead, 2006, p. 14). In addition to the racial implications, there are also concerns about the gender implications of a boy crisis for girls. Education Sector, a nonpartisan Washington, D.C.-based think tank, has challenged the media reports of a "boy crisis."

> The truth is far different from what these accounts suggest. The real story is not bad news about boys doing worse; it's good news about girls doing better. In fact, with a few exceptions, American boys are scoring higher and achieving more than they ever have before. But girls have just improved their performance on some measures even faster. As a

> result, girls have narrowed or even closed some academic gaps that previously favored boys, while other long-standing gaps that favored girls have widened, leading to the belief that boys are falling behind....
>
> The hysteria about boys is partly a matter of perspective. While most of society has finally embraced the idea of equality for women, the idea that women might actually surpass men in some areas (even as they remain behind in others) seems hard for many people to swallow. Thus, boys are routinely characterized as "falling behind" even as they improve in absolute terms. (Mead, 2006, p. 3)

Education Sector noted that the portrayal of the issue as a "crisis"

> touches on Americans' deepest insecurities, ambivalences, and fears about changing gender roles and the "battle of the sexes." It troubles not only parents of boys, who fear their sons are falling behind, but also parents of girls, who fear boys' academic deficits will undermine their daughters' chances of finding suitable mates.... Unfortunately, the current boy crisis hype and the debate around it are based more on hopes and fears than on evidence.

This conclusion is consistent with others who challenge the discourse and narrative of a boy crisis and its resulting justification for single-sex schools, noting how the discourse perpetuates an essentialist myth of masculinity (Cohen, 2009). It also legitimizes ideologies around gender privilege for males. The dominant media coverage of the "boy crisis" in the 2000s has created significant concern for feminist organizations. The "boy crisis" has replaced the 1990s discourse of a "girl crisis."

About 20 years ago, the social problem in education, according to the American Association of University Women, was that schools were shortchanging girls. In 1992, the American Association of University Women (AAUW) published "How Schools Shortchange Girls." They documented that "girls receive significantly less attention from classroom teachers than do boys; African-American girls have fewer interactions with teachers than do white girls, despite evidence that they attempt to initiative interactions more frequently; and sexual harassment of girls by boys was increasing" (AAUW, 1991, p. 2). Seventeen years later, in 2008, the AAUW re-examined girls' and boys' educational achievement and challenged the popular media reports of a boy crisis in their report "Where the Girls Are" (2008).

> In part, the idea of a boys' crisis in education has garnered so much media attention because many of the ideas put forth by its proponents—for

example that boys are disadvantaged by the "feminized" classroom—are based on a nostalgic idea that boys and girls have very different roles, are fundamentally very different, and by extension learn very differently. There is no boys' crisis in education. The true crisis is that American schoolchildren are deeply divided across race/ethnicity and family income level, and improvement has been slow and unsteady. This crisis is not a new phenomenon, but it is no less urgent simply because it has been around for a long time.

"Where the Girls Are" was a comprehensive examination of girls' educational achievement in the past 35 years on a variety of measures, including national standardized test scores, degree attainment, and high school graduation, among others. Almost universally, African-Americans were at the bottom, below Hispanics, Whites, and Asians. Although there were areas where Black girl achievement was higher than Black boys, such as college graduation rates and reading test scores, there were also areas where Black boy achievement was higher, for example in math. The report also revealed the significant impact of class and economic income on educational attainment. Although the class data was not incorporated into the data by race and gender, it is likely that minority achievement continues to be affected by race and class, more than gender.

Similar conclusions were documented in the National Women's Law Center report, *When Girls Don't Graduate, We All Fail: A Call to Improve High School Graduation Rates for Girls* (2007). The report noted that about half of the estimated dropouts from the Class of 2007 were female students and that there was long-standing gender segregation in career and technical education with women segregated in cosmetology, child-care, and health care fields and underrepresented in the trades. They also found that Blacks had the highest percentage of dropouts for the class of 2003–2004 among all racial groups. Black males represented 54 percent of the dropouts and Black girls were 40 percent. Though the rate was significantly higher for Black males, the statistics clearly document a problem for both genders. The National Coalition for Women and Girls in Education (2008) also challenged the "boy crisis" and claims that the academic gains of girls had been at the expense of boys. They noted that the educational performance of both sexes has continued to improve. They mentioned that both boys and girls face problems such as low high school graduation rates, sexual harassment, and sex stereotyping. The AAUW asserted that "the crisis is not specific to boys; rather it is a crisis for African-American, Hispanic, and low-income children" (2008, p. 4). Other reports confirm this conclusion (Mathews, 2006; Mead, 2006; Weis, 1988; Weis & Fine, 1993).

Feminist organizations, then, not only challenge the "boy crisis," they also challenge the proposed solution of single-sex schools, believing that the best environment is a co-educational one informed by a commitment to equity (Gandy, 2006b). They are concerned that the "boy crisis" will result in increased funding and attention for boys' initiatives at the expense of girls. This concern is exemplified by the recent launch of an investigation by the U.S. Commission on Civil Rights to assess the possible discrimination against girls in college admissions. The U.S. Commission on Civil Rights is investigating whether some colleges are admitting less qualified men over more qualified women to prevent their campuses from becoming predominantly female (Sanchez, 2009; Bailey, 2009). Women, on average, represent almost two-thirds of the college population, even higher at historical Black colleges, so some colleges are engaged in initiatives to address the underrepresentation of males on college campuses. One such initiative involves creating targeted higher education intervention efforts, such as African-American Male Academy at James Madison University. The JMU program is a three-week program for African-American males that focuses on self-esteem and college preparation. Similar programs exist at the University of Cincinnati, the University of Toledo, and Florida A&M University (Morgan, 1995). In Virginia, a female companion program was started at another institution to complement the male program. Though not exclusively for Black females, it was designed to fulfill legal mandates in Virginia for equality.

These initiatives are precisely those that concern feminists, as they fear that the gains that women have made will be eroded through new initiatives, inequitable funding, and unclear policies and procedures. They are concerned that the support that is needed to prevent bias against women and increase and encourage the participation of women in historically underrepresented areas may be affected (AAUW, 1998a, 1998b, 2001, 2008; Gandy, 2006a; Michigan National Organization for Women, 2007; National Women's Law Center, 2007). Sensitive to the historical past, the AAUW (1998) notes "Historically, public single-sex education has often harmed girls by depriving them of equal educational opportunities. Where programs are established separately for both boys and girls, they have tended to be distinctly unequal, with fewer resources allocated for girls' programs." Neuborne (1991),

Executive Director of NOWLDF, noted "In American history, whenever educational resources were scarce, the first ones pushed out of the lifeboat were women." She (1991) continues, "The attitude was always been the same: educate boys first—and better they need the opportunity more than girls."

These concerns have led feminist organizations to focus on the disciplinary domain and challenging practices related to creating single-sex environments. They are also engaged in activism in the hegemonic domain—challenging ideology and assumptions, ideas, attitudes, and stereotypes about women, and the tendency to subtly cast blame on girls for the underperformance or differential achievement of boys (Gongwer News Service, 2006b). The goal is to impact the experiences of girls in the structural domain of the education system. The irony is that proponents of single-sex schools are also engaged in the same activism. They are creating reports, books, and publications about single-sex schools and their benefits. They are guiding and assisting schools in creating single-sex programs with suggested policies, procedures, and practices (Gurian, 2007, 2009). Their goal is to influence the experiences of students in the classrooms and schools. These efforts have been extremely successful.

The growth of single-sex public schools has been astonishing. In 1995, there were three single-sex schools. In October 2007, there were 363 schools in 38 states. As of November 2009, there were at least 547 public schools that offered single-sex educational opportunities, with 91 of the schools operating as single-sex schools, according to the National Association for Single Sex Public Education (NASSPE) website created by Sax (Meyer, 2008; Sax, n.d.; Adcox, 2007). South Carolina has had the most dramatic increase, with a state-wide coordinator. Many schools in the south, with more conservative gender attitudes, are leading the increase (Weil, 2008).

There are several success stories, however, about single-sex schools. The Young Women's Leadership School in Harlem, which opened in 1996, is an all-girl public school. Founded and supported by Ann Rubenstein Tisch, a former correspondent for NBC and wife of the co-chairman of the Loews Corporation, the school was created to provide minority girls with the same path that "wealthy girls and parochial-school girls and yeshiva girls are offered" (Weil, 2008). The success of the school is evidenced by the fact that every senior has graduated and has been accepted to college. Whether its success can solely be attributed to the single-gender environment is unknown. However, the girls at the school value the "desexualized—or at least less-sexualized—environment" (Weil, 2008). A female YWLC student commented, "It's not that I don't want to be with boys...I just think it will be better with girls. Most boys get a lot of attention, and girls are kind of shy. With all girls we can speak up and talk to each other and the teachers can help us" (Steinberg, 1996). Tisch's Young Women's Leadership Foundation is expanding outside of New York and opening schools in other large metropolitan cities, including Chicago, Philadelphia, Dallas, and Austin. The Young Women's Charter School in Chicago, opened August 2000, is the only all-girls public school for urban girls in 7–12 grade. It ranks first among 77 Chicago public schools in students entering college or post-secondary education (Young Women's Leadership Charter School, March 13, 2010). The school has a college preparatory focus in math, science, and technology and there is a waiting list of over 400.

Complementing the Young Women's Charter School in Chicago is the Urban Prep Academy for Young Men, which opened in 2006. In 2010, all 107 of its first senior class were accepted at four-year colleges (Eldeib, 2010). Urban Prep Academies was founded in 2002 as a nonprofit organization with the goal of providing "comprehensive high quality college preparatory education to young men that results in graduates succeeding in college" (Urban Prep Academies, 2008). In addition to the Englewood campus school that opened in 2006, the East Garfield Park location opened in 2009, and a South Shore location will open in 2010. The CEO, Tim King, indicated that his desire was to improve the "educational opportunities available to urban boys" based on "extensive research on the academic benefits of same sex schools" (Urban Prep Will Focus, November 16, 2009). The curriculum includes a strong focus on literacy, languages arts, and community service, and a dress code.

Albany, New York, is also promoting single-sex public urban elementary education through its Bright Choice Charter Schools. Since 2002, the schools—one for girls and one for boys—have longer class days and school year, computers in every classroom, specialized teachers, and school uniforms (Brighter Choice Charter School, n.d.). Boys and girls are educated in separate classrooms within the same school and the primary population that the schools serve is "at-risk students from low-income backgrounds." Its website states "Most educators finally acknowledge the learning and behavioral differences between boys and girls which is why so many private schools are single-sex. This school will finally give at-risk children those same opportunities."

Philadelphia and Wilmington have also implemented single-sex charter schools. In 2008, Wilmington, Delaware, opened Prestige Academy, an all-boys public charter school, to serve low-income Black and Latino boys (Silva, March 16, 2008). It provides a single-gender college preparation middle school education. It also includes a focus on discipline and respect, character development, literacy and math, extended day and year, Saturday classes, and parent and community involvement (Prestige Academy, 2010). The Delaware legislation approving the school required that a "substantially equal" all-girls school be approved within two years (Silva, March 16, 2008). Reach Academy for Girls (2009) will open in Fall 2010, as an all-girls charter school in Wilmington, to complement its all-boys charter public school. The Boys' Latin of Philadelphia is another charter public single-sex high school that opened in 2007 with uniforms, longer school hours, and required Latin classes with an all-black male class of 130 students. The school has a focus on classics and traditional college preparatory curriculum (Matheson, 2008).

From the recent growth in single-sex schools, it is clear that this movement is in its infancy. The number of single-sex schools, particularly in the inner city, is likely to continue increasing. The controversy about single-sex schools is likely to continue as well. The controversy is fueled, in part, by the lack of conclusive findings on the benefits of single-sex schools. In the past 20 years, there has been extensive research on single-sex schools. The findings, however, are largely inconclusive, with a few studies showing small benefits to girls. The research challenge is compounded by the difficulty of isolating whether benefits are caused by a single-gender environment, or the myriad of other factors that can influence outcomes, including socioeconomic status, curriculum, quality of teachers and principals, and funding, among other variables (Grooms, n.d.; Hurst and Johansen, 2006; Kiselwich, 2008; Kuklenski, 2007; Lee & Bryk, 1986; Lee & Lockheed, 1990; Marsh, 1989; McCloskey, 1994; Protheroe, 2009; Salomone, 2004; Silva, 2008; Spielhagen, 2008; Weil, 2008; Zwerling, 2001). There is also very little research about minorities.

The most recent report from Linda Sax (2009), based largely on research in Catholic high schools and White female environments, finds small but statistically significant benefits for girls from single-sex high school environments: "distinctions extend across multiple categories, including self-confidence, political and social activism, life goals, career orientation, academic engagement and achievement." She notes that though the benefits of single-sex education are "fairly small," they are in areas that have historically favored men and therefore represent a potentially effective vehicle for mitigating longstanding gender gaps. Streitmater (1999) also asserts that single-sex schools benefit girls. Yet, the report acknowledges that unilateral conclusions about single-sex education cannot be determined, because "such determinations depend on which populations are studied, which student and school characteristics are considered, and which outcomes are examined." Her conclusion suggests several questions that need to be addressed involving single-sex research: "How and why do single-sex schools produce positive outcomes and which conditions could be transferred to coeducational schools? Which types of students benefit most from single-sex education? Do the benefits of single-sex education persist throughout college and beyond? In addition, how do the effects of single-sex education compare for males versus females?"

This conclusion is consistent with other work analyzing research on single-sex schools. The Canadian Centre for Knowledge Moblisation Report (2004) on single-sex schools concluded that "given that few studies were identified as meeting the criteria of rigorous research, we cannot make conclusive statements about the effects of single-sex school." They did, however, identify the following common themes in the research:

> single-sex schooling benefits certain (typically disadvantaged) students' academic achievement; there are psychological and social benefits for girls in single-sex classes; when given the choice, girls generally prefer single-sex classes whereas boys typically prefer coeducational classes; there are no measurable differences between single-sex and mixed-sex schooling on a variety of variables; single-sex classes assist in breaking down sex-role stereotypes and 'genderization' of subject areas, whereas coeducational settings reinforce them.

They concluded that "the research we reviewed is too tenuous to support the organization of single-sex classrooms or schools." They do, however, recommend that "schools need to implement policies and practices which ensure equality of opportunity for males and females and eliminate sex discrimination in instruction and the management of student behaviour." The study warns that 'curriculum-as-usual' single-sex classes "may do nothing to challenge the macho or 'laddish' cultures inherent in schools; indeed, it may be the case that they actually exacerbate them. As such, curriculum-as-usual single-sex boys' classes are unlikely to offer the solution that many schools are hoping for."

The American Institutes for Research study in 2004 (Mael et al., 2004) concluded that "the actual research evidence, although suggestive that SS schools can benefit some students in some realms of academic and socio-emotional accomplishment, is equivocal. As a result of the obstacles to conducting true randomized experiments, few or no studies have provided definitive evidence for or against SS schooling" (Mael et al., 2004, p. 2). Similarly, the U.S. Department of Education report in 2005 reviewed research comparing single-sex and co-educational schooling. The general conclusion was that despite the presence of research supporting both coed and single-sex schools, "it is more common to come across studies that report no differences between SS and CE schooling than to find outcomes with support for the superiority of CE" (United States Department of Education, 2005, p. 106). Noting that most of the research was in Catholic single-sex high schools, with few in the public or private elementary sector, they ultimately concluded that "there is a death of quality studies across all outcomes" because only 40 of the 2,221 quantitative studies met the relaxed standard for methodologically adequacy (United States Department of Education, 2005, p. 19).

In the absence of clear research, Bracey (2006) suggested the following specific questions should be asked of any proposal for single-sex schools or classes.

1. What are the goals of the program? (For example, they could be cognitive, affective, and/or behavioral outcomes.)
2. Are single-sex schools or classes the *best* way to accomplish the goals?
3. What might be lost if co-education were generally abandoned? What are the costs and tradeoffs of establishing a single-sex school or class?
4. When single-sex schools have been found to be effective, what factors produce that effectiveness? Does the proposal take these factors into account?
5. What policy obstacles lie in the way of or conflict with the stated goals? Is sex segregation a means of reaching gender equity or a tool for increasing test scores?
6. What are the rationales for the program? Gender equity? Differential brain function? Recruitment of girls into curriculum areas historically avoided?
7. Has the program been well thought through?
8. Where did the program come from? Are its sources external to the school? Is the reform expedient or, in the word of Datnow and Hubbard, inauthentic? There is a long and sorry history of attempts to impose educational change of many kinds from without.

9. Has the school administration bought in? Has the faculty? Have the parents?
10. Will a program of professional development built around the goals of the program be provided for administration and faculty?
11. Is there a sound plan to evaluate the outcomes of the program as described in #1 above?

These questions, in large part, reflect that more and better research is necessary (Cable and Spradlin, 2008). As public inner-city single-sex schools continue to be created, it will be important to assess the results and analyze the experiences of students.

The reality, then, is that the legal changes have had a tremendous impact. This legal activism can be viewed through the lens of TASJ. The legal and education systems represent interlocking social systems within the structural domain. The legislative initiative authorizing single-sex schools involved policies, procedures, and practices within the disciplinary domain. The legal changes set forth how single-sex schools could be implemented. The legal changes led to changes in the education system. Following closely on the heels of the legislative activity was the boy crisis—and extensive media coverage about the differences in academic achievement between boys and girls. The claim that boys were in crisis and deserved attention became a widely supported and accepted principle in the hegemonic domain. The crisis was widely publicized by the media in the structural domain and as a result, influenced the education system and the rapid growth of single-sex schools and classrooms. At the same time that feminist organizations and others are challenging the ideology of a boy crisis and the justification for single-sex schools, some single-sex inner-city schools such as YWLC and Urban Prep are producing impressive results. What is not clear is whether the results are due to the separation of the sexes, or the other critical components for school success, such as smaller classes, longer days, the college preparatory curriculum, uniforms, the discipline and character focus, the leadership emphasis, and parent, teacher, and community involvement.

The success of these schools and others continues to raise questions about issues of race, class, and gender. How does the intersection of race, class, and gendered discourse about education influence social justice activism? Can separate be equal? What about the long-standing Black male crisis? What about White male activism against affirmative action regulations? Is there a middle/upper class White male crisis?

What about Black girls? The voice of Black girls and women continues to be soft, a largely unheard voice and perspective. The next section, then, remembers the Black girls in Detroit and reflects on the lessons learned from Detroit.

5.3 Remembering Our Black Girls

In 1991, the original male academies, Malcolm X, Paul Robeson, and Marcus Garvey, became African-centered immersion schools (Lockhart, 2002). Though for many years there was a particular focus on boys and the Academies had a dominant male enrollment (Newcomb, 2000), the gender ratio as of November 2009 is more equitable, though majority is still male, with 825 males and 783 females. The ratio varies of males to females varies by school, with a 187 to 134 ratio at Malcolm X; a 285 to 318 ratio at Robeson, and 353 to 331 ratio at Garvey (Marcus Garvey, n.d.; Malcolm X, n.d.; Paul Robeson, n.d.).

Twenty years after the DMA initiative, Detroit has two single-sex college preparatory high schools: the Detroit International Academy for girls and the Frederick Douglass School for boys. As of 2009, the Detroit International Academy (n.d.) is a girls high school with 540 girls enrolled in grades 6–12. The Detroit International Academy has extensive academic programming, extracurricular activities, and relationships with business partners and community organizations. The school focuses on character development, anger management and conflict resolution, leadership skills, finances, and community service projects. The Frederick Douglass School (Douglass Academy for Young Men, n.d.) for boys, as of 2009, had 298 students in grades 6–12. The Douglass Academy has parental involvement, dress code, uniforms, JROTC, "smaller classes, academic discipline, conduct codes, hands-on learning, and dedicated teachers who love and push them to stay on the grind" (Gerritt, November 12, 2009). Principal Sean Vann mentioned the benefits and justification for the single-sex environment: "In programs where you don't have girls, boys tend to be more collegial and work with each other.... Boys have a tendency to be more hands-on and exploratory, but with girls you don't have that. And when you have girls, boys tend to evaluate the girls' response before they initiate a response on their own" (Mrozowski, 2007). The difference, though, in enrollment is startling. The girls' high school has twice the number of students as the boys'. This clearly reflects the need and desire of parents of girls to secure strong educational opportunities for their daughters when provided the opportunity.

Detroit still has the Catherine Ferguson Academy, an alternative Detroit public school for teen moms, serving students in grades 6–12, with 310 students (Catherine Ferguson Academy, n.d.). It provides nursery service and offers middle- and high-school courses, hands-on interactive technique, choir, sports, college-prep, and tutoring programs, and an urban farming course. The principal reflected on the benefit of the Ferguson Academy's single-sex approach.

> Women fight over two things: boys and clothes. We don't have any boys over the age of 3, so we only had to deal with the clothes issue. We tried the boys thing once. We had three boys here. But girls give power away too readily, as do women. They were wonderful boys and their stock will never be that high. When they graduated, they held two of six elected leadership positions. You're telling me these boys were better than 80 girls? We as women abdicate our power so easily. We haven't had boys apply since then.

A sixteen-year-old female student concurred: "It's better here because all there is to do is work. There's no boys, boys, boys" (Collins, 2004, p. 204).

These comments by principals and students reflect widely accepted views about the benefits of single-sex education. So as the country seems to be moving toward single-sex education, it is important to realize that almost all of the schools have instituted additional reforms besides separation based on gender. It will be difficult, then, to determine whether their success can be attributed to the single-gender environment, or the myriad of other necessary programs for a successful school. At the same time, it will be interesting to monitor these schools, and TASJ is one method. It would allow schools to be assessed from many standpoints and domains. What are ideas and attitudes about gender within the school (the hegemonic domain)? What about the curriculum, the policies and procedures, and practices in the school (disciplinary domain)? What is the relationship between students, between students and teachers, between teachers and administrators, between teachers, parents, and community members (interpersonal domain?) What is the interaction between the different social structures: the local community, the school district, the school, the colleges, the employment and labor markets (structural domain)?

It will also be important for individuals, organizations, and entities involved to be mindful of the lessons from the Detroit Male Academy. Social justice activism often involves advocacy on behalf of marginalized and disenfranchised individuals and groups who have multiple intersecting identities. These individuals and groups experience oppression based on their intersecting identities, often through the operation of interlocking social structures. These social structures and systems embody the hegemonic, structural, interpersonal, and disciplinary domains of power. As a result, advocacy must challenge the domains of power and the operation of existing social systems. Advocates and activists must, then, be strategic and sophisticated in their approach to social problems; must recognize the complex interaction among individuals, social structures, and domains of power; and must craft advocacy solutions that are responsive to these challenges. The language of those associated with these schools reflects the power of the hegemonic domain and ideologies associated with gender roles. It is precisely the ideology reflected in the discourse that raises concerns for opponents of single-sex schools (Cohen, 2009; Copeland, n.d.). Notions of masculinity, such as heteronormativity, aggression, activity, competitiveness, sports obsession, stoicism, and "not feminine," must be challenged (Cohen, 2009). Ideas and discourse such as those by Sewell (2010)—"More than racism, I now firmly believe that the main problem holding back black boys academically is their over-feminised upbringing"—must be challenged. This discourse blames females and simplifies a very complex issue. As Page (1991b) continued to ask: "are girls the problem or is it more complex than that?"

Twenty years later, there is still a critical need for alternative advocacy strategies for Black feminist political and social issues. There is still a need for social justice advocacy that encourages the Black community, in particular, to embrace and support (rather than marginalize and ostracize) Black females in their efforts to address and remedy the complex manifestations of racism, sexism, and classism. Inclusive, rather than exclusive, strategies for addressing issues of power, privilege, and oppression must be developed. Strategies must also address the power of oppressive discourse and its consequences for Black females, including their marginalization from opportunities, the perpetuation of stereotypes, and the continuation of sexism. The effective representation and protection of the interests of Black females can only be accomplished by understanding and recognizing the complex dynamics of race, class, and gender politics in the Black community.

The antagonism of Black males and Black females to "feminism" and the absence of politically powerful Black feminist organizations suggests that, in the absence of new strategies, Black females may continue to be marginalized, disenfranchised, and excluded from the struggle for race, gender, and class equality. Black women must find a voice and a forum to address issues that affect them, including their gendered racial interests, and racialized gender interests.

Black women still need to support each other to form organizations to advocate for Black girls and develop a strategy of political advocacy and social justice activism, using the tenets of critical race feminism and Black feminist thoughts as guides. Ransby (2000) asked the following:

> after mourning the loss of several stillborn black feminist organizations over the course of the 1990s... why did we seem unable to sustain a national organization beyond the moment of crisis or celebration that inspired its conception... After all of our meetings, conferences, mobilizations, listservs, draft documents, retreats, and rallies, what did we have to show for our efforts? There was no name, no structure, no office, no badge, not even a voicemail or post-office box.

But she concludes, "we do exist." She discusses how black feminists operate in a decentralized manner with informal leadership and nonhierarchical organizational structures with committees and working groups. This structure enabled them to create the African-American Women in Defense of Ourselves—1600 women who responded to the Hill-Thomas hearing and the Million Man March. However, these coalitions, without "support of a national body or solidly planted roots," died after their work. Hamer and Neville (2001) mention the excitement of the Black Feminist Caucus at the Black Radical Congress. Yet in 2009, the website mentioned in the article, *www.blackradicalcongress.org*, does not include any visible mention of the Black Feminist Caucus.

Other national Black female organizations do not appear to have a feminist focus. Sororities and organizations such as Alpha Kappa Alpha, Delta Sigma Theta, the National Council of Negro Women, the Links, and other Black women's groups did not comment on the Male Academy or openly support Garrett and Doe. The work of these groups, though valuable, does not often address political issues of empowerment. The silence of Black females, or rather, "silencing" because most feel forced to take this position, reflects a central theme in Black feminist thought—the concept of voice and Black women's struggle to find their voice. Black women activists and scholars also have attempted to refute images of powerlessness of Black women by portraying Black women as "empowered individuals," documenting their activism, and by bringing to the forefront voices and experiences of Black women, most often in the literary tradition, in the form of biographical or autobiographical work, or critical essays (Dill, 1983; Davis, 1981, Guy-Sheftall, 1995; hooks, 1981; Paul, 2003). Though Black women's voices advocating on behalf of Black women are present in the "safe spaces," this work has illustrated the need for their voices to be heard in the public and official spheres, in addition to the private discourses.

The daily lives of Black women are based on mastering the "habits of survival." K. Scott (1991, p. 147) notes that one habit of survival Black women have adopted is the "abandonment of feminism." A sociological consequence of this abandonment of feminism has been Black women's inability to fully value their femaleness, to advocate on behalf of issues affecting Black women, and to speak out against sexism in the Black community. The silence of many Black women about Black male sexism, their loyalty to the "racial" issue, their acceptance of Black male privilege, their participation in the male-dominated and paternalistic Black liberation movement, and their acquiescence in a male-centered definition of "African-American" culture has resulted in the isolation of Black women from the struggle for equality.

It is essential that feminism, Black feminism, and womanism be re-defined to promote and encourage the participation of all groups in addressing the multiple effects of racism, classism, and sexism in the Black community (Springer, 2002). Johnetta Cole (1995, p. 550) notes that there is a "dread" among contemporary African-American women "of being called feminist." She notes that this is a result of stereotypes about feminism, including having to choose one "ism" against another, the racism of many White women in the feminist movement, a perception that feminism means to hate men, and an assumption that feminism is synonymous with lesbianism (Collins, 2006, p. 172). Feminism is often associated with individualism, materialism, personal choice, and class privilege. (Collins, 2006, p. 195). It does not incorporate a sense of group-based social justice. Cole (1995) notes that some choose to define their position in Alice Walker's terms as "womanist."

Many African-Americans experience uneasiness with the idea of feminism, simultaneously supporting and rejecting it, as Collins notes.

> It is important to stress that African-Americans (women and many men) reject not the ideas of feminism but the label of feminism. Given this receptivity [among black men and black women], the lack of knowledge about Black feminism even among women who have had access to college education is troubling. Whether Black women and other women of color call themselves "feminists" is not important. The power of a stigmatized label to shut down radical protest and keep young Black women from learning their own history for fear of being labeled "feminists" is a much larger problem for African-Americans as a collectivity than the continued racism or elitism of any individual White American feminist." Collins (2006, p. 190–191)

Collins encourages the African-American community to address these challenges through "new grassroots feminist organizations within African-American communities" and "infusing churches, recreational activities, and civil-rights organizations of Black civil society with a feminist sensibility" (Collins, 2006, p. 193). Hamer & Neville (2001) encourage "revolutionary Black feminist to develop study groups, to be involved with campaigns on issues affecting Black women, to develop strategic approaches to guide efforts, and to continually re-evaluate efforts, thus linking theory to practice." Zerai and Campbell (2005) also encourage using radical black feminism to develop political strategies to address multiple and intersecting oppressions.

Hip-hop, too, is an area that can blend theory and practice and may allow for transformative applied research (Akom, 2009; Brown, 2009). Brown's (2009) articulation of a hip-hop feminist pedagogy includes a recognition of the importance of Black feminist political organizing, understanding cultural practices, recognizing the role of masculinity and patriarchy, and creating new knowledge. It is about power at the borders and boundaries of hip-hop, feminism, and education (Brown, 2009). Sharpley-Whiting (2007) calls us to recognize the complexity of hip-hop culture and to address the contradictory themes rather than ignore them. Hip-hop has the potential to be transdisciplinary, with a focus on social justice, oppression based on intersectionality, and narrative experiences (Akom, 2009).

Black women's community work and Black feminism need to be recontextualized "within a new framework of Black feminist nationalism/Black nationalist feminism" (Collins, 2006, p. 137). Theory must be merged with activism and gender must be at the center of the Black political agenda (Collins, 2006, p. 25), given the number of Black families headed by women and the incarceration of Black men. An ark of gender relations must be created (Cole & Sheftall, 2003). This ark includes the very small, but growing, body of work on the educational experiences of Black girls (Brown, 2009; Evans-Winters, 2006; Fordham, 1993; Grant; 1994; Lei, 2003; Paul, 2003; Morris, 2007).

We remain, unfortunately, invisible in much scholarship about education, education experiences, and education policy. Rollock (2007) notes the "invisible or absent presence" of girls. It is rare that quantitative data on educational achievement contains data disaggregated by race and gender. Most of the data is aggregated by singular categories. The American Association for University Women (AAUW) has produced extensive reports on the educational experiences of girls (1992; 1998; 2001; 2008). Only in its most recent report of 2008 is there data specifically on Black girls.

The research, though, illustrates that Black girls experience many challenges in the educational system because of their intersecting race, gender, and class identities; the challenges of self-identification and self-expression within insensitive and unexpressive classroom environments; and challenges with each other, with boys and men, with teachers, and with school administration. There must be more quantitative data disaggregated by race and gender, so that the unique experiences of students based on their intersecting race and gender identity can be analyzed. There must also be more qualitative studies of the classroom experiences of Black girls, including teacher and administrator perceptions. The roles of stereotypes and expectations of appropriate conduct must be examined, as well as the dynamics in the classroom between different races and genders.

Of course, the research should not be limited to Black females, as there is also a significant paucity of research on the educational experiences of Black males. Their education performance and experiences in the classroom should be examined as well to determine best practices for both genders and all races. Administrators' assumptions about race and gender are guiding and influencing education practice (Fergus, Sciurba, Martin & Noguera, 2009). These beliefs and assumptions must be scrutinized, researched, validated, or challenged (Mead, 2006, p. 19). They cannot be taken for granted assumptions, particularly if they include stereotypes or are rooted in sexism.

There is a crisis of Black boys (Noguera, 2008). Being a feminist does not mean that the problems cannot be acknowledged. As Rollock (2007) noted

> The concerns expressed about the educational attainment of Black boys remains a valid area of address for policymakers and practitioners but should not exist in place of, or overshadow, the sets of equally important educational issues surrounding Black girls and how they can become included in debates on schooling.

At the same time, there may be opportunities provided by single-sex environments for both boys and girls that should not automatically be discarded (Salomone, 2004). As Salomone notes,

> feminists, armed with their unique perspectives, can here play a significant role, not as shrill uncompromising critics, nor simply as vigilant watchdogs, nor even as distantly supportive cheering squads, but rather as reasoned voices, in discussion and not debate, constructively helping educators determine how best to provide an appropriate education for girls and boys, based not on group stereotypes, but on informed understandings of individual needs as they sometimes coalesce around gender.

The potential benefits, however, must be carefully scrutinized against the potential risks. If we acknowledge gender-related tension in the Black community, misunderstandings, deep-rooted sexism, notions of privilege and entitlement based on gender, we must ask ourselves whether schools can address these issues in sex-segregated environments. NOW (2006) notes that "separating our daughters from our sons is an ineffective response to a complex problem" and fails to prepare boys and girls to "interact with and work along side each other." Page (1991b) notes that one of the problems that Black females have "are the misconceptions that males (black and otherwise) have about them." He questions whether boys will really learn lessons of manhood "any better in an environment that in subtle ways treats girls as mysterious aliens instead of lifelong companions." Even more importantly, we must ask what lessons of manhood are being taught. How can issues of mutual respect, understanding, and acceptance of differences based on race, religion, ethnicity, and gender be taught? With an already polarized community around gender, will single-sex schools further polarize our community and lessen our ability to deal collaboratively with large-scale structural issues?

As the discourse continues, then, this work encourages us to remember Black girls in all aspects of society. We must make sure that the message is not communicated that "black boys are special, but black girls are not" (Malveaux, n.d.). Britt's (1992) article title reflects this concern: "What about the Sisters?; With All the Focus on the Problems of Black Men, Someone Got Left Out." Black girls must be remembered in discussions about Black boys, not by parentheticals or footnotes, but as part of the team and part of the solution. Black women are the teachers, mothers, educators, principals, sisters, aunts, grandmothers, and classmates. We have to be part of the solution. The language, rhetoric, and discourse must be sensitive to this issue. The perpetuation of dominant discourse in schools and the media must continue to be challenged, the perpetuation of traditional leadership in education institutions must change, and the perpetuation of standard curriculum in schools must be transformed, and Black women must be involved in those changes.

We must remember ourselves: "much of the work to change patriarchy to partnership must begin within ourselves as women" (Cole & Sheftall, 2003, p. 218). We must work on our relationships with each other (Springer, 2002). We must "fall in love with the sounds of our voices" (Springer, 2002). We need to be unafraid to be angry. We need to be unafraid to speak our anger. "Within Black feminism, the passion of anger is crucial to what gives us the 'energy' to react against the deep investment that exists in forms of racism, as well as sexism" (Ahmed, 2009, p. 51). Quoting Lorde, on the power of speaking anger, "My fear of anger taught me nothing. Anger expressed and translated into action in the service of our vision and our future is a liberating and strengthening act of clarification. Anger is loaded with information and energy" (Ahmed, 2009, p. 51). We must be pioneers "clearing a path for ourselves and our sisters" (hooks, 1986 , p. 196). We must be prepared for a revolution and take time, as suggested by Toni Cade Bambara, to "fashion revolutionary selves, revolutionary lives, and revolutionary relationships" (Cole & Guy-Sheftall, 2003, p. 219).

Though we must start with ourselves, we must end with others. We must be involved as lawyers, as councilwomen, as CEOs, senators, as businesswomen, and as professors. We must become journalists and writers. We must pursue degrees in higher education. We must be scholar-activists. We must have several seats at the table where policy decisions are made and we must be willing to be fearless and courageous in speaking out, mobilizing support, and educating to create the change. We must know that our battles and fights do make a difference. We must fight and be fearless feminists (Onwuachi-Willig, 2007). We must continue the struggle against oppression and work diligently to determine effective and strategic approaches to advancing and improving society. Ultimately, we must gift ourselves, our knowledge, our experiences, and our understanding to the larger community, and in the sacrifice of gifting (Rabouin, 2000), realize the ultimate salvation of ourselves and our communities. As Black women continue to gift and sacrifice ourselves, "we must believe that as others see us reach our goals—no longer victimized, no longer unrecognized, no longer afraid—they will take courage and follow" (hooks, 1981, p. 196). Our guiding principle, then, must be the same as the motto that has guided the National Association of Colored Women since 1896 (Giddings, 1984, p. 97–98): lifting as we climb.

Appendix A

List of Major Social Actors in *Garrett*

From December 1990 to December 1991

1. Asante, Molefi. Professor and Chairperson of the Department of African American Studies at Temple University (Board's expert witness).
2. Carter, Arthur. Interim Deputy Superintendent for Community Confidence of the Board of Education and Chair of the Male Academy Task Force.
3. Davis, Martha. Staff attorney at NOW Legal Defense and Education Fund, representing Shawn Garrett and her daughter and Nancy Doe and her daughters.
4. Doe, Nancy. 34-year-old Black female plaintiff and mother of three girls, ages 11, 6, and 5 (Jane, Judy and Jessica Doe).
5. Garrett, Shawn. 24-year-old Black female plaintiff and mother of a four-year old girl, Crystal Garrett.
6. Hale, Janice. Professor at Wayne State University in early childhood development (Board's expert witness).
7. Hambrick, Harvey. Principal for the Marcus Garvey Academy.
8. Hayden, Frank. Vice-President of the Board of Education, Chairman of the Community Confidence Committee.
9. Holland, Spencer. Director of the Center for Education of African-American Males at Morgan State University.
10. Johnson, Ray. Principal for the Paul Robeson Academy.
11. Jones, Cloyzelle. Professor at the University of Michigan, Division of Education (Board's expert witness).
12. Kenyatta, Kwame. Director of the Malcolm X Center in Detroit.
13. McGriff, Deborah. Superintendent of Detroit Public Schools as of July 1, 1991.
14. Patrick, Lawrence. President of the Detroit Board of Education.
15. Porter, John. Interim General Superintendent of Schools from July 1, 1989, to July 1, 1991.

16. Reid, Pamela. Professor of Psychology at the City University of New York (Garrett's expert witness).
17. Scott-Jones, Diane. Associate Professor in the Department of Educational Psychology and the Department of Psychology at the University of Illinois (Garrett's expert witness).
18. Sedler, Robert. Professor of Law, Wayne State University and Legal Consultant to the Detroit Public Schools on the Male Academy.
19. Simon, Howard. Executive Director of the Michigan American Civil Liberties Union.
20. Smitherman, Geneva. Professor and Director of the African-American Language and Literacy Program, Department of English at Michigan State University (Board's expert witness).
21. Watson, Clifford. Principal of Woodward Elementary School and principal of the Malcolm X Academy.
22. Willie, Charles. Professor of Education and Urban Studies at Harvard University (Garrett's expert witness).

Bibliography

Academies graduate first women. (1980, May 29). *Oakland Post*, 532, 1.

ACLU directors oppose all-male academy. (1991, May 30). *United Press International*. Retrieved from www.lexisnexis.com.

Adams, J. (1979). *Report of the Admission of Women to the U.S. Military Academy (Project Athena III)*. Westpoint, New York: U.S. Military Academy.

Adcox, S. (2007, October 1). SC leading nation in public schools offering single-gender classes. *The Associated Press*. Retrieved November 27, 2009, from www.lexisnexis.com.

Ad Hoc Group of Concerned Educators. (1990). *Report on saving the black male conference*. Detroit School Board.

African-American Male Task Force, Milwaukee Public Schools (1990). *Educating African-American males: A dream deferred*. Milwaukee: Milwaukee Public Schools.

Ahmed, S. (2009). Embodying diversity: Problems and paradoxes for Black feminists. *Race Ethnicity and Education*, 12(1), 41–52.

Akom, A. (2009). Critical hip hop pedagogy as a form of libratory praxis. *Equity and Excellence in Education*, 42(1), 52–66.

Allan, E. (2008). *Policy discourses, gender, and education: Constructing women's status*. New York: Routledge.

All-girl schools: Detroit counters lawsuit. (1991, August 8). *Daily Report Card*. Retrieved from www.lexisnexis.com.

All-male school gets green light in Detroit. (1991, March 1). *New York Times*, p. A16. Retrieved from www.lexisnexis.com.

All-male schools: Change laws to save a generation in trouble [Editorial]. (1991, September 12). *Atlanta Constitution*, p. A14. Retrieved from www.lexisnexis.com.

All-male schools: McGriff's inflammatory remarks don't aid her cause [Editorial]. (1991, August 15). *Detroit Free Press*, p. 12A. Retrieved from www.lexisnexis.com.

American Association of University Women. (1991). *Shortchanging Girls, Shortchanging America*. Retrieved January 2, 2010, from *www.aauw.org/research*.

American Association of University Women Educational Fund. (1992). *How schools shortchange girls: The AAUW Report*. Retrieved January 2, 2010, from *www.aauw.org/research*.

American Association of University Women Educational Fund. (1998a). *Gender gaps: Where schools still fail our children.* Retrieved January 2, 2010, from *www.aauw.org/research.*

———. (1998b). *Separated by Sex: A critical look at single-sex education for girls.* Retrieved January 2, 2010, from *www.aauw.org/research.*

———. (2001). *Beyond 'gender wars': A conversation about girls, boys, and education.* Retrieved January 2, 2010, from *www.aauw.org/research.*

———. (2008). *Where the girls are: The facts about gender equity in education.* Retrieved January 2, 2010, from *www.aauw.org/research.*

American Civil Liberties Union. (1991). ACLU answers: Issue all-black male schools. New York Office.

———. (2004, April 23). *ACLU letter to the Department of Education on single-sex proposed regulations comments.* Retrieved November 24, 2009, from http://www.aclu.org.

———. (2006, October 24). New Education Department Regulations Violated Title IX, Constitution. Retrieved November 24, 2009, from www.aclu.org.

American Historical Association. (1998). *Why Study History?* Retrieved September 15, 2008, from www.historians.org.

American Institutes for Research. (2004, November 9). *Theoretical Arguments For and Against Single-Sex Schools: A critical analysis of the explanations.* Retrieved January 2, 2010, from www.air.org.

American Political Science Association. (n.d.) *What is political science?* Retrieved September 15, 2008, from http://www.apsanet.org.

American Sociological Association. (n.d.) *Society and social life.* Retrieved September 15, 2008, from *http://www.asanet.org.*

Anthias, F. (1990). Race and class revisited—conceptualising race and racisms. *The Sociological Review*, 38, 19–42.

Anthias, F. & Yuval-Davis, N. (1992). *Racialized boundaries: Race, nation, gender, colour, and class and the anti-racist struggle.* London: Routledge.

Asante, M. (1991). Affidavit. [*Garrett* legal briefs].

Austin, R. (1989). Sapphire bound. *Wisconsin Law Review*,539–569.

———. (1992). Black woman, sisterhood, and the difference/deviance divide. *New England Law Review*, 26, 877–887.

Bailey, R. (2009, November 11). Affirmative action for males—Gender discrimination in college admissions. Message posted to http://reason.com/blog/11/11/affirmative-action-for-males-g/print.

Balibar, E. (1990). Paradoxes of universality. In T. Goldberg (Ed.), *Anatomy of racism*, pp. 283–294. Minneapolis: University of Minnesota Press.

Barnes, R. (1990). Race Consciousness: The Thematic Content of Racial Distinctiveness in Critical Race Scholarship. *Harvard Law Review*,103, 1864–1871.

Barnett, B. (1993). Invisible southern black women leaders in the Civil Rights Movement: The triple constraints of gender, race, and class. *Gender and Society*, 7(2), 162–182.

Barrett, D. (1991, September 16). Racist curriculum [Letter to Editor]. *Detroit Free Press*, p. 8A.

Barriers and opportunities for America's young black men. (1990). Hearing Before the House Select Committee on Children Youth and Families.

Becher, T. (1989). *Academic tribes and territories: Intellectual enquiry and the cultures of disciplines.* Bristol, PA: Open University Press.

Biglan, A. (1973). The characteristics of subject matter in different academic areas. *Journal of Applied Psychology*,57, 195–203.

Bivins, L. (1990, October 28). Rescuing an endangered generation; mentors try to save youths sinking in violence. *Detroit Free Press*, p. 1F.

Black male dropouts lead nation in incarceration. (2009, October 9). *PR Newswire.* Retrieved December 5, 2009, from http://www.prnewswire.com.

Bouffard, K. (2008, February 25). *The Detroit News.* Retrieved November 27, 2009, from *www.bridges4kids.org.*

Bracey, G. (2006). *Separate but Superior?: A review of issues and data bearing on single-sex education.* Retrieved December 2009, from www.greatlakescenter.org.

Brewer, R. (1989). Black women and feminist sociology: The emerging perspective. *American Sociologist*, 20(1), 57–70.

———. (1993). Theorizing race, class, and gender: The new scholarship of Black feminist intellectual and Black women's labor. In S. James and A. Busia (Eds.), *Theorizing Black feminisms: The visionary pragmatism of Black women.* New York: Routledge.

Brighter Choice Charter Schools. (n.d.). Retrieved March 13, 2010, from www.brighterchoice.org.

Briscoe, S. (1991, August 21–27). We will have a male academy. *Michigan Chronicle*, 54 (50).

Britt, D. (1992, February 2). What about the sisters? *Washington Post*, p. F1. Retrieved from www.lexisnexis.com.

Brown v. Board of Education of Topeka Kansas, 347 US 482 (1954).

Brown, K. (1994). The dilemma of legal discourse for public education responses to the "crisis" facing African-American males. *Capitol University Law Review*, 23, 63.

Brown, R. (2009). *Black girlhood celebration: Toward a hip-hop feminist pedagogy.* New York: Peter Lang.

Bruni, F. (1991, September 5). Academy deadline for females extended. *Detroit Free Press.*

Buanes, A. & Jentoft, S. (2009). Building bridges: Institutional perspectives on interdisciplinarity. *Futures*,41, 446–454.

Cable, K. & Spradlin, T. (2008). Single-Sex education in the 21st century. *Center for Evaluation and Education Policy.* Retrieved January 3, 2010 from ceep.indiana.edu.

Calce, C. (Ed.). (2009). Tenth Annual Review of Gender and Sexuality Law: Education Law Chapter: Single-Sex Education. *Georgetown Journal of Gender and the Law*, 10:573.

Califano v. Webster, 430 U.S. 313 (1977).

Canadian Centre for Knowledge Mobilisation. (2004, November 30). *Single sex schooling final report.* Retrieved January 2, 2010 from *www.cckm.ca/single_sex.htm.*

Caplice, K. (1994). The case for public single-sex education. *Harvard Journal of Law and Public Policy*, 18, 277.

Carter, A. (1991a). Affidavit. [*Garrett* legal briefs].

———. (1991b). A developmental account of the creation of the Male Academy concept for the Detroit Public Schools.

Catherine Ferguson Academy. (n.d.). *Detroit Public Schools*. Retrieved November 28, 2009, from www.detroitk12.org.

Chrisman, R. & Allen, R. (1992). *Court of appeal: The Black community speaks out on the racial and sexual politics of Thomas vs. Hill*. New York: Ballantine Books.

Citadel gets a way out. (1995, May 19). *Time*. Retrived November 28, 2009 from *www.time.com*.

Clay, R. (n.d). Retrieved January 10, 2010 from blackboysincrisis.com.

Coed Citadel still a work in progress. (2006, August 12). *USA Today*. Retrieved November 28, 2009 from *www.usatoday.com*.

Cohen, D. (2009, Winter). No boy left behind? + single-sex education and the essentialist myth of masculinity. *Indiana Law Journal*, 84, 135.

Cohn, A. (n.d.). Good social policy not always good law. *Detroit News*.

Cole, J. (1995). Epilogue. In B. Guy-Sheftall (Ed.), *Words of Fire* (pp. 549–551). New York: The New Press.

Cole, J. & Guy-Sheftall, B. (2003). *Gender talk: The struggle for women's equality in African American communities*. New York: One World.

Collins, L. (2004, November 24). School of life: A place for teen moms to find success. *Metro Times*. Retrieved November 25, 2009, from metrotimes.com.

Collins, P. (1986). Learning from the outsider within: The sociological significance of Black feminist thought. *Social Problems*, 33(6):14–32.

———. (1991)(2000)(2009). *Black feminist thought: Knowledge, consciousness and the politics of empowerment*. New York: Routledge.

———. (2006). *From Black power to hip hop: Racism, nationalism, and feminism*. Philadelphia: Temple University Press.

Committee to Study the Status of the Black Male in the New Orleans Public Schools. (1988). *Educating Black male youth: A moral and civil imperative*. New Orleans: Orleans Parish Board.

Coleman, W. (2006, December 13). Special Bulletin. *The Detroit Public Schools Report Card*. Retrieved January 1, 2010, from *http://www.detroit.k12.mi.us/admin/ceo/reportCard.php*.

Coleman, W. (2007, February 8). Special Bulletin: State of the Detroit Public Schools: We are turning the corner. *The Detroit Public Schools Report Card*. Retrieved, January 1, 2010, from *http://www.detroit.k12.mi.us/admin/ceo/reportCard.php*.

Cooper, K. J. (1990, December 5). Three Rs and role model in Baltimore third grade; single-sex class harnesses boys' instincts. *Washington Post*. Retrieved from www.lexisnexis.com.

Copeland, L. (n.d.) Single-sex schools: A flawed plan for Michigan. Retrieved November 24, 2009, from *www.associatedcontent.com*

Creamer, E. (2003). Exploring the Link Between Inquiry paradigm and the Process of Collaboration. *The Review of Higher Education*, 26.4, 447–465.

Crenshaw, K. (1989). Demarginalizing the intersection of race and sex: A Black feminist critique of antidiscrimination doctrine, feminist theory and antiracist politics. *The University of Chicago Legal Forum*, 139–167.

Crenshaw, K., Gotanda, N, Peller, G., & Thomas, K. (Eds.) (1995). *Critical race theory: The key writings that formed the movement.* New York: New Press.

Crossfire. (1991, August 16). Transcript #378. Retrieved from www.lexisnexis.com.

Cummings, R. (1993). All-male Black schools: Equal protection, the new separatism and *Brown v. Board of Education. Hastings Constitutional Law Quarterly*, 20, 725–782.

Dardis, F. (2007). The role of issue-framing functions in affecting beliefs and opinions about a sociopolitical issue. *Communication Quarterly* 55(2), 247–265.

Davis, A. (1981). *Women, race & class.* New York: Random House.

Davis, M. (1991a). Affidavit. [*Garrett* legal briefs].

———. (1991b). Declaration. [*Garrett* legal briefs].

Deal reportedly reached to eliminate all-male academies. (1991, August 25). *United Press International.* Retrieved from www.lexisnexis.com.

Deitch, C. (1993). Gender, race, and class politics and the inclusion of women in Title VII of the 1964 Civil Rights Act. *Gender and Society*, 7(2), 183–203.

Delgado, R. & Stefancic, J. (1993). Critical race theory: An annotated bibliography. *Virginia Law Review*, 79, 461–516.

Denenfeld. P. (1991, June 14). *Letter to Fund Board Trustees.* [ACLU Correspondence].

DeRamus, B. (1991, September 10). All-male academies offer Black youths a slice of light, a ray of hope; to reject the idea is to bury yet another dream. *Detroit News*, p. 1B.

Detroit Academies: Any plan to accept girls must be in good faith [Editorial]. (1992, August 27). *Detroit Free Press*, p. 8A.

Detroit agrees to let females into all-male schools. (1991, August 27). *The Reuter Library Report.* Retrieved from www.lexisnexis.com.

Detroit Association of Black Organizations. (April 16, 1991). Letter to Mr. Larry Patrick, President.

——— (August 26, 1991). Letter to Mr. Larry Patrick, President.

Detroit Board of Education. (February 26,1991). Male Academy Resolution.

Detroit Board of Education President speaks on male academies compromise. (1991, November 8). *PR Newswire.* Retrieved from www.lexisnexis.com.

Detroit Board of Education President vows to review male academy options. (1991, August 15). *PR Newswire.* Retrieved from www.lexisnexis.com.

Detroit City Council. (1991, June 5). Resolution relative to all-male academies in the City of Detroit.

Detroit International Academy for Young Women. (n.d.). Detroit Public Schools. Retrieved November 25, 2009, from www.detroit.k.12.mi.us.

Detroit News Staff and Wires. (1991, September 10). Bush supports all-male academies. *The Detroit News*, 3A.

Detroit OKs school aimed at Black males. (1991, February 28). *Chicago Tribune.* Retrieved from www.lexisnexis.com.

Detroit Public Schools—News. Retrieved November 23, 2009, from *www.detroit.k12.mi.us*.

Detroit School Board committee approves male academy proposal. (1991, January 11). *PR Newswire*. Retrieved from www.lexisnexis.com.

Detroit Schools "ground zero." (2009, May 14). *The Washington Times*. Retrieved November 25, 2009, from www.washingtontimes.com.

Detroit tosses plan for same-sex schools. (2005, August 11). *The Detroit News*. Retrieved November 29, 2009 from nl.newsbank.com.

de Vise, D. (2009, October 15). A Slow March to Change: VMI is Steeped in Traditions Dating to 1839. Until 1997, Female Cadets Weren't Part of Them." *Washington Post*, pg. A01. Retrieved November 28, 2009, from *www.lexisnexis.com*.

Dill, B. (1983). Race, class, and gender: Prospects for an all-inclusive sisterhood. *Feminist Studies*, 9, 131–138.

Dillon, N. (2006, August 8). Detroit school leaders pin hopes on single-gender schools. *School Board News*. Retrieved November 25, 2009, from www.nsba.com.

District halts plans to open single sex high schools. (2005, August 10).

Dixson, A. and Rousseau, C. (2006). *Critical race theory in education: All God's children got a song*. New York: Routledge.

Doe, N. (1991). Affidavit. [*Garrett* legal briefs].

Dog the Bounty Hunter Racist Rant—Caught on Tape. (2007, October 31). *National Enquirer*. Retrieved January 9, 2010, from www.nationalenquirer.com.

Dolling, I. & Hark, S. (2000). She who speaks shadow speaks truth: Transdisciplinarity in women's and gender studies. *Signs: Journal of Women in Culture and Society*, 25(4), 1195–1198.

Dominguez, V. (1987). *White by definition*. New Brunswick, NJ: Rutgers University Press.

Douglass Academy for Young Men. *Detroit Public Schools*. Retrieved November 25, 2009, from www.detroit.k12.mi.us.

Dozier, M. (1991, August 30). Lone white among those academy seeks to save. *Detroit Free Press*, p. 1B.

DPS Chief comments on male academies. (1991, August 13). *PR Newswire* Retrieved from www.lexisnexis.com.

Dressen-Hammouda, D. (2008). From novice to disciplinary expert: Disciplinary identity and genre mastery. *English for Specific Purposes*, 27, 233–252.

Dybis, K. (2009, September 21). A disturbing trend for Detroit's schools. *Time Magazine*. Retrieved November 27, 2009, from Detroit.blogs.time.com.

Dyson, M. (1993). *Reflecting black: African American cultural criticism*. Minneapolis: University of Minnesota Press.

Eckholm, E. (2006, March 20). Plight Deepens for Black Men, Studies Warn. *The New York Times*. Retrieved December 5, 2009 from www.nytimes.com.

Editorial Projects in Education Research Center. (2008, April 1). *Cities in crisis: A special analytic report on high school graduation*. Retrieved January 2, 2010, from www.edweek.org.

Editorial Projects in Education Research Center. (2009, April). *Closing the graduation gap: Educational and economic conditions in America's largest cities.* Retrieved January 2, 2010, from www.edweek.org.

Eldeib, D. (2010, March 5). Every Urban Prep senior is college-bound. *Chicago Tribune.* Retrieved March 13, 2010 from www.chicago.tribune.com.

Elliott-Larsen Civil Rights Act. Act 453. 37.2101 (1976).

Eng, S. (1991, August 13). Parents hope all-male schools will inspire kids. *Detroit News* Retrieved from www.lexisnexis.com.

Equal Education Opportunities Act, 20 U.S.C. 1701 *et. seq.*

Evans-Winters, V. (2005). *Teaching black girls: Resiliency in urban classrooms.* New York: Lang.

Farhi, P. (2007, April 12). MSNBC drops simulcast of Imus show: Growing outrage over slur by CBS radio host. *The Boston Globe.* Retrieved January 6, 2009, from bostonglobe.com

Feldman, M. (1995). *Strategies for interpreting qualitative data.* Thousand Oaks, CA: Sage.

Fergus, E., Sciurba, K., Martin, M., Noguera, P. (2009, October 31). Single-sex schools for Black and Latino boys: An intervention in search of theory. *In Motion Magazine.* Retrieved March 13, 2010 from www.inmotionmagazine.com.

Ferguson, A. (1990). The intersection of race, gender, and class in the United States today. *Rethinking Marxism, 3*(3), 45–64.

Ferguson Academy for Young Women. (n.d.) *Detroit Public Schools.* Retrieved November 25, 2009, from www.detroit.k12.mi.us.

Fitzgerald, J. (1991, September 4). Officials need to grow up in attitudes about Detroit. *Detroit Free Press*, p. 8F.

Fordham, S. (1993). "Those loud Black girls": (Black) women silence, and gender "passing" in the academy. *Anthropology and Educational Quarterly*, 32: 3–32.

Francois, C. (2006). Transdisciplinary Unified Theory. *Systems Research and Behavioral Science*, 23, 617–624.

Franklin, C. (1994). Men's studies, the men's movement, and the study of Black masculinities in the 1990s. In R.Majors & J. Gordon (Eds.), The American Black male: His present status and his future (pp. 271–283). Chicago: Nelson-Hall.

Gamson, W. (1992). The social psychology of collective action. In A. Morris & C. Mueller (Eds.), *Frontiers in social movement theory* (pp. 53–76). New Haven: Yale University.

Gandy, K. (2006a, March 28). Separation threatens girls. *USA Today.* Retrieved November 24, 2009, www.usatoday.com.

———. (2006b, June 28). On Title IX Anniversary, Michigan poised to remove girls' equal education guarantee. www.now.org.

———. (2006c, October 12). There is no boy crisis. *USA Today.* Retrieved March 26, 2010, *www.now.org.*

Gardenswartz, D. (1993). Public education: An inner-city crisis! Single-sex schools: An inner-city answer? *Emory Law Journal*, 42, 591–646.

Gardner, L. (1991). *Affidavit.* [*Garrett* legal briefs].

Garibaldi, A. (1992). Educating and motivating African-American males to succeed. *Journal of Negro Education*, 61(1), 4–11.

Garrett v. Board of Educ. of School D. of Detroit, 775 F.Supp. 1004 (E.D. Mich. 1991).

Garrett v. Board of Educ. of School D. of Detroit legal briefs. (1991). [Legal briefs]. United States District Court: Detroit, Michigan.

Garrett, S. (1991a). *Affidavit*. [*Garrett* legal briefs].

———. (1991b, August 15). Statement of Shawn Garrett. [Garrett legal briefs].

Gates, H. Jr. (Ed.). (1987). *Race, writing and difference*. Chicago: University of Chicago Press.

Gender matters: Boys will be boys. (2006, June 20). *The Seattle Times*. Retrieved December 5, 2009, from http://www.thefreelibrary.com.

Gerritt, J. (2009, November 12). No boys left behind at Detroit pubic school. *Free Press*. Retrieved November 23, 2009, from www.freep.com.

Giddings, P. (1984). *When and where I enter: The impact of Black women on race and sex in America*. New York: William Morrow.

Gilchrist, B. (1991, August 6). Lawsuit challenges all-male academies: District charged with sex discrimination. *Detroit Free Press*, p. 3A.

———. (1991, August 16). Single-sex schools are unconstitutional: Judge stops all-male programs in Detroit. *Detroit Free Press*, p. 1A.

———. (1991, August 19). Leaders start organizing protest for male schools. *Detroit Free Press*, p. 1B.

———. (1991, August 27). Deal may admit girls to male academies. *Detroit Free Press*, p. 1A.

———. (1991, August 29). Boys academy opens with rules; Friendly principal sets tone at disputed Detroit school. *Detroit Free Press*, p. 6A.

———. (1991, September 3). All-male schools anguish civil rights veterans. *Detroit Free Press*, p.1A.

———. (1991, September 10). The few girls adjust to mostly male schools. *Detroit Free Press*, p. 8A.

———. (1991, November 7). Detroit Board yields on male school fight; Court case abandoned; Change in law sought. *Detroit Free Press*, p. 1A.

Gilchrist, B. & Musial, R. (1991, August 28). Detroit Board allows girls into academies: It plans to keep fighting for all-male schools. *Detroit Free Press*, p. 1A.

Gilchrist, B., Richardson, J., Trimer-Hartley, M., & Brum, F. (1991, September 10). Bush backs single-sex schools; Change laws if need be, he says. *Detroit Free Press*, p. 1A.

Give single-sex schools a try. (2008, November 16). *Boston Globe Editorial*. Retrieved November 28, 2009 from www.boston.com/bostonglobe.

Gladden, M. (1992). The constitutionality of African-American male schools and programs. *Columbia Human Rights Law Review*, 24, 239–271.

GMA Exclusive: Anita Hill. (2007, October 2). *ABC News*. Retrieved January 5, 2010, from abcnews.go.com/gma.

Goldberg, T. (Ed.). (1990). *Anatomy of racism*. Minneapolis: University of Minnesota Press.

Gongwer News Service. (2006a, June 14). Panel Ok's single gender schooling. Retrieved November 27, 2009, from http://www.bridges4kids.org.

Gongwer News Service. (2006b, June 15). Michigan Senate passes single gender school bill. Retrieved November 27, 2009, from *www.bridges4kids.org.*

Grant, L. (1984). Black females `place' in desegregated classrooms. *Sociology of Education*, 57, 98–111.

Gratz v. Bollinger, 539 U.S. 244 (2003).

Graves, E. (2006, January 1). Saving our young black men. *Black Enterprise.* Retrieved December 5, 2009, from www.thefreelibrary.com.

Green, R. & Wright, D. (1991). *African-American males: A demographic study and analysis.* W.K. Kellogg Foundation National Workshop on African-American Men and Boys.

Gregory, S. (1993). Race, rubbish, and resistance: Empowering difference in community politics. *Cultural Anthropology*, 8(1), 24–48.

Griffin, L. (1995). How is sociology informed by history? *Social Forces*, 73(4), 1245–1254.

Griffin, L. & Korstad, R. (1995). Class as race and gender: Making and breaking a labor union in the Jim Crow South. *Social Science History*, 19(4), 425–454.

Grooms, A. (n.d.). Single sex education. Retrieved January 1, 2010, from http://www.vanderbilt.edu/VIPPS/C&FPC.

Grossman, R. (2001, September). It's not easy being green...and female. *HRMagazine*, 46(9).

Grutter v. Bollinger, 539 US 306 (2003).

Guba, E. & Lincoln, Y. (1994). Competing paradigms in qualitative research. In N. Denzin & Y. Lincoln (Eds.), *Handbook of qualitative research* (pp. 105–117). Thousand Oaks, CA: Sage.

Gurian, M. (2007). *The minds of boys: Saving our sons from falling behind in school and life.* San Francisco: Jossey-Bass.

———. (2009). *The purpose of boys: Helping our sons find meaning, significance and direction in their lives.* San Francisco: Jossey-Bass.

Guy-Sheftall, B. (Ed). (1995). *Words of Fire.* New York: New Press.

Hale, J. (1991). *Affidavit.* [*Garrett* legal briefs].

Hall, S. (1980). Race, articulation and societies structured in dominance. In *UNESCO, sociological theories: Race and colonialism* (pp. 305–345). Paris: UNESCO.

Hamer, J. & Neville, H. (2001). Revolutionary Black feminism: Toward a theory of unity and liberation. *The Black Scholar*, 28(3/4), 22–29.

Harding, S. & Norberg, K. (2005). New feminist approaches to social science methodologies: An introduction. *Signs: Journal of Women in Culture and Society*, 30(4), 2009–2015.

Harmon, A. (1991, August 22). 300 rally in support of all-male schools. *Los Angeles Times*, p. A4. Retrieved from www.lexisnexis.com.

Harris, A. (1990). Race and essentialism in feminist legal theory. *Stanford Law Review*, 42, 581–616.

Hawke, P. (2007, July 12). Dismal Drop- Out Rates for Detroit Schools. *EzineArticles.com*, Retrieved November 25, 2009.

Hayden, F. (1991, September 9). Rationale behind male academies dictates legal pursuit of that goal. *Detroit Free Press*, p. 11A.

——— (n.d.) Statement of Frank Hayden, Vice-President, Detroit Board of Education regarding settlement of All-Male Academy case.

Haymes, S. (1995). Race, culture, and the city: A pedagogy for urban black struggle. Albany: State University of New York Press.

Henry, A. (1998). 'Invisible' and 'Womanish': Black girls negotiating their lives in an African-centered school in the USA. *Race Ethnicity and Education*, 1(2), 151–170.

Herbert, J. (1988). Otherness and the Black woman. *Canadian Journal of Women and the Law*, 3, 269–279.

Higginbotham, E. (1992). African-American women's history and the metalanguage of race. *Signs*, 17(2), 251–274.

Hill, D. (1993). Afrocentric movements in education: Examining equity, culture, and power relations in the public schools. *Hastings Constitutional Law Quarterly*, 20, 681–724.

Holland, S. (1989, September/October). Fighting the epidemic of failure: A radical strategy for educating inner-city boys. *Viewpoint.*

Holland, S. (1991). Positive role models for primary grade Black inner city males. *Equity and Excellence*, 25(1), 41–44.

hooks, b. (1981). *Ain't I a woman*. Boston: South End Press.

———. (1984). *Feminist theory: From margin to center.* Boston: South End Press.

———. (1990). *Yearning: Race, gender, and cultural politics.* Boston: South End Press.

Hopkins, R. (1997). *Educating Black males: Critical lessons in schooling, community, and power.* Albany: State University of New York Press.

Hostility greets students at Black school in White area of Detroit. (1992, December 2). *New York Times.* Retrieved November 27, 2009, www.lexis-nexis.com.

Howard-Hamilton, M. (2003, Winter). Theoretical Frameworks for African American Women. *New Directions for Student Services*, 104:19.

Hsiao, L. (1992). "Separate but equa"' revisited: The Detroit male academies case. *Annual Survey of American Law*, 85–115.

Hulett, S. (2009, June 6). Report: State graduate rate slides slightly; Detroit's drops. Retrieved November 27, 2009, from www.publicbroadcasting.net/michigan.

Hull, G., Scott, P., & Smith, B. (1982). *All the women are White, all the Blacks are men, but some of us are brave: Black women's studies.* Old Westbury, New York: Feminist Press.

Hunter, A. & Davis, J. (1992). Constructing gender: An exploration of Afro-American men's conceptualization of manhood. *Gender and Society*, 6(3), 464–479.

Hurst, J. & Johansen, I. (2006). The changing landscape of single-sex education. *School Law Bulletin, 37(2).*

education. Chapel Hill: The University of North Carolina School of Government., Retrieved January 3, 2010 from http://www.sog.unc.edu/pubs.

Huskisson, G. (1991a, January 29). Preserving manhood: Civic, political leaders unite to rescue young black males at-risk. *Detroit Free Press*, p. 1B.

———. (1991b, February 9). Invest time in Black males, witnesses urge; hearings seek better future for those at-risk. *Detroit Free Press*, p. 3A.

Ilka, D. (1991, August 14). School chief say ACLU, NOW meddling in all-male debate. *The Detroit News* Retrieved from www.lexisnexis.com.

Innerst, C. (1991, September 3). School geared to Black boys attracts girls. *The Washington Times*, p. A3.

Irvine, J. (1990). *Black students and school failure: Politics, practices, and prescriptions.* Westport, CT: Greenwood Press.

Iverson, S. (2005, August 12). The discursive construction of diversity: A policy discourse analysis of U.S. university diversity action plans." Paper presented at the annual meeting of the American Sociological Association, Marriott Hotel, Loews Philadelphia Hotel, Philadelphia, PA. Retrieved from *http://www.allacademic.com/meta/p21545_index.html*

James, S. & Busia, A. (1993). *Theorizing Black feminisms: The visionary pragmatism of Black women.* New York: Routledge.

Janofsky, M. (1996, June 29). Citadel, Bowing to Court, Says It Will Admit Women. *The New York Times.* Retrieved November 27, 2009 from www.nytimes.com.

Jerven, T. (2010, March 9). Navy submarines: What's really in the way of women serving? *The Christian Science Monitor.* Retrieved from news.yahoo.com.

Johnson, J. (1989). *The Black male: The new bald eagle.* Silver Spring, MD: Management Plus.

Johnson, R. (1991). Affidavit. [*Garrett* legal briefs].

Jones, C. (1991). *Affidavit.* [*Garrett* legal briefs].

Joseph, G. & Lewis, J. (1981). *Common differences: Conflicts in Black and White feminist perspectives.* Garden City, New York: Doubleday.

Kahn, C. (2001, May 19). VMI graduates its first class of female cadets. *Associated Press State and Local Wire.* Retrieved November 28, 2009, from www.lexisnexis.com.

Katz, D. (1991, August 5). Boarding schools proposed to get youths off mean streets. *Detroit News-Gannet News Service.* Retrieved from lexisnexis.com.

Kelly, D. (1991, August 8). All-girls school pushed in Detroit. *USA Today*, pg. 1D. Retrieved from www.lexisnexis.com

———. (1992, January 15). Detroit academies develop Black males. *USA Today.* Retrieved from www.lexisnexis.com.

Ken, I. (2007). Race-Class-Gender theory: An Image(ry) Problem. *Gender Issues*, 24, 1–20.

———. (2008). Beyond the intersection: A new culinary metaphor for race-class-gender studies. *Sociological Theory*, 26(2), 152–172.

King, D. (1988). Multiple jeopardy, multiple consciousness: The context of a Black feminist ideology. *Signs: Journal of Women in Culture and Society*, 11(1).

———. (1992). Unraveling fabric, missing the beat: Class and gender in Afro-American social issues. *Black Scholar*, 22(3), 36–44.

Kiselewich, R. (2008). Note: In Defense of the 2006 Title IX Regulations for Single-Sex Public Education: How Separate Can Be Equal. *Boston College Law Review*, 49, 217.

Klandermans, B. (1992). The social construction of protest and multiorganizational fields. In A. Morris & C. Mueller (Eds.), *Frontiers in social movement theory* (pp. 77–103). New Haven: Yale University.

Kolb, D. (1981). Learning styles and disciplinary differences. In A. Chickering (Ed)., *The Modern American College*, San Francisco: Jossey Bass.

Kuklenski, V. (2007, February 1). Divide and conquer single sex education sends girls, boys to head of the class. *Daily News*. Retrieved December 5, 2009, from www.thefreelibrary.com.

Kuzmic, J. 2000. Textbooks, knowledge and masculinity: Examining patriarchy from within. 105–126. In N. Lesko, ed. *Masculinities at school* (pp. 49–74). Thousand Oaks, CA: Sage Publications.

Lack of female students may keep academies segregated. (1991, September 9). *Detroit News* Retrieved from www.lexisnexis.com.

Ladner, J. (1986). Black women face the 21st century: Major issues and problems. *Black Scholar*, 17(5), 12–19.

Lattuca, L. & Stark, J. (1995). Modifying the major: Discretionary thoughts from ten disciplines. *The Review of Higher Education*,18(3), 315–344.

Leake, D. and Leake. B. (1992). Islands of hope: Milwaukee's African-American immersion schools. *Journal of Negro Education*, 61(1), 24–29.

Lee, J. (2004). Comparing Institutional Relationships with Academic Departments: A Study of Five Academic Fields. *Research in Higher Education*, 45(6), 603–624.

Lee, V. & Byrk, A. (1986). Effects of single-sex secondary schools on student achievement and attitudes. *Journal of Educational Psychology*, 78(5), 381–395.

Lee, V. & Lockheed, M. (1990). The effects of single-sex schooling on achievement and attitudes in Nigeria. *Comparative Education Review*, 34(2), 209–231.

Lei, J. (2003). (Un)necessary toughness? Those "loud black girls" and those "quiet Asian boys." *Anthropology and Education Quarterly*, 42(2), 158–181.

Lemelle, A. (1995). Black male deviance. Westport, CT: Praeger.

Lesko, N. 2000. Introduction. In N. Lesko (Ed.). *Masculinities at school*. Thousand Oaks, CA: Sage Publications.

Lindsey, S. (2009, November 22). Federal probe levies sexism charge against VMI. *Marine Corps Times*. Retrieved November 28, 2009 from www.marinecorpstimes.com.

Lockhart, V. (2002, February 6). Black schools take lead: African-centered classrooms report rise in student achievement, self-esteem. *Michigan Chronicle*, pg. A1. Retrieved, November 27, 2009, from proquest.umi.com.

Lorde, A. (1984). *Sister outsider: Essays and speeches*. Freedom, CA: The Crossing Press.

Lynn, M. & Parker, L. (2006, November). Critical race studies in education: Examining a decade of research on U.S. Schools. *The Urban Review*, 38(4), 257.

Mace, N. (2001). *In the Company of Men: A woman at the Citadel.* New York: Simon and Schuster.

Mael, F., Smith, M., Alonso, A., Rogers, K., & Gibson, D. (2004, November 9). Theoretical Arguments for and against single-sex schools: A critical analysis of the explanation. *American Institutes for Research.*

Malcolm X Academy. (n.d.). Retrieved November 28, 2009, from *www.detroitk12.org.*

Male academies court reversal a blow, but a better plan is needed. [Editorial] (1991, August 17). *Detroit Free Press*, p. 6A.

Male academies' support group to defy court order; will hold demonstration. (1991, August 19). *PR Newswire.* Retrieved from www.lexisnexis.com.

Male academy despite roadblocks, innovative school is worth a try [Editorial]. (1991, February 2). *Detroit Free Press,* p. 8A.

Male academy grades K-8: A demonstration program for at-risk males. (1991). Detroit School Board. [Task Force Report].

Male academy to be discussed at Detroit's community confidence meeting Thursday, January 10, 1991. *PR Newswire* Retrieved from www.lexisnexis.com.

Malveaux, J. (n.d.). All-boy school ignore girls' problems. *Burrelle's.*

Marable, M. (1983). Groundings with my sisters: Patriarchy and the exploitation of Black women. In *How capitalism underdeveloped Black America: Problems in race, political economy and society.* Boston: South End Press.

Marcus Garvey Academy. (n.d.). Retrieved November 28, 2009, from www.detroitk12.org.

Marsh, H. (1989). Effects of attending single-sex and coeducational high schools on achievement, attitudes, behaviors, and sex differences. *Journal of Educational Psychology*, 81(1), 70–85.

Martin, M. (2007, October 4). Anucha Browne Sanders speaks out in Knicks case. *NPR Transcript.* Retrieved January 6, 2010 from www.npr.org.

Martin, T. (2006, November 8). Michigan voters approving banning some affirmative action programs. *Associated Press State and Local Wire.* Retrieved November 28, 2009, from *www.lexisnexis.com.*

Matheson, K. (2008, September 6). Philly school rekindles same-sex education debate. *USA Today.* Retrieved March 13, 2010, from www.usatoday.com.

Mathews, J. (2006, June 26). Boys in crisis? Actually, they're doing just fine, new report says. *The Seattle Times.* Retrieved December 5, 2009, from www.thefreelibrary.com.

Matsuda, P. & C. Tary. (2007). Voice in academic writing: The rhetorical construction of author identity in blind manuscript review. *English for Specific Purposes Journal*, 26, 235–249.

MBC Celebrates VWIL's 10th Anniversary March 18, 2004 (2005, March 1). Mary Baldwin College News. Retrieved January 23, 2010 from www.mbc.edu.

McCammon, H., Newman, H., Muse, C. & Terrell, T. (2007). *American Sociological Review*, 72, 725–749.

McCloskey, L. (1994, June 17). Boys & Girls together: But not everywhere & all the time. Retrieved December 5, 2009, from www.thefreelibrary.com.

McGriff, D. (1991a). Affidavit. [*Garrett* legal briefs].

———. (1991b, November 6). Statement by Dr. Deborah M. McGriff, General Superintendent, Detroit Public Schools Regarding Settlement of Male Academy Case. [*Garrett* legal briefs].

McWilliam, E., Hearn, G., & Haseman, B. (2008, August). Transdisciplinarity for creative futures: what barriers and opportunities? *Innovations in Education and Teaching International*, 45(3), 247–253.

Mead, S. (2006). The truth about boys and girls. *Education Sector.* Retrieved January 10, 2010 from www.educationsector.org.

Memorandum of law in opposition to plaintiffs' motion for a temporary restraining order and preliminary injunction. (1991). [*Garrett* legal briefs]. [DM].

Memorandum of law in support of plaintiffs' motion for a temporary restraining order and preliminary injunction. (1991). [*Garrett* legal briefs]. [PM].

Meyer, P. (2008, January 1). Learning separately: The case for single-sex schools. *Education Next.* Retrieved December 5, 2009, from www.thefreelibrary.com.

Michigan House Fiscal Agency. (2007, January 25). Legislative Analysis. HB 4264 and HB 6247. Retrieved from http://www.legislature.mi.gov.

Michigan Information and Research Service. (2006, June 13). Michigan Gov likes same-sex schools. Retrieved November 27, 2009, from *www.bridges4kids.org.*

Michigan National Organization for Women. (2007, November). Why we oppose sex-segregated education. Retrieved January 3, 2010, from www.michnow.org/public_html/MINOW1sexsch.pdf

Michigan Public Act 303 of 2006.

Michigan Public Act 347 of 2006.

Michigan Public Act 348 of 2006.

Michigan Revised School Code. (1976). Act 451.

Michigan Senate Fiscal Agency. (2006a, June 21). Bill Analysis. S.B. 1305. Floor Analysis. Retrieved from www.senate.michigan.gov/sfa.

Michigan Senate Fiscal Agency. (2006b, July 19). Bill Analysis. S.B. 1305. First Analysis. Retrieved from *www.senate.michigan.gov/sfa.*

Michigan Senate Fiscal Agency. (2006c, July 25). Bill Analysis. H.B. 4264 and H.B. 6247. Committee Summary. Retrieved from www.senate.michigan.gov/sfa.

Milliken v. Bradley, 433 U.S. 267 (1977).

Mincy, R., ed. (2006). *Black males left behind.* Urban Institute Press, Washington, DC.

Mirel, J. (1993). *The Rise and fall of an urban school system: Detroit, 1907–1981.* University of Michigan.

———. (1998). After the fall: Continuity and change in Detroit, 1981–1995. *History of Education Quarterly*, 38(3), 23–267.

Mississippi University for Women School of Nursing v. Hogan, 458 U.S. 718 (1982).

Moore & Associates. (1993). *1991–1992 African-Centered Academies Evaluation Final Report.* Detroit: Michigan.

Morgan, J. (1995). Black males on campus: Early intervention single-gender 'academies' show promise. *Black Issues in Higher Education*, 12(14).

Morial, M. (2007). Empowering Black Males to Reach Their Full Potential. In *National Urban League: The State of Black America* (pp. 13–15). Silver Springs, MD: The Beckman Publications Group.

Morris, E. (2007). "Ladies" or "Loudies"?: Perceptions and experiences of black girls in classrooms. *Youth and Society*, 38(4), 490–515.

Morrison, T. (Ed.). (1992). *Race-ing justice, en-gendering power: Essays on Anita Hill, Clarence Thomas and the construction of social reality.* New York: Pantheon Books.

Moss, D. (1991, August 13). New chief backs all-male school. *USA Today*, p. 2A. Retrieved from www.lexisnexis.com.

Mrozowski, J. (2007, November 13). Single-sex schools make comeback. *The Detroit News*. Retrieved November 23, 2009, from www.detnews.com.

Murtadha-Watts, K. (2000). *Theorizing Urban Black Masculinity Construction in an African-Centered School.* In N. Lesko (Ed.), *Masculinities at School* (pp. 49–74). Thousand Oaks, CA: Sage Publications.

Murray, P. (1975). The liberation of Black women. In J. Freeman (Ed.), *Women: A Feminist Perspective* (pp. 351–363). Palo Alto, CA: Mayfield,

Mutua, A. (Ed). (2006). *Progressive Black masculinities.* New York: Routledge.

Nagel, J. (1984). Constructing ethnicity: Creating and recreating ethnic identity and culture. *Social Problems* 41(1), 152–176.

National Association for the Advancement of Colored People. (1991a). *Resolutions on Education: 1970–1991.*

National Association for the Advancement of Colored People Legal Defense Fund, Inc. (1991b). Statement on proposals for African-American pupils. *Reply Brief*, Appendix B [*Garrett* legal briefs].

National Coalition for Women and Girls in Education. (2008). Title IX at 35: Beyond the headlines. Retrieved November 27, 2009, from www.ncwge.org.

National Organization for Women. (2004, April 23). Single sex proposed regulation comments. Retrieved January 3, 2010 from www.now.org.

——— (October 24, 2006). NOW opposes single-sex public education as "separate and unequal." Retrieved August 21, 2010 from www.now.org.

National Organization for Women Legal Defense and Education Fund. (1991). *Public education programs for African American males.* 99 Hudson Street, New York: New York.

National Urban League. (2007a). The State of Black America 2007. Silver Springs, MD: The Beckman Publications Group.

National Urban League report cites nation's Black male crisis. (2007b, May 17). *Jet Magazine*. Retrieved December 5, 2009, at http://findarticles.com.

National Women's Law Center. (2004, April. 22). Letter to the US Department of Education re: single-sex proposed regulations comments. Retrieved January 10, 2010, from *www.nwlc.org.*

———. (2006, October 24). Administration's single-sex regulations violate Constitution and Title IX. Retrieved January 10, 2010, from *www.nwlc.org.*

———. (2007). *When girls don't graduate we all fail: A call to improve high school graduation rates for girls.* Retrieved January 10, 2010, from *www.nwlc.org.*

Navy welcomes women to serve in submarines. (April 30, 2010). Retrieved August 20, 2010, from www.navy.mil.

Neuborne, H. (1991, August 16). Girls are drowning, too. *The New York Times.*
Newcomb, A. (2000, August 13). Teaching boys that "all the answers are within." *Zoom information.* Retrieved November 25, 2009, from cache.zoominfo.com.
New solution or segregation. (1992, January 15). *USA Today*, pg. 7A. Retrieved from www.lexisnexis.com.
Nightline: Detroit Black male academies ruled unfair. (1991, August 15). ABC News.
No Child Left Behind Act of 2001. Pub. L. 107–100, 115 Stat. 1425.
Noguera, P. (2008). *The trouble with Black boys... and other reflections on race, equity, and the future of public education.* San Francisco: Jossey-Bass.
Nondiscrimination on the Basis of Sex, 34 CFR 106 (2006).
Note (1991). Invisible man: Black and male under Title VII. *Harvard Law Review*, 104, 749–768.
NOW opposes single-sex public education as "separate and unequal." *www.now.org.*
Omi, M. & Winant, H. (1986). *Racial formation in the United States from the 1960s to the 1980s.* New York: Routledge.
O'Neill, W. (1998). Sex scandals in the gender-integrated military. *Gender Issues*, 16(1–2).
Onwuachi-Willig, A. (2006). Foreword: This bridge called our backs: An introduction to "The Future of Critical Race Feminism." *U.C. Davis L. Rev.* 39, 733–742.
———. (2007). GIRL, Fight! (Review of *Fight Like A Girl: How to be a fearless feminist. Berkeley Journal of Gender, Law, & Justice*, 22, 254–274.
———. (2009). Celebrating critical race theory at 20. *Iowa Law Review* 94, 1497.
Ore, T. (2006). Book review. *Making sense of race, class, and gender: Commonsense, Power and Privilege in the United States* by Pascale, C. (2006), in *Contemptorary Sociology*, 37(1).
Paechter, C. (1998). *Educating the Other: Gender, Power, and Schooling.* Washington, DC: Falmer Press.
Page, C. (1991a, August 18). The trouble with all-male schools. *The Chicago Tribune*, pg. 3C.
———. (1991b, August 19). What do male schools fix. *The Ann Arbor News.*
———. (2008, August 20). Helping boys without hurting girls. Retrieved from *www.realclearpolitics.com.*
Parents Involved in Community Schools v. Seattle School District. 551 U.S. 701 (2007).
Parks, C. (1991, August 5). Detroit schools sued over all-male academies. *United Press International* Retrieved from www.lexisnexis.com.
Pascale, C. (2006). *Making sense of race, class, and gender: Commonsense, power, and privilege in the United States.* New York: Routledge.
Patrick, L. (1991a, October 29). Detroit parents should have right to choose. *Detroit Free Press*, 9A.
———. (1991b, November 6). Statement of Lawrence C. Patrick, Jr., President, Detroit Board of Education Regarding Settlement of Male Academy Case.

Paul, D. (2003). Talkin' back: Raising and educating resilient Black girls. Westport, CT: Praeger.

Paul Robeson Academy (n.d.). *Detroit Public Schools*. Retrieved November 28, 2009, from *www.detroitk12.org*.

Pollock, M. (2006, December 18). Testimony Concerning Implementation of Article I, Section 26 of the Michigan Constitution before the Michigan Law Revision Commission. Retrieved November 25, 2009 from www.michnow.org.

Porter, J. (1990, December 19). *Memorandum*. [*Garrett* legal briefs].

———. (1991). *Affidavit*. [*Garrett* legal briefs].

Pratt, M. (1997). Where are the Black girls? The marginalization of Black females in the single-sex school debate in Detroit. [dissertation]. Ann Arbor: UMI Company.

Preliminary Statement. (1991). [*Garrett* legal briefs].

Prestige Academy. (2007–2010). Retrieved March 13, 2010, from www.prestigeacademy.cs.org.

Protheroe, N. (2009, May- June). Single-sex classrooms. *Principal*, 88(5), 32–35.

Provisional Charter for Male Academy Program of the Detroit Public Schools at Cooper School. (1991, June 25). [Exhibit D, *Garrett* legal briefs].

Rabouin, E. (2000). "Gifting children of promise": Re-imagining the academic margins as transformative legal space. *Journal Gender Race and Justice*, 3, 581.

Radford-Hill, S. (1986). Considering feminism as a model for social change. In T. de Lauretis (Ed.), *Feminist studies/critical studies* (pp. 157–172). Bloomington: Indiana University Press.

Ransby, B. (2000). Black Feminism at twenty-one: Reflections on the evolution of a national community. *Signs: Journal of Women in Culture and Society*, 25(4), 1215–1221.

Ransby, B. & Matthews, T. (1995). Black popular culture and the transcendence of patriarchal illusions. In B. Guy-Sheftall (Ed.), *Words of fire* (pp. 526–535). New York: The New Press.

Raspberry, W. (1991, August 30). Opponents are missing the point of all-male Academies. *Chicago Tribune*, p. 23. Retrieved from www.lexisnexis.com.

Ray, E. (1991, September 1). All-male black schools put on hold in Detroit; Girls will be admitted after court challenge. *Boston Globe* Retrieved from www.lexisnexis.com.

Reach Academy for Girls (2009). Retrieved March 13, 2010 from www.reachacademyforgirls.org.

Reply Brief in Support of Plaintiff's Motion for a Temporary Restraining Order and Preliminary Injunction. (1991). [Garrett legal brief, RB].

Reverse discrimination suits flourish: Courts see a growing number of reverse discrimination cases. (2009, April 28). *The Associated Press*. Retrieved December 5, 2009 from www.msnbc.com.

Ricci v. DeStefano, 2009 US Lexis 4945.

Robinson, J. (2008). The African-centered school movement and the Detroit Public School system. (Doctoral Dissertation, Michigan State University, 2008).

Rollock, N. (2007). Why Black girls don't matter: Exploring how race and gender shape academic success in an inner city school. *Support for Learning*, 22(4).

Russell, R. (1991a, August 5). All-male schools sued for excluding females. *Detroit News*. Retrieved from www.lexisnexis.com.

———. (1991b, August 5). Girls' schools proposed to balance all-male academies. *Detroit News*. Retrieved from www.lexisnexis.com.

———. (1991, August 7). Push on for all-girl academy. *Detroit News*. Retrieved from www.lexisnexis.com.

———. (1991, August 15). Detroit may admit girls, on appeal all-male ruling. *Detroit News*. Retrieved from www.lexisnexis.com.

———. (1991, August 16). Detroit may let girls enroll in all-boy schools. *Detroit News*, 2A.

———. (1991, August 21). NAACP Fund might join in opposing all-male schools. *Detroit News*. Retrieved from www.lexisnexis.com.

———. (1991, August 27). Catholic academy to separate girls, boys. *Detroit News*. Retrieved from www.lexisnexis.com.

———. (1991, September 5). Lack of female students may keep academies segregated. *Detroit News*, 2B.

———. (1991, November 7). All-male schools plans dropped by Detroit Board. *Detroit News*. Retrieved from www.lexisnexis.com.

Russell, R. & Hamada, T. (1991, August 25). Agreement will allow girls in Detroit all-male schools. *Detroit News*. Retrieved from www.lexisnexis.com.

Russell, R. & Skwira, G. (1991, August 29). Supporters of all-male schools organize to continue fight. *Detroit News*. Retrieved from www.lexisnexis.com.

Russell, A., Wickson, F., & Carew, A. (2008). Transdisciplinarity: Context, contradictions, and capacity. *Futures*, 40, 460–472.

Ryan, W. (1971). *Blaming the victim*. New York: Pantheon Books.

Sacks, K. (1989). Toward a unified theory of class, race, and gender. *American Ethnologist, 16*,(3), 534–550.

Sadker, M. & Sadker, D. (1994). *Failing at fairness: How America's schools cheat girls*. New York: C. Scribner's Sons.

Salomone, R. (2003). *Same, different, equal: Rethinking single-sex schooling*. New Haven: Yale University Press.

———. (2004). Feminist voices in the debate over single-sex schooling: Finding common ground. *Michigan Journal of Gender and Law*, 11, 63.

Sanchez, C. (2009, November 11). Do Colleges favor male applicants? *National Public Radio*. Retrieved December 11, 2009 from www.npr.org.

Satyanarayana, M. (2009, November 15). Summit aims to keep young men in school. *Detroit Free Press*. Retrieved November 27, 2009 from www.freep.com.

Sax, L. (2006). *Why gender matters: What parents and teachers need to know about the emerging science of sex differences*. New York: Basic Books.

———. (2007). *Boys Adrift: The five factors driving the growing epidemic of unmotivated boys and underachieving young men*. New York: Basic Books.

———. (n.d.) National Association for Single Sex Public Education. Retrieved November 23, 20009, from *www.singlesexschools.org*

——— (2009). *Women Graduates of Single-Sex and Coeducational High Schools: Differences in their Characteristics and the Transition to College.* Los Angeles: UCLA Graduate School of Education and Information Studies.

Scales-Trent, J. (1989). Black women and the Constitution: Finding our place, assessing our rights. *Harvard Civil Rights-Civil Liberties Law Review*, 24, 9–44.

Schmidt, P. (1990, September 26). Movement grows to rescue black males in crisis. *Education Week*, p. 9.

School board vows to pursue fight for all-male schools. (1991, August 28). *UPI Lexis-Nexis.*

Schott Foundation for Public Education. (2008). *Given half a chance: The Schott 50 state report on public education and Black males.* Retrieved November 27, 2009, from blackboysreport.org.

Schlesinger v. Ballard, 419 U.S. 498 (1975).

Schriver, K. (2003, Spring). Rhetorical pathologies and gender difference: An ideological examination of cultural discourse in *Faulkner v. Citadel. Women's Studies in Communication* 26, 27.

Scott, D. (1997). *Contempt and Pity: Social policy and the image of the Damaged Black Psyche, 1880–1996.* Chapel Hill: University of North Carolina Press.

Scott, J. (1986). Gender: A useful category of historical analysis. *American Historical Review*, 91,(5), 1053–1076.

Scott, K. (1991). *The habit of surviving: Black women's strategies for life.* New Brunswick: Rutgers University Press.

Sedler, R. (1991). *Memorandum of Law.* [*Garrett* legal briefs].

Sewell, T. (2010, March 15). *Black boys are too feminised.* Retrieved March 29, 2010 from www.guardian.co.uk.

Shandor, M. (1991, August 28). Racist, not sexist. *Detroit Free Press*, p. 8A.

Sharpley-Whiting, T. (2007). *Pimps up, ho's down: Hip Hop's hold on young Black women.* New York: New York University Press.

Silva, E. (2008, March 16). Boys and girls are more alike in school than they are different. *Delaware News Journal.* Retrieved November 27, 2009 from www.educationsector.org.

Simmons, W. & Grady, M. (1990). *Black male achievement: From peril to promise.* Report of the Superintendent's Advisory Committee on Black Male Achievement for Prince George's County Public Schools.

Singleton, K. (1991, September 16). Be fair about academies: Letter to editor. *Detroit Free Press*, 8A.

Smith, B. (1995). Some home truths on the contemporary Black feminist movement. In B. Guy-Sheftall (Ed.), *Words of Fire* (pp. 254–267). New York: The New Press.

———. (2002, May 8). First Black female cadets to graduate from The Citadel. *Associated Press State and Local Wire.* Retrieved November 28, 2009, from *www.lexisnexis.com.*

Smith, P. (1992). All-male Black schools and the equal protection clause: A step forward toward education. *Tulane Law Review*, 66, 2004–2055.

Smitherman, G. (1991). *Affidavit.* [*Garrett* legal briefs].

Smitherman, G. (ed). (1995). *African-American women speak out on Anita Hill-Clarence Thomas*. Detroit: Wayne State University Press.

Snow, D. & Benford, R. (1992). Master frames and cycles of protest. In A. Morris & C. Mueller (Eds.), *Frontiers in Social Movement Theory* (pp. 133–155). New Haven: Yale University.

———. (2000). Clarifying the relationship between framing and ideology. *Mobilization: An International* Journal 5, 55–60.

Snow, D., Rochford, E., Worden, S., & Benford, R. (1986). Frame alignment process, micromobilization, and movement participation. *American Sociological* Review, 51, 464–481.

Sommers, C. (2000, August 22). Fair treatment for boys. *Washington Post Op-ed*. p. A19.

Spector, M. & Kitsuse, J. (1987). *Constructing social problems*. New York: Aldine de Gruyter.

Spielhagen, F. (ed.) (2008). *Debating single-sex education: Separate and equal?* Lanham, MD: Rowman and Littlefield Education.

Springer, K. (2002). Third wave Black feminism? *Signs: Journal of Women in Culture and Society*, 27(4), 1059–1082.

Staples, R. (1979). The myth of Black macho: A response to angry Black feminists. *Black Scholar*, 10(6), 24–33.

Statement of the Metropolitan Detroit Branch American Civil Liberties Union regarding the Detroit School Board's plan for an "all-male" Academy (1991).

Steinberg, J. (1996, July 16). Plan for Harlem girls school faces concern over sex bias. *New York Times*, p. A1, A2.

Stewart, L. (1991, August 16). Perfect answer erased by ruling, parents say. *Detroit Free Press*, p. 8A.

Stipulation and Agreement (November 7, 1991), *Nancy Doe v. The Board of Education of the School District of the City of Detroit*. No. 91-CV-73821.

Streitmater, J. (1999). *For girls only: Making a case for single-sex schooling*. Albany: State University of New York Press.

Sundberg, K. (1991a, June 9). All-male academy is built on sexist myths [Letter to Editor]. *Detroit Free Press*, p. 2F.

———. (1991b, November 8). Gender apartheid [Letter to Editor]. *Detroit Free Press*, p. 10A.

Tanay, E. (1991, August 25). Ill-advised comments [Letter to Editor]. *Detroit Free Press*, p. 2F.

Task Force to Address the Decline in Enrollment and Graduation of the Black Male From Institutions of Higher Education. (1990). *African-American men and higher education in Maryland*. Montgomery County: NAACP.

Tatar, M. (2005, January 14). Resistance to "Interdisciplinarity." *Chronicle of Higher Education*, 51, 19.

Taylor-Gibbs, J. (1988). *Young, Black and male in America*. Dover, MA: Auburn House Publishing Company.

Terrolonge-Stone, P. (1995). Feminist consciousness and Black women. In B. Guy Sheftall (Ed.), *Words of Fire* (pp. 490–501). New York, the New Press.

Tetzeli, R. (1992, August 10). Most dangerous and endangered. *Fortune*, p. 78 Retrieved from *www.lexisnexis.com*.

The Male Academy compromise [Editorial]. (1991, August 27) *Detroit News*. Retrieved from www.lexisnexis.com.

Theoharis, G. (2007). Social Justice Educational Leaders and Resistance:

Thomas, B. (2006, June 23). Editorial: Single-gender schools increase choices of Michigan parents, students, and teachers. *Detroit Free Press*. Retrieved November 24, 2009, from www.detbuzz.com.

Tilly, C. (1978). *From mobilization to revolution*. New York: Random House.

Title IX, Education Amendments of 1972, 20 USC 1681–1688.

Toma, J. (1996). Scholars and Their Inquiry Paradigms: Exploring a Conceptual Framework for Classifying Inquiry and Inquirers Based upon Paradigmatic Assumptions. *Educational Resources Information Center*. Paper presented at the Annual Meeting of the American Educational Research Association, New York, NY, 1–41.

Toward a theory of social justice leadership. *Educational Administration Quarterly* 43(2), p. 221–258.

Transcript of *Garrett*. [*Garrett* legal briefs].

Trashing Detroit's initiative [Editorial]. (1991, August 19). *Washington Times*, p. D2.

Tuchman, G. (1996, July 1). West Point marks 20 years as co-ed school. *CNN*. Retreived March 13, 2010, from www.cnn.com.

Twenty-seven female applicants apply for Detroit's African-centered schools. (1991, September 4). *PR Newswire*. Retrieved November 27, 2009, from www.lexisnexis.com.

United Community Services of Metropolitan Detroit, Research Division. (1989). *The social and economic status of young black males and the impact on the formation of Detroit area families*.

United States Department of Education. (2002, May 3). Guidelines on current Title IX requirements related to single-sex classes and schools and Notice of intent to regulate. Retrieved November 25, 2009 from *www.ed.gov*.

———. (2005). *Single-Sex Versus coeducational schooling: A systematic review*. Retrieved January 2, 2010, from www.air.org.

———. (2006, October 25). Federal Register, 71, 206.

United States v. Hinds, 560 F.2d 691 (5th Cir. 1977).

United States v. Virginia, 518 US 515 (1996).

Urban Prep Academies. (2008). Retrieved March 13, 2010 from www.urbanprep.org.

Urban Prep will focus on reversing dismal graduation rates of young urban men by providing high quality college prep education. (November 16, 2009). Retrieved August 20, 2010, from ccsr.uchicago.edu.

Van Dijk, T. (Eds.). (1993). Analyzing racism through discourse analysis: Some methodological reflections. In J. Stanfield, II and R. Dennis (Eds.), *Race and Ethnicity in Research Methods*. Newbury Park, CA: Sage.

Vaznis, J. (2008, October 29). School Revamp hits a snag. Single-sex center may be illegal. *The Boston Globe*. Retrieved November 25, 2009, from Retrieved from www.lexisnexis.com.

———. (2009, January 2). In Detroit a lesson in same-sex schools. *The Boston Globe*. Retrieved November 23, 2009, from www.boston.com.

Vergon, C. (1993). Male Academies for at-risk urban youth: Legal and policy lessons from the Detroit experience." *Ed. Law Rep.* 79, 351.

Vernon-Chesley, M. (1991, February 27). Board clears the way for all-male academies. *Detroit Free Press-Gannett News Service*. Retrieved from www.lexisnexis.com.

Vojdik, V. (2002, January 31). Gender Outlaws: Challenging Masculinity in Traditionally Male Institutions. *Berkeley Women's Law* Journal, 17, 68.

Vorchhiemer v. School District of Philadelphia, 532 F.2d 880 (3rd Cir. 1976).

Wallace, M. (1995). Anger in isolation: A Black feminist search for sisterhood. In B. Guy-Sheftall (Ed.), *Words of Fire* (pp. 220–227). New York: The New Press.

Walters, L. (1991, September 9). The plight of Black male schools. *Christian Science Monitor*. Retrieved from www.lexisnexis.com.

Watson, C. (1991). *Affidavit*. [*Garrett* legal briefs].

Watson, C. & Smitherman, G. (1996). *Educating African-American Males*: Detroit's Malcolm X Academy solution. Chicago: Third World Press.

———. (2003). Educating African American Males: Detroit's Malcolm X Academy Solution. *Urban Education*, 38(4), 380–397.

Watson, S. (1991a, June 2). Waiting for equality won't solve black males' problems. *Detroit Free Press*, p. 4F.

———. (1991b, August 21). Male academy deserves chance. *Detroit Free Press*, p. 1B.

Webb, J. (2006). When 'law and sociology' is not enough: Transdisciplinarity and the problem of complexity. In Freeman, M. (ed). *Law and Sociology: Current legal issues*. London: Oxford University Press.

Weber, M. (1993). Immersed in an educational crisis: Alternative programs for African-American males. *Stanford Law Review*, 45, 1099.

Weil, E. (2008, March 2). Teaching boys and girls separately. *The New York Times*. Retrieved January 23, 2010 from www.nytimes.com.

Weis, L. (Ed.). (1988). *Class, race, and gender in American education*. Albany, New York: State University of New York Press.

Weis, L. & Fine, M. (Eds.). (1993). *Beyond silenced voices: Class, race, and gender in United States schools*. Albany, New York: State University of New York Press.

We will have a male academy: Detroiters vow to do whatever is necessary to save concept…blast ACLU and NOW. (1991, August 21–17). *Michigan Chronicle*, p. 1A-4A.

Whitehead, T. & Reid, B. (1992). *Gender constructs and social issues*. Chicago: University of Illinois Press.

Whitley, R. (1984). *The Intellectual and Social Organization of the Sciences*. Oxford: Clarendon Press.

Whitmire, R. (n.d.) Why Boys Fail Website. Retrieved November 27, 2009, from *www.whyboysfail.com*

Williams, B. (1989). A class act: Anthropology and the race to nation across ethnic terrain. *Annual Review of Anthropology*, 18, 401–444.

Williams, C. (1991, August 22). "We're fed up" say 300 protesters supporting all-male academies. *Detroit News*.

Williams, J. (1991). Dissolving the sameness/ difference debate: A post-modern path beyond essentialism in feminist and critical race theory. 1991 *Duke Law Journal*, 296–323.

Williams, L. (1984, November 8). On the ethics of research on the triple oppression of Black American women." *Humanity and Society*, 506–513.

Williams, V. (2004). Reform or Retrenchment? Single Sex Education and the Construction of Race and Gender. *WILR* 2004, 15.

Wilson, J. (1992, February 24). Expert dislikes all-male schools: he played a key role in '54 Brown ruling. *Detroit Free Press,* p. 1B.

Wilson, W. (1987). *The truly disadvantaged: The inner city, the underclass and public policy.* Chicago: University of Chicago Press.

———. (1996). *When work disappears: The world of the new urban poor.* New York: Knopf

Wimberley, M. (1991, August 7–13). Male Academy critics sue. *Michigan Chronicle*, 1A, 4A.

Wing, A. (1990). Brief reflections toward a multiplicative theory and praxis of being. *Berkeley Women's Law Journal*, 6, 181.

———. (ed.) (2003). *Critical Race Feminism: A reader.* New York: New York University Press.

Wing, A. & Willis, C. (1999). From Theory to Praxis: Black women, gangs, and critical race feminism. *La Raza Law Journal*, 11(1).

Wisconsin Department of Public Instruction. (2006, November). Changes in state law to allow single-sex schools and courses. Retrieved November 27, 2009 from dpi.wi.gov.

Wolf, E. (1981). *Trial and error: The Detroit school segregation case.* Detroit: Wayne State University.

Wolffe, J. (1991, September 4). ACLU disappointed at efforts to recruit girls to academies. *United Press International* Retrieved from www.lexisnexis.com.

Women flock to VWIL as female enrollment levels off at VMI. (2001, August 25). *Associated Press State and Local Wire.* Retrieved November 28, 2009, from Retrieved from www.lexisnexis.com.

Worth, S. (1991, August 14). All in favor of the male academy. *Michigan Chronicle,* pp.1C-9C.

Wright, W. (n.d.). *The at-risk endangered species: The Black male child.* Miami: Dade County Public Schools.

Yosso, T. (2006). Whose culture has capital? A critical race theory discussion of community cultural wealth. In A. Dixson & C. Rousseau (Eds). *Critical race theory in education: All God's children got a song* (pp. 167–189). New York: Routledge.

Young Women's Leadership Charter School of Chicago. (2009). Retrieved March 13, 2010 from ywlcs.org.

Zerai, A. & Campbell, H. (2005). The Black Radical Congress and Black Feminist Organizing. *Socialism and Democracy*, 19(2), 147–156.

Zerai, A. & Salime, Z. (2006). A Black feminist analysis of responses to war, racism, and repression. *Critical Sociology*, 32(2–3), 501.

Zwerling, E. (2001, June 3). California study: Single-sex schools no cure-all. *Womensenews.org.* Retrieved December 5, 2009.

Index